AF541057

WOMEN'S ROLE IN FAMILY

Women's Role in Family

KANTA SHARMA

ANMOL PUBLICATIONS PVT. LTD.
NEW DELHI - 110 002 (INDIA)

ANMOL PUBLICATIONS PVT. LTD.
4374/4B, Ansari Road, Daryaganj
New Delhi - 110 002
Ph.: 23261597, 23278000
Visit us at: www.anmolpublications.com

Women's Role in Family

First Published, 2004

ISBN 81-261-1979-9

PRINTED IN INDIA

Published by J.L. Kumar for Anmol Publications Pvt. Ltd., New Delhi - 110 002 and Printed at Mehra Offset Press, Delhi.

Contents

Preface

A woman's role in her family is very significant. She begins to act at a very early stage of her life. To start with, she behaves as a daughter and sister; then she becomes wife and after that a mother. In all these capacities, she has to fulfill vital responsibilities in maintaining peace in the household and shaping the future of the family.

The family expands to become a society and thus woman's role is also extended automatically. She influences the growth and development of society and in that course, also plays a decisive role, which causes many a change.

In India, particularly, the women—though neglected and sidelined—play electrifying roles and share all sorts of responsibilities, which make her a pillar of society and culture and the real creator of civilization, known as Indian civilization.

Marriage is an institution in our society. The woman is the plank of a marital bond, like her life partner—the man. In sociologists' view, real life begins with marriage only. Hence, the tragedy of a marriage-break up—divorce to say precisely—is considered to be a sin, as per our traditions. Needless to say that it's woman and woman only, who guards marital bonds and who helps build a happy household. She, in fact, is the champion.

Gone are the days, when women were at the receiving end. Today, they are part and parcel of society and active in all fields.

Thanks to the sustained efforts of the women-lib organisations and a constant movement, now, women's issues have gained ascendence. However, much is still there, to be done.

One more interesting factor is also there. Today, women's movements or the feminist movements are not run by womenfolk alone. The men are equally concerned and many a gentleman steer the feminist movements. After all, they also stand to gain for women's liberation, emancipation and empowerment.

This book, a timely one, deals with all issues concerning women and family. Hopefully, this modest effort of the undersigned should fill the vacuum for a comprehensive and exhaustive (and not very bulky) book on the subject. The editor is confident that this endeavour would be acknowledged by concerned circles.

Editor

1

Introduction

Significantly, the word 'gender' means much more than 'sex'. The gender of a man is masculine and that of a woman feminine. Neither a man nor a woman is sex alone or a biological species. So, the concept of gender may be said to be more inclusive than that of sex. But this distinction as such says nothing as to which of the two is inferior or superior. A bigger circle is only bigger than - not necessarily superior to — the smaller one, which it may include. In other words, the word gender in my view is a value-free concept. Differences of value arise only when we take genders in relation to their functions in society and, what is more important, when our way of looking at the matter is merely external. The point may be brought out as follows:

When female child becomes a wife, she acquires the functions of a mother, similarly a male child becomes a father. Now the functions of a mother are mostly confined to activities which quietly take place within the house. The father, on the other hand, earns a living by working in the outer world. What takes place in the open is noticed easily. What happens at home does not strike the public eye. So by the average man, whose way of looking is confined to the externals - that is, whose *drishti* is *bahirmukhi*-the male is taken to be superior to the female. Those who are careful enough to take a comprehensive view of the human life, attach as much value to the mother's activities of producing and nursing children and keeping a family together as to the bread winners outdoor activity of earning a living. It is really a defect in our ways of looking at things, and not the fact of gender as such, which is at the root of prevailing bias against women.

However, in the contemporary feminist literature, gender is not a value-free concept. It is a value-loaded term. It has acquired new dimensions and greater significance. It now refers to the social institutionalisation of sexual difference . It aims at exposing the present masculinist hegemony in the name of natural sexual differences, and also at uncovering the male connotations of the existing vocabulary of reason, morality, autonomy, justice and history. It, therefore, aims at suggesting an alternative epistemology and methodology, which can uncover the present gender bias, and may reflect more accurately the experiences and needs of all human beings. Feminists assert that any discrimination based on the basis of sexual differences is unjust; the body differences do not warrant such discriminatory differentiation; and, that they are only socially produced. Catharine A Mackinnon says:

> "Our issue is not the gender difference, but the difference gender makes, the social meaning imposed upon our bodies - what it means to be a woman or man is a social process and, as such, a subject to change. Feminists do not seek sameness with men. We more criticise what men have made of themselves and the world that we, too, inhabit. We do not seek dominance over men. To us, it is a male notion that power means someone must dominate. We seek a transformation in the terms and conditions of power itself."

It would be relevant here to discuss how political theorists in the past have neglected gender. John Locke defines political power as distinct from the power relations operating within the household. Rousseau and Hegel have clearly contrasted the two spheres and have justified this contrast in legitimising male rule in the domestic sphere. Locke has categorically mentioned that when "women hold the helm of government, the state is at once in jeopardy". Rousseau believes that women pose a permanent threat to political order. The natural morality of women fits them only for the 'natural society' of domestic life. He argues in Politics and the Arts, "even if it could be denied that a special sentiment of chasteness was natural to women, would it be less true that in society ... they ought to be raised in principles appropriate to it? If the timidity, chasteness and modesty, which are proper to them are social inventions, it is in society's interest that women acquire these qualities....."

Freud offers remarkably similar justification for women's confinement to domesticity. He writes, "for women the level of what is ethically normal is different from what it is in men. Their superego is never so inexorable, so impersonal, so independent of its emotional origins as we require it to be in men... They show less sense of justice than men, they are more often influenced in their judgements by feeling of affection of hostility..." Hence, Freud insists that the difference in moral capacity between the two sexes must be accepted.

Ironically, most contemporary political theorists continue the same neglect of gender by ignoring the family. Susan Moller Okin has rightly claimed, "the judgement that the family is 'non-political' is implicit in the very fact that it is not discussed in most works of political theory today". A number of examples can be cited.

However, there are a few exceptions. The works of Michael L Walzer, Philip Green, Allen Bloom and Michael J Sandel can be cited here.

Contemporary feminist scholars have used the word 'gender' after two decades of intensive thought and research. To them gender is a social and political construct, related to and not determined by, biological sex difference.

In its most recent usage, gender seems to have first appeared among American feminists, who wanted to reject biological determinism implicated in the use of such terms as 'sex' or 'sexual difference'. Two major theories of gender are prevalent today-the psychologically focused theory of gender; and the historically and anthropologically focused explanation of gender.

Simone de Beauvoir, in her work *The Second Sex*, a quintessential example of modern feminist inquiry and critique, claims that "one is not born but rather becomes a woman". She claims that It is a whole process by which femininity is manufactured in society. To quote her, "she is defined and differentiated with reference to men and not he with reference to her; she is the incidental, the inessential as opposed to the essential. He is the subject, he is the Absolute - she is the Other".

Beauvoir argues that it is the child-bearing role of women which excluded them from the productive process, and prevented them from seeing themselves as subjects in their own right. Thus, an artificial idea of womanhood was created by society. She exhorts: "No biological, psychological or economic fate determines the figure that the human female presents in society; it is civilisation as a whole that produces this creation, intermediate between male and eunuch, who is described female."

Nancy Chodorow also subscribes to the above viewpoint and substantiates her argument from a psychoanalytical point of view. She argues that since women have always been assigned the responsibility of primary parenting and nurturing, they develop a psychology of being more suited to the task of nurturing and caring. Thus she chooses the role of a caregiver and confinement to the private. On the other hand, man from the very beginning is encouraged for more and more individuation and attaining status leading to personality traits impelling him to associate himself with the pubic.

Chodorow's use of the notion of gender identity presupposes three major premises: First, everyone has a deep sense of self, which is constituted in early childhood through one's interaction with his/her primary parent, and which remains relatively constant thereafter. The second premise is that this deep self differs significantly for men and women, but is roughly similar among women and among men both across cultures and within cultures across lines of class, race and ethnicity The third premise is that, this deep self colours everything one does.

The second theory of gender proclaims that in most societies across cultures, so far, gender has been a socially constructed category rather than biologically determined. However the proponents of this theory have also stressed that the nature of this social construction differs from one society to the other. So, there cannot be any unicausal, universalist and a historical explanation of it. Anthropologist Michelle A Rosaldo supports this theory on the basis of her cross-cultural research, which reveals that women are subjected to the authority due to the existing dichotomy between the public and the private.

Historian Linda J Nicholson also rejects the unicausal explanation of inequality of the sexes. She emphasises that it has been affected by various causal factors in different social contexts. She stresses the need to fight against the powerful tendency present in political theory to rectify the public-private distinction and to perceive it as rigid. She believes that one can comprehend this distinctly only through the study of history, for the gender structure of a particular time and place is less affected by other contemporary structures, such as political, economic, etc., more by the previous history of gender. Joan W Scott also stresses the centrality of history in analysing different aspects of the social construction of gender. She explains (a)how cultural myths and symbols reify the suppression of women: (b)how these symbols create the 'binary opposition of masculine and feminine male and female; (c)how social institutions like family, labour markets, educational institutions and polity reinforce this dichotomy; and, (d)how the subjective identity formation of individuals is psychologically determined. She, therefore, emphasises the need to expose the social construction of gender by deconstructing it. This calls for:

> "a refusal of the fixed and permanent quality of binary opposition, a genuine historicization and deconstruction of the terms of sexual difference... (we must) reversel and displace its hierarchical construction, rather than accepting it as real or self-evident or in the nature of things."

In fact, all of them are unequivocal in proclaiming that the public sphere till today, has been constructed under the assumption of male superiority and dominance. It has avoided a number of compelling questions such as that of incorporating the responsibilities of child-bearing and child rearing into the fabric of job-structure.

The above analysis of gender has helped feminists in rejecting many of the existing dominant paradigms. First, they reject the claim that separation of the public and the private follows inevitably from the natural characteristics of the sexes. They argue that a proper understanding of social life is possible only when it is accepted that the two spheres, the private and the public, are inextricably interrelated. Unless the separation of the two worlds is not destroyed, the public life would always be conceptualised as the sphere of men. Carole Pateman has aptly remarked:

> "In popular (and academic) consciousness the duality of female and male often serves to encapsulate or represent the series (or circle) of liberal separations and oppositions: female, or-nature, personal, emotional love, private intuition, morality, ascription, particular, subjection; male, or-culture, political, reason, justice, public, philosophy, power, achievement, universal, freedom."

The most fundamental and general of these opinions associate women with nature and men with culture. Nature is always seen in a lower order than culture. The feminists like Ortner argue that the opposition between women/nature and men/culture is itself a cultural construct and does not exist in nature. S.Firestone in her work *Dialectic of Sex*, argues against this separation of private and public. Women necessarily suffer from a fundamentally oppressive biological condition. It is their role as reproducers that has handicapped women over the centuries and made possible men's patriarchal power.

The consequences of this public-private dichotomy are disastrous. Due to this, women have been deprived of political power and effective participation. Citizenship for women is always seen as 'an elaboration of their private domestic tasks'. Thinkers like Ruskin could argue that "man's duty as a member of the commonwealth, is to assist the maintenance, in the advance and in the defence of the state. The women's duty, as a member of the commonwealth, is to assist in the ordering, in the comforting, and in the beautiful adornment of the state."

This has eventually led to the dichotomy between morality and poor. Women, in the name of being more moral, have been excluded from the public realm. Even the suffragists argued in favour of women's franchise by claiming women's superior morality as it would usher the state in a reign of peace. This is why J B Elshtain alleges that suffragists instead of challenging the separation of the public and private, merely "perpetuated the very mystifications and unexamined presumptions, which served to rig the system against them."

Against this background, one can understand the significance of the feminist slogan:

The feminists argue that public realm of politics can be so rational, noble and universal only because like the messy content of the human body, meeting its needs for production, care-taking and attending to birth and death, as too in politics are taken care of elsewhere.

So, a modern reflective political theory should recognise that the glory of the public is dialectically entwined with exploitation and repression of the private and the people restricted to that sphere so that they can take care of the people's needs. In view of this, the feminist political theory concludes that the 20th century politics requires a basic rethinking of this distinction and its meaning for politics.

The feminists are trying to develop a theory of social practice on the following premises. First, there should be no sexual division of labour at work place and in political organisations of all ideological persuasions; second, there should be a differentiated social order within which various dimensions are distinct but not separate or opposed, and which rests on social conception of individuality, which includes both women and men as biologically differentiated but not unequal creatures.

Third, there is a need to base and expand the conception of politics on the understanding that power relations between men and women are not confined to the 'public' world of law, the state and economics, but pervade all areas of life. This means that contrary to the assumptions of traditional political theory, the family, reproduction and sexuality must be included in political analysis.

The question arises how far this public/private dichotomy and its deconstruction is relevant to the women of the Third World? Can this empowerment epistomology rooted in white women's experiences, subjectivity and identity, fulfil the interest of the Third World women?

However, in the post colonial discourse, women of the North have understood the significance of the Third World women's realities, and they themselves have rejected the monolithic nature of the earlier feminist discourse on the grounds that it ignores difference, indigenous knowledge, and local expertise. For example, modernity is equated with westernisation, industrialisation and superiority, whereas non-modernity is equated with non-western countries, tradition and inferiority. In the 1970s, Eshter Boserup's pioneering work *Women's Role in Economic Development*, asserted that modernisation had marginalised women and their contributions in the Third World. Chandra Mohanty also questions the western approach, when she asks:

> "Is it possible to refer to the sexual division of labour when the content of this division changes radically from one environment to the next, from one historical juncture to another? At its most abstract level ... concepts such as the sexual division of labour can be useful only if they are generated through local, contextual analyses. If such concepts are assumed to be universally applicable, the resultant homogenisation of class, race, religion, and daily material practices of women in the Third World can create a false sense of the commonality of oppressions, interests, and struggles between and among women globally.

G Sen, and Crown too, are cautious against adopting a concept of gender that ignores differences and diversities. They believe that this diversity is built on gender oppression and hierarchy. He exclaims:

> "Feminism cannot be monolithic in its issues, goals and strategies, since it constitutes the political expression of the concerns of women from different regions, classes, nationalities, and ethnic backgrounds. There is and must be a diversity of feminism, responsive to the different needs and concerns of different women, and defined by them for themselves."

The most positive part of the whole discourse is that these concerns are reflected in practice also. Women involved in different social movements are fighting against injustice on their own cultural terms. Environmental activists like Vandana Shival are speaking of the need to decolonise northern assumptions such as the concept of sustainable development, and appeal to save environment through knowledge based on poor women's experience.

Thus, feminist scholarship has brought sweeping changes to social and political theory. It has cautioned us against constituting gender as a superordinate category of analysis. It should neither be an automatic starting point of analysis of adjustment, nor should it be ignored as a potential starting point. We must avoid approaches that are gender-blinded or gender-blind. Then only we can have true meaning of democracy and participation.

2

Fundamental Problems

Issues involving women are closely related to supportive services. These refer to the gamut of services and amenities that make the women more functional and productive, while at the same time reduce the overburdening drudgery of the daily chores which she is expected to perform for the survival of her family. The major supportive services that require attention are fuel, fodder, water, creche and housing services. One of the major hurdles to women's development activities is the difficulty of providing economically viable means of releasing them from day to day drudgery and survival activities which are neither awarded an economic value nor are shared by men. Data indicate that women are unable to avail of tubectomy services in the absence of a substitute who can care for the children while the woman is away. Similarly, the education of girls is impeded because they are invariably required to help the mother to look after younger children. It is well known that besides adult women, children are also expected to fetch fodder, fuel and water. Cooking also accounts for a large chunk of the woman's time. The use of inefficient smoky chulhas affect their lungs, eyes and health in general. This also interferes with social interaction.

The factors affecting women's advancement are thus critically linked to the socio-cultural environment. In keeping, with her sex stereotyped role as a housewife and home maker, an Indian woman irrespective of clan, creed, region, religion, spends, most of her time on household chores. While the actual time distribution would vary from place to place, undoubtedly many women are subjected to the drudgery of a day to day subsistence working up to 16-18 hours per day. Unfortunately, such 'shadow work' brings her no monetary returns nor does it enhance her prestige in the family or society which is necessary for her to participate in decision making.

In addition, women are often left to fend for the household's basic needs and sanitation, especially in the rural context. The Seventh Plan notes that women play an important role in agriculture, animal husbandry and other related activities such as storage, marketing of produce, food processing, etc. About 54 per cent of rural women and 26 per cent urban women are engaged in marginal occupations in order to supplement family income by collection of fodder, firewood, cowdung, maintenance of kitchen gardens, tailoring, weaving, teaching, etc. It is not easy for a woman to take up employment, unless there are alternative ways to saving time at home and sufficient remuneration to justify her employment outside. Thus all programmes for women, be it education, health, family planning, nutrition, social welfare or legislation are necessarily interrelated support structures for reducing the household drudgery.

Since drinking water, fuel and fodder are the basic requirements especially in the rural areas, a major portion of women's time is spent on collecting these. Strategies which help overcome such problems by providing the necessary support services need to be carefully devised and effectively integrated in development strategies/ plans for women.

In the previous plan periods, the emphasis was mainly on issues concerning education, employment and social aspects, without giving commensurate attention to supportive services. For example, the section dealing with the 'Infrastructure for

Women's Participation in a Modernizing Economy', the Report on the Status of Women, touched only upon childcare services. The National Plan of Action (1976) was also silent on the structuring of various supportive services. However, the Sixth Five-Year Plan recommended separate Science and Technology (S&T) inputs for women (Item 19.35) as a part of Science & Technology for Human Resource Development. The Plan suggested the setting up of special cells for promotion of Science and Technology for women under the aegis of different organizations such as the University Grants Commission (UGC, Council of Scientific and Industrial Research (CSIR), Indian Council for Medical Research (ICMR), Department of Adult Education (DAE), etc. Although it was proposed to apply Science and Technology for the improvement of the living conditions and status of women, support services were not specifically discussed. The Seventh Plan is more emphatic on women's development and has a separate section on 'Socio-Economic Programmes for Women'. It notes that in giving Science and Technology inputs for women, special efforts have to be made to reduce their drudgery.

The interlinkages between various sectoral and support services have to be fully understood so that an integrated purposeful view is taken of women development. The programmes have to be planned on the basis of a detailed analysis both at micro and macro levels. The analysis should identify critical factors including resource availability, appropriate technologies, skill constraints, public awareness and organizational, institutional and policy supports.

Fuel and fodder are best taken up together since they are bio-mass based and often the same plant provides both. This system also integrates with food which, in turn, is linked to fuel through cooking. Hence the discussion here also touches upon forestry and wasteland utilization for growing a variety of biomass in the broader perspective.

Women participate in fodder production as a part of their activities in agriculture and in cutting and fetching fodder for feeding the animals. Generally green fodder is raised as one of the crops or in grasslands and is gathered from the fields as and when required. Alternatively a variety of straws and other agricultural residues are collected and stored as fodder or converted into silage or hay. Often women also have to visit the nearby forests to cut fodder from trees and bushes. This is generally done along with fuel collection. The harder biomass like twigs and firewood are used as fuel and the palatable leaves, as fodder. As for fuels, as indicated by a number of studies, cowdung (gobar) and agricultural residues and firewood form the major fuel for cooking and are gathered and stored mainly by women. The act of making and storing cowdung cakes has developed into an art, with 'bitodas' (cowdung storage structures) prominently standing out in the rural landscape. Cowdung cakes are preferred for slow cooking on low fires or heating milk, while firewoods and agricultural residues serve to produce more intensive heat. Depending on resource availability, the utilization pattern varies with cowdung being more prominent in the northern regions. The major portion of total energy, consumed is through such 'non-conventional' sources which, in rural areas, accounts for 90 per cent of the domestic energy expenditure.

The three plans (Fifth, Sixth and Seventh) had generally discussed the fodder under 'Animal Husbandry', fuel under 'Energy', and biomass under 'Forestry'. The Fifth Plan observed that the 'forestry' development has assumed a significant dimension as a source of timber and fuel and for the maintenance of the natural ecological system. Special plantations have been given high priority. Under the section 'Energy' it has been proposed to adopt a multipronged approach to develop biogas technology and tap new sources such as solar energy, tidal and wing power. The Sixth Plan noted that feed and fodder constitute 60 to 70 per cent of the cost of production of various livestock products and that the area under fodder crops has remained more or less static during the last two decades. It also stated that emphasis will continue to be placed on the promotion of fodder production as an integral part of crop husbandry through a mixed farming system, particularly, on the small landholdings. Effective farmer-oriented extension programmes will be taken up by the Government for evolving and popularizing high yielding varieties of fodder crops, and introduction of leguminous fodders in existing crop rotations. Production and distribution of high quality fodder seeds will also receive priority attention. Accordingly, a Central Fodder Seed Production Farm and Centres for Forage Production and Demonstration were set up during this plan. The development of extensive grasslands and creation of grass reserves were taken up by the State Forest Departments. Under the social forestry programmes marginal and degraded forests were allocated for cultivation on fodder trees.

As for fuel, the Sixth Plan (item 9.248 under social forestry) proposed: (i) Mixed plantation of wasteland; (ii) Reforestation of degraded forests and raising of shelter belts. In the districts where shortage of fuel wood was particularly acute, new centrally sponsored schemes of social forestry including Rural Fuel Wood Plantation and Farm Forestry were introduced in selected areas. New thrusts in the form of Tree for Every Child Programme, Economic Development Force, Eco-development Camps and Agro Forestry programmes were devised during the Sixth Plan. The concept of organic recycling (Item 9.36) and the propagation of biogas technology (Item 9.40, 9.41) were also envisaged. Further, this plan dealt with the new and renewable energy sources and suggested that energy forestry, biogas and biomass conversion technologies have to be taken up along with solar and wind energy and a variety of other technologies. For example, item 15.95 on 'Energy Forestry' notes that firewood is the most important traditional fuel accounting for two-thirds of the total energy contribution from non-commercial sources and is becoming scarce. In view of the pressure on land, all available unutilized pockets of land could be used for energy plantations. Considering that rural communities will continue to depend heavily on such resources, it was proposed to decentralize energy production and distribution as a part of an Integrated Rural Energy System (Item 15.105) which considers all energy resources in a given area.

In the Seventh Plan also, emphasis has been given to social forestry, agro forestry and various renewable energy technologies and the necessity of creating awareness among people through mass media. The Plan notes that a proper implementation of some components of forestry programmes may be entrusted to local and voluntary bodies (NGOs). Concepts like 'social fencing' may be tested. Infact the revised 20-Point Programme (1986) has advocated a "New Strategy for Forestry" (Point No. 16).

In recognition of the importance of renewable resources, a Department of Non-conventional Energy Sources has been set up. Also a National Wasteland Development Board was created with the objective of bringing 5 million hectares of land every year under fuelwood and fodder plantation.

In many of the above programmes, the role of women in the production, collection and utilization of fuel and fodder and the related problems are not adequately emphasized. However, it is heartening to note that the Department of Science and Technology set up a cell on "Science & Technology for Women" in 1982. This cell divided the various technologies required for women into the following four areas: Technologies for Drudgery Reduction; Employment Generation Technologies; Health and Sanitation Technologies; and Technologies for Minimizing Occupational Hazards.

Under the first category, the problems of fuel, fodder and drinking water were perceived from the point of view of women. Besides a number of projects funded through individual institutions, an All India Coordinated Project was also undertaken on 'Fuel and Cooking Aspects' through Science and Technology Department. More than 20 institutions from all over the country participated, analysing the data based on micro level surveys.

The local specific and general problems of women in dealing with fuels were identified and the viability of a variety of technologies were field tested. Similarly, some of the selected technologies like the improved chulha, biogas solar cooking biogas based technologies, etc., are being taken to the people through the Department of Non-Conventional Energy Sources. Apart from various governmental institutions like Department of Science and Technology (DST), Indian Council of Agricultural Research (ICAR) Council for Scientific and Industrial Research (CSIR) and Department of Non-Conventional Energy Sources, a number of relevant State departments are also taking up the implementation of such projects. Some reports analysing the reasons for the success as well as failures of experiments undertaken are available.

It is encouraging to know that recently a number of NGOs have taken up programmes with funding support from the various Government bodies noted above. A Bio-energy Society of India has also been established with a view to promote research and development as well as public awareness. Bio-energy education dealing with the production, conversion and utilization of biomass with special emphasis on fuel aspects is being given prominence. People's participation is being promoted through social forestry and other programmes. However, the linking of women with these activities is still weak. A few movements like 'Chipko' stand out, emphasizing that much can be achieved by organizing women at the local levels.

The agricultural universities, dairy development institutions and forest institutes undertake research in fodder and fuel production and have a network of extension centres such as Krishi Vigyan Kendras for taking these technologies from the lab to land. While agriculture provides fodder crops, special attention is also paid to trees and plant species like 'subabool' which can cater to both fuel and fodder needs. Researchers on social forestry and agro-forestry all over the country now recognize the need for integrating the food, fodder, fuel, fertilizer, fibre and other biomass based production and utilization aspects.

The various technologies developed are being compiled into suitable directories for dissemination, e.g., the Science and Technology Women's Cell has listed a number of technologies for women. Council for Advancement of People's Action and Rural Technology (CAPART) has undertaken the publication of several volumes of *National Directory of Rural Technologies*, the first volume titles '*Post-Harvest Technologies*' has already been printed.

However, the scope exists for designing and developing more technologies appropriate to women taking into consideration the agronomy, ease of handling, economics, etc. A special mention must be made of Agricultural Tool Research Centre at Bardoli, which has tried to make efficient agricultural tools especially suited for women.

Although India is one of the wettest countries in the world with an average annual rainfall of 1170 mm, it still faces and is expected to face in future the threat of acute water shortage. Among the various usages of water in rural areas, drinking water followed by irrigation, sanitation and agriculture are of importance for the overall developmental process.

Water resources are generally dealt with as a part of irrigation in agriculture. In addition to this, the Sixth Plan laid special stress on rural water supply as a part of the 'Minimum Needs Programme'. As in the Sixth Plan, the Seventh Plan also highlights the importance of drinking water. The supply of drinking water to all problem villages features at Point 7 of the Twenty-Point Programme (1986). A 'Technology Mission on Drinking water in Villages and Related Water Management' was established in 1986-87 under the Department of Rural Development, Ministry of Agriculture, Government of India. The collaborating agencies identified were Council of Scientific and Industrial Research, Ministry of Science and Technology, Department of Environment and Forests, Department of Defence Research and Development, Ministry of Health and Family Welfare, Ministry of Water Resources and State Governments. The 'problem' villages were identified as those with: (i) No source of water; (ii) Water sources more than 1.6 km. distance, 15 km depth and 100 metres elevation difference; (iii) Biological contamination (guinea worm, cholera, typhoid); and (iv) Chemical contamination (fluoride, brackishness, iron). The number of such problem villages amounts to 39 per cent of the total villages (2.27 lakh out of 5.57 lakh).

Apart from these, the strategy has focused on 50 project areas (Mini missions) to evolve new, cost effective science and technology techniques, to apply and replicate these techniques in the rest of the problem villages and to implement an integrated approach to water conservation.

A booklet outlining the project objectives, background, strategy, management structure, targets, methodology, milestones, accomplishment, resources and policy needs, has been brought out by the Ministry of Agriculture. Already this mission has started working with the State Departments concerned. In addition, universities, research institutions and voluntary organizations are also being involved. A first Regional Seminar to focus on these issues for Southern States and Union Territories was held at Gandhigram in Tamil Nadu in July 1987.

Most of the above efforts, however, are not directly addressed to women. Although in the Sixth Plan, special mention has been made about assuring the weaker sections of their due share of water, only a few organizations like the Science and Technology Women's Cell have looked at this problem from the women's development angle. In addition to sanctioning some institutional level projects on various aspects of potable water, an "All India Coordinated Project on Drinking Water" has also been proposed by this department.

Ideally, as in the case of urban services, the Government should be in a position to supply potable water to all households through pipelines and taps right at the doorsteps. However, considering the current constraints of finance and non-availability of suitable water sources, problem terrains, etc., this may not be feasible in the near future. Hence constructing and maintaining smaller water sources like wells, water tanks, hand pumps, etc., are to be given due consideration.

As with the implementation of any project, there is always the problem of ensuring people's participation in both maintenance and the distribution systems. Merely installing different kinds of units and equipment does not lead to sustained water supply. Thus, organizing women to adopt different technologies is a key issue. In this context, a successful experiment by a voluntary agency in Rajasthan could be considered as a model for replication. In this case, the people were involved in identifying the locations for tube-wells. A few persons were then trained in their actual construction and maintenance. The system of giving due remuneration for subsequent management to these trained personnel was also evolved. This ensured sustained working of the pumps/tube-wells and equitable distribution of water. Other case-studies worthy of note are the "Water Harvesting Systems" employed at Banwasi Sewa Ashram and the "Water Sharing System" evolved at Sukhamajari.

Although a number of technologies are available, only a few have reached the villages. More research and development is needed on issues like devices for carrying water in hilly terrain, water purification techniques suitable for different problem areas, storage at home levels, and rapid methods of water testing.

A list of available technologies have been compiled in a volume brought out by the Cell on Science and Technology for Women. The CAPART has also brought out publications on drinking water and the third volume of its National Directory of Rural Technologies will be on Drinking Water. The Technology Mission on Drinking Water has brought out two publications entitled *Sub-Mission on Desalination of Water and Sub-Mission on Eradication of Guineaworm.*

Child Care

With the advent of industrialization and modernization, and with the gradual disappearance of the traditional joint family and with its in-built security system, the problem of working mothers has become increasingly serious. Although it is mainly an urban phenomenon, rural India is beginning to experience it too. With increasing economic pressures more and more women have to take out of home jobs. The situation is serious because the majority of women who need daycare for their children are from economically backward strata of society.

Working mothers of low-income groups need day care most as they cannot afford to hire or pay for labour-saving devices. Thus, in addition to the general need for child care for all working mother's, there is also a more specific and strong need for child care for those belonging to the poorest sections of the society.

Rural mothers struggle hard not only in the fields but also to collect fuel, fodder and water. Thus their time 'out of home' is much more and the majority of them are forced to either take their infants along or to leave them under the 'supervision' of elder children who stay at home, or even alone. This situation not only keeps older children away from the educational system, but endangers the health of infants and small children. The need for childcare services had already been accepted, but the legal provision exists only for women in the organized sector, which comprise approximately 10 per cent of the working women.

After the submission of the CSWI report (1974), and the International Women's Year, childcare has been recognized as an important and essential support service in women's development. The CSWI report has stated that despite the laws and ILO Convention, maternity and childcare benefits are available only to 3-5 per cent of Indian women workers in the organized sector. The other 3-5 per cent of the organized sector (mainly in services) do not get creche facilities because they are not covered by labour laws. To the 90 per cent of women workers who are in the informal sector, these facilities have so far never been provided as highlighted in the report of the National Commission on Self-Employed Women and Women in the Informal Sector.

In 1950, creches were run by four national level voluntary organizations - The Indian Council for Child Welfare, Bhartiya Grameen Mahila Sangh, Bhartiya Adimjati Sevak Sangh and Harijan Sevak Sangh. The then Ministry of Social Welfare launched a scheme of creches/day care centres for children of working and ailing mothers in February 1975. The aim of the scheme was to promote healthy all round development of such children. The scheme caters to the basic needs of young children of poor working and ailing women in the unorganized sector. The services under the scheme include health care, supplementary nutrition, sleeping facilities, immunization, entertainment and nursery school facilities for children. Starting in 1974-75 with 247 creches to cover 6175 beneficiaries, the scheme has been considerably expanded since then. In the year 1987-88 there were 3,137 agencies running 10,210 creches in the country which included both permanent and mobile units. The Department of Women and Child Development which now deals with the scheme had on its plan that by the end of 1988-89, 12,000 creches would cover 2,82,800 children. The training of creche workers under this programme commenced from September, 1986. Grants-in-aid to certain all-India level institutions were released for conducting training courses. In the statutory sector, around 55,000 children are taken care of in creches/day care centres.

The Balwadi Nutrition Programme is another programme being implemented since 1970-71 which looks after the social and emotional development of children in the age group of 3-5 years, apart from providing supplementary nutrition to them. About 5,045 balwadi centres are functioning in the country covering about 2.29 lakh children.

The Integrated Child Development Services (ICDS) scheme launched by the government in 1975 is designed both as a preventive and developmental effort. It extends beyond the existing health and education systems to reach children below six years and their mothers in villages and slums and delivers to them an integrated package of services - non-formal pre-school education., immunization, health checkups, supplementary nutrition, medical referral services and nutrition and health education for women. As on 31 March, 1988 information received from 1,455 ICDS projects indicate that 1,46,693 Anganwadis were providing supplementary nutrition to 96.10 lakh children. In these Anganwadis, 18.40 lakh nursing mothers were receiving supplementary nutrition. Though focused on the all round development of the pre-school child, it is also the largest scheme providing part time creche facilities to children in rural and tribal areas and in slums. As an employment generation scheme for women, it employs nearly 2,00,000 women at the Anganwadi level.

The National Policy on Education' 1986 (NPE), for the first time took note of the growing awareness that the performance of household chores, specially care of younger siblings, is a major reason for the stagnation in enrolment of girls in schools. At two, places in the policy document, (vide para 5.2 in Early Childhood Care and Education (ECCE) and para 4.3 in Education for Women's Equality, reference is made to the need for child care, attached to or near primary schools, as a support service to encourage and allow girls to attend school.

Habitation

The rapid rate of urbanization in India, coupled with large scale migration of people into the metropolitan cities, has created a tremendous pressure on the housing situation in the country. On the one hand, is the ever increasing shortage of housing which is estimated to be to the tune of 5.1 million dwelling units in urban areas alone (NBO 1981), and on the other, is the steep cost of housing and new construction which is unable to keep pace with the increasing demand and is beyond the reach of the urban dwellers.

In the successive Five-Year Plans, the Government of India has launched several social housing schemes for different income groups under which, loan/ subsidy is given to the low income and economically weaker section families. The implementation of these schemes on a countrywide basis has created great awareness of the desirability of improving the housing and environmental conditions among all sections of the populations including women.

Several other measures which have been taken include providing house building advance, housing finance at low rates of interest through financial institutions, fiscal incentives, bulk acquisition and development of land and ceiling on land, land use regulations, promotion of housing through cooperatives, setting up of Housing Boards and City Development Authorities and Slum Clearance Boards to augment the housing stock.

A Central Scheme of assistance for construction of hostel buildings for working women was initiated in 1972. The scope of the scheme was widened in 1980 by including a provision for daycare centres for children. Financial assistance is given to voluntary organizations for construction/expansion of hostel buildings for working women. Local bodies are also eligible for taking up these programmes. The total number of hostels sanctioned so far is 429 with a total capacity of 27,292 working women with day-care centre facilities for 2,920 children, since the inception of the scheme in 1972. It has been decided to reserve 5 per cent seats in the hostels for widows and other women in distress who are otherwise, eligible for hostel accommodation.

Under the Minimum Needs Programme to ameliorate housing and environment conditions, the Government of India has been implementing various schemes, viz., Slum Clearance

Improvement Scheme, Scheme for Environmental Improvement in Slum Areas and the Schemes for Provision of House Sites to landless workers in rural areas and other social housing schemes for improving the living conditions of the urban and rural poor. The benefits of the schemes accrue to women also.

In the Twenty Point Programme (1986) high priority was accorded to provision of drinking water supply (Point No. 7), improvement of housing conditions for 14.6 million rural landless families (Point No. 14) and those living in slums and squatter settlements (Point No. 15).

Large-scale housing programmes were taken up in different states under the National Rural Employment Programme (NREP) and Rural Landless Employment Guarantee Programme (RLEGP). Housing schemes with employment as the main feature have also been taken up in many States. For implementing the Indira Gandhi Grih Nirman Awas Yojna, an allocation of Rs. 125 crore annually has been provided in the Seventh Five-Year Plan to build one million houses for Scheduled Castes and tribal families.

Improvement in the quality of life of people depends to a great extent on the quality of housing and related facilities which determine the physical environment. It is in recognition of this fact that the world conference of the International Women's Year adopted a World Plan of Action in 1975 which included aspects related to housing amongst its recommendations. The Plan suggested that settlement planning and policies should be formulated keeping in view the trend to recognize women's role in the development process and should prioritize investments in infrastructure therein according to the needs of women. Subsequently, following the declaration of 1987 by the United Nations as the International Year of Shelter for the Homeless, the Ministry of Urban Development of the Government of India formulated a Draft National Housing Policy (March, 1987) with a view to ensuring every family a shelter by the end of this century. Nowhere in its text, however, had the draft acknowledged that housing and women's needs required to be closely linked. Passing references to women were made only at page 12 para 13.4 of the draft wherein it stated that special efforts would be made to improve women's skills and working conditions in the housing sector.

For women, housing has a wider meaning. It implies their working and living environment to which they are confined for a greater portion of their lives, performing their multiple roles that of production which is often home based and therefore implies the use of the shelter and its environs as the working space; that of reproduction which is traditionally viewed as their primary role and includes child rearing activities linked to domestic chores; and that of management of resources and assets within the family unit which includes activities such as storage, managing domestic provisions, processing, etc.

Women's housing needs, arising from their multiple roles, have been listed as follows; as child bearers, they need access to sanitary facilities and a healthy living environment; as child rearers, they need space for childcare and recreation within or outside the house; as managers of households, they need water, fuel, waste and garbage disposal, proper light and ventilation and space to perform domestic chores; and as producers, they need a working space as well as space for storage of raw materials and finished products, besides space for processing of materials. In addition, women also need privacy and security as well as facilities for education, recreation, production and training within the housing space. Housing thus, implies space beyond the confines of the immediate shelter.

An effective public distribution system for essential commodities like rations and cloth is a necessary support for women, especially women workers in the unorganized sector. Poor women are denied ration cards which forces them to purchase basic necessities from the open market at exorbitant prices. Even women with ration cards are often denied rations due to understocking or diversion of stocks.

Each of the above roles indicates that women's efficiency and effectiveness in performing the productive and reproductive tasks are linked to the quality of housing. Since they are in effect the primary users of housing, women must have a role to play in decisions regarding housing as well as ensure that they have access to ownership of the same.

In planning for women's development, priority needs to be given to creating access to assets for single women and female headed households. An estimated 30-35 per cent of households in rural India are headed by women according to available micro studies. Women have hitherto had no rights to ownership or inheritance of property within the framework of customary law. Recent legislative provisions have tried to remedy this situation but ancestral property still remains inaccessible to women. By and large, the patriarchal patterns of land ownership and transfer have implied that land is transferred to males. This pattern has been adopted by the planners in formulation of housing programmes so that men are recognized as heads of: households and land is distributed in their names. Although distribution of land deeds or pattas has been legally sanctioned for men and women jointly, in effect, women are not given land titles. Where women are able to gain access to land or assets, they are often required to have a man stand surety for the same, as also for loans and credit.

Within the patriarchal norm, women may not customarily claim ownership of the matrimonial home. This has often denied women access to shelter in times of crisis. In cases where women have been deserted and are destitute, they have not had any legal right to claim access to shelter, housing or any such assets. Only recently have policy makers and legislators realized that, it is imperative to accord priority to the provision of housing for single and women headed households.

Various strategies have been evolved to augment the housing stock in the country by urban planners and specialists especially for economically weaker sections. The target groups have however seldom been involved in planning for such housing. The norms applied to make such houses affordable for the identified target groups have ignored women's needs for space in the dwelling unit. It is necessary to scrutinize established standards and develop norms in housing especially for economically weaker sections, and to determine their adequacy for women. There must also be visible participation of women in the planning and execution of housing programmes in order to ensure that women's needs are adequately considered in the housing designs.

Women have had no traditional access to capital assets or to institutional finance and credit for housing. They have had to resort to borrowing from traditional credit sources at exorbitant rates of interest. Institutional sources of credit such as banks have not recognized women as credit-worthy individuals in their own right so that they may borrow through existing schemes at differential rates of interest. Various agencies have tried to play an intermediary role in creating access for women to institutional credit but their out reach has been limited. It is essential, therefore, that institutions such as HDFC and HUDCO recognize women in their individual capacities as beneficiaries for housing credit and finance.

The housing market also offers a vast potential for employment, especially in the rural areas. Expanding construction activity in housing would ensure that greater opportunities for employment are created, while also creating shelter for the rural populace.

Problems specific to women have to be highlighted in considering issues like fodder, fuel and drinking water. Since these directly concern women, their involvement in the programmes related to such issues must be given prominence. The interlinkages among fuel, fodder and drinking water with other aspects of the development of women such as education, employment, food and nutrition, health and sanitation must be recognized and integrated programmes worked out on a holistic basis for optimal utilization of personnel and financial inputs.

As had been stressed by the Seventh Plan, the government must ensure public participation and draw upon the resources of voluntary agencies, educational (especially Science and Technology) institutions, industries and financial organizations in implementing various programmes for the development of women. Various funding agencies may consider sponsoring All India or regional projects on a coordinated basis wherein, Science and Technology experts could collaborate with the NGOs and the people in designing and implementing programmes based on micro-level surveys.

Women must be specifically organized by involving the NGOs wherever necessary to participate in the implementation of social forestry programmes, water sharing projects and in the maintenance of various gadgets and devices. The necessary formal and non-formal education has to be appropriately matched with their time schedules, seasonal occupations and socio-cultural constraints.

In training programmes, in addition to NGOs, educational institutions could play an important role. Agricultural extension centres, home science colleges, and youth forums like NSS should be purposefully involved. Science and Technology institutions can take up the task of training and provide the technical back up in technology transfer as well as monitoring and evaluation.

A data bank may be set up with such resource centres, where information may be made available not only on technologies but also on manufacturing availability of training facilities, etc. These centres must have working models readily available for demonstrations, and requisite resource persons. Interaction among the centres will enable them to serve as a national network.

Research must be undertaken both in improving and developing hardware and software systems. All the necessary technologies on collection, processing, storage and utilization of fodder, fuel and drinking water may be carefully analysed and gaps identified. Many issues are regional and location specific and tackled best at the micro level. For example, carrying water is more problematic in hills than in plains and fuel problem is more acute in arid zones. The choice of fuel and fodder generating plants would depend on the agroclimate and terrains. The type of improved chulha required depends on the food and cooking practices. Perhaps an area based approach can be taken combining locations with similar type of problems into groups or clusters.

The necessary industrial support in the manufacturing of various small equipments should be created, e.g., manufacture of small water storage systems, forage harvesting system, etc. Women and small entrepreneurs should be involved in such ventures with suitable subsidies.

The decision makers both at the bureaucratic and political levels should be sensitized to the importance of programmes specifically targeted for women in the context of national development.

The socio-cultural and traditional practices must be suitably modified for conservation of various resources and more efficient utilization of time, energy and capital. For example, cooking recipes which require more fuel and time in cooking have to be pointed out and corrected. Where possible, community kitchens should be encouraged. Especially in the periphery of towns, the food prepared in neighbouring areas can be brought in packages. This would reduce the load on fuel, provide employment to women in the surrounding areas while benefiting many working women.

Many of the local hardware and software problems especially with respect to fuel and drinking water are not easily solved at the household level. The right level of scaling has to be planned, keeping in view both the economic viability and the consumer's convenience. For instance, in a biogas system, a 80m' community biogas plant is more economical than a 2m' household plant but the former calls for a more elaborate management system. Perhaps a subcommunity biogas plant of 15-20M3 for 15-20 families could be a solution. Thus for each problem, a suitable community or sub-community system has to be worked out.

Some of the above recommendations have been noted both in the 'Country Report of 1985' presented at Nairobi and "Forward Looking Strategies for the Year 2000". However, at the level of implementation, the programmes of various governmental departments tend to get superimposed. Hence it is important to identify one of the Ministeries as the 'Nodal Ministry' for coordination and keeping abreast of all programmes related to women. The Ministry of Human Resource Development could perhaps take this up so that a Master Table could be prepared of all action/projects having a bearing on women, noting the time schedules - for implementation, and the agencies involved in planning and action at the central, state, regional local levels. This "Nodal Ministry" for women may constitute sub-committee with members drawn not only from government but also from other participating agencies to discuss the various issues and evolve strategies.

Infrastructure

Creche services must be universally provided to all women, especially in the poverty sector. This would enable some of them to augment their family income and, at the same time, ensure proper care of their children. The children's health, sanitation, nutrition and early stimulation would get attention. Increasing the number of creches would also generate more employment opportunities for women. In view of the above, it is recommended that in rural areas, wherever ICDS infrastructure already exists, creches should be opened and attached to the Anganwadis. These creches should make provision for babies below 3 years age. The timings of Anganwadis which provide pre-school services for children of 3-6 years, should be adjusted according to the working hours of rural women. These creches will help in containing morbidity and mortality rates and malnutrition of infants and small children. They will also relieve the children in the school going age group from child care responsibilities, and give an opportunity to them to utilize the ICDS pre-school services.

The existing law that stipulates provision of a creche for employment of thirty or more women should be changed to thirty persons (men and women). This would ensure that employers do not use loopholes in the law to their advantage and would extend creche facilities to children of men workers whose wives, if they are not in the organized sector do not otherwise have access to such facilities.

The Government of India, being an employer of a large number of women, must provide creche facilities in or near all workplaces.

Creche service must follow an integrated approach to childcare.

Creche workers should preferably be local women to whom appropriate skill-oriented, on the job training should be imparted.

Technical institutions and home-science colleges should be utilized to train creche workers and also provide inputs for systematic monitoring and supervision of the creche programmes.

Organizations running creches should be given flexibility to adopt timings suitable to the needs of the working mothers.

Local women's groups and mothers of the children attending creches must be given training in preparation of toys, play materials out of low cost/no cost indigenous material.

Employment for women can be generated by employing local women to prepare the midday meals, etc.

Action research projects, such as, a study of the impact of day care services on the education of girls should be initiated.

The Household

Traditionally, women have had a significant role in resource management including housing management. It is important to recognize this role and provide for women's participation in development programmes, and for incorporating their needs in schemes for improvement of housing and environmental conditions in the following manner:

Identify the needs of women in relation to housing and community facilities and build them in an integrated manner into housing development programmes.

Integrate environmental factors into development planning for women including their requirements in settlement planning.

Involve women at all levels of decision making and bring about their participation in programme implementation so as to ensure that the benefits of housing, essential services, and community facilities are directed to women in general and to the poor and vulnerable among them in particular.

The special needs of women should be identified and adequately catered to while formulating minimum housing standards.

Necessary facilities in homes should be provided to lessen the burden and drudgery of women in performing productive and reproductive roles.

Priority investment in infrastructure such as water supply, sanitation, energy, transportation, working women's hostels, public distribution of basic needs, etc., should take into consideration the needs of women.

Provision of housing for working and/or single women is recommended on priority basis. In addition, women in difficult circumstances such as widows, refugees, destitutes, victims of social oppression, seasonal migrant workers, victims of natural disasters, etc., must be provided shelter as part of an integrated rehabilitation programme.

The National Housing Policy which has been formulated, must pay adequate attention to the special needs and roles of women in the implementation of housing programme.

The social and economic constraints which come in the way of women's participation should be removed and their active involvement in housing should be promoted by:

- Allotting house-sites in the joint name of wife and husband;
- Mobilizing savings of women for housing;
- Organizing self-help in undertaking house construction work;
- Imparting training so that women could become skilled labour (including masons and other skilled labour); and
- Ensuring access for women to institutional credit at low rates interest without collateral.

In India, rural women constitute nearly 80 per cent of the female population. They contribute largely to the country's economy which is mainly agriculture based. Although distributive justice has been categorically underlined in all the development plans, the needs of women have not been adequately addressed. While laying emphasis, on enhanced agriculture production in which the involvement of women is high, the plans have fostered a target group and area oriented approach to reduce regional and ecological imbalances disregarding women's equality as embodied in the Constitution. Rural development programmes for women have only in recent decades recognized the crucial role of organization and mobilization as strategies for women's empowerment and development. Rural women's organizations are also mechanisms for restructuring and redistributing power and have been utilized pressure groups that influence and/or bargain on behalf of rural women.

Conditions and Issues

The launching of the Community Development Programme in 1952 was a landmark in the history of India and ushered in an era of development with the participation of the people. The Community Development Programme adopted a systematic integrated approach to rural development with a hierarchy of village level workers and block level workers drawn from various fields to enrich rural life. Agriculture, animal husbandry, public health, women's development, rural industries, etc., found a special niche in the framework cast for this purpose. Five thousand National Extension Service Blocks were created under the Community Development Programmes by the end of the Second Five-Year Plan. During the Third Five-Year Plan the momentum was maintained through a series of developmental schemes though allocations under the NES programme tapered. This was succeeded by the Small Farmers Development Agencies followed by Marginal Farmers Development Agencies, Crash Schemes for Rural Employment, Food for Work Programme, Drought Prone Areas Programme and Desert Development Programme in the early seventies. The contents of all these programmes were to strengthen the rural base of the economy, specifically the primary sector comprising agriculture, animal husbandry, etc., and employment through labour intensive works that would create the infrastructure of roads and other community assets for the benefit of the rural people.

It was recognized that the skewed pattern of landholdings stood in the way of creating an egalitarian society and obstructed modernization and intensification of agriculture. Land reform measures for abolition of intermediary tenures, tenancy reforms, imposition of land ceiling on agricultural holdings, distribution of surplus land to the landless agricultural workers and consolidation of landholdings were introduced through a series of State Legislations under Central guidelines.

Certain areas of the country are characterized by soil-erosion, water stress and environmental degradation. The Drought Prone Areas Programme was started in 1973 aiming at an integrated area development for optimum utilization of land, water, livestock and human resources through a watershed management approach to mitigate the effects of drought. A few years later the Desert Development Programme, a wholly centrally funded scheme, specifically to cover extremely arid areas for controlling desertification and restoration of ecological balance, was also started.

The emphasis shifted to fulfilling minimum needs of the people during the Fifth Five-Year Plan.

A systematic analysis and examination of the status and role of women within the agriculture and rural development strategies in India started with the National Plan of Action (NPA) for women which followed the report of the Committee on the Status of Women in India (CSWI). Subsequently, efforts of women activists, social science institutions and researchers produced enough documentary support to persuade the Sixth Plan document to include a chapter on 'Women and Development' for the first time in the country's history of planned development.

A strategy of direct attack on poverty was adopted in the Sixth Plan as the theory of trickle down benefits of general development programmes had not proved as a successful strategy for the removal of poverty. Forty-eight per cent of the population were found to be living below the poverty line at the beginning of the Sixth Five-Year Plan.

One positive outcome of these developments has been the recognition that rural women are not a homogeneous group to justify a uniform development strategy. The development plans in the case of women must be based on the assessment of their actual role and participation in socio-economic activities.

Women's employment has been recognized as the 'critical entry point' for Women's integration in mainstream development. The low and deteriorating status of rural women is attributed to their declining economic participation and other factors like the modernization of the agricultural sector. The need for giving a better deal to the rural women is beginning to be widely recognized. It is now accepted that the participation of women themselves in the development activities is the most effective tool for the promotion of the access of women to the benefits of development. A working group set up by the Deptt. of Rural Development, Ministry of Agriculture and Rural Development in 1978 recommended that the major objectives of the development plan for rural women should be: (i) The improvement of their economic status, and (ii) The promotion of women's organization to have the collective strength to articulate their needs and promote their participation in the development process.

The Integrated Rural Development Programme initiated in 1978-79 and extended to all the development blocks in the country in 1980-81 was conceived as one of the instruments for a direct attack on poverty. It dealt with individual rural families below the poverty line. Credit from banking institutions and subsidy from the Government were given to the families for self-employment and income generation. Under IRDP, a special place was accorded for training rural unemployed youth for employment with the introduction of TRYSEM. An exclusive scheme for the social and economic uplift of women belonging to families below the poverty line, DWCRA (Development of Women and Children in Rural Areas) was launched in 1982 as a sub-component of IRDR '

The Sixth Plan accepted poor rural women to be targets of rural development strategies. The specific problems identified concerning rural poor women were:

(i) Marginality of attention and services to them in rural and agricultural development;

(ii) Special constraints that obstruct their access to available assistance and services such as, lack of training to develop their awareness and skills; lack of information and lack of bargaining power;

(iii) Low productivity and narrow occupational choices;

(iv) Low level of participation in decision making;

(v) Inadequate finance and expert guidance for promoting socio-economic activity of rural women and their participation;

(vi) Inadequate monitoring of women's participation in different sectors;

(vii) Wage discrimination;

(viii) Inadequate application of science and technology to remove drudgery; and

(ix) Low health and nutrition status.

The Sixth Plan document stated that one of the most important means of achieving improvements in the status of women would be to secure for them a fair share of employment opportunities, to earmark a percentage of allocation for women, and to fix for them a quota in all the poverty alleviation programmes. The Seventh Plan reiterated the strategies suggested in the Sixth Plan with a sharper focus on the increased coverage of women in various rural development programmes.

Simultaneously, the National Rural Employment Programme (NREP), assuring wage employment to the unemployed rural population was introduced in 1980. Subsequently, concentration on the rural landless was attempted by the introduction of the Rural Landless Employment Guarantee Programme (RLEGP) in 1983. The Indira Awas Yojana was added as an important component of the programme in the Seventh Plan for constructing houses for SC/STs and free bonded labourers. Social Forestry was added as another component of the RLEGP with national emphasis on greening fuel and fodder.

The establishment of the Technology Mission on Drinking Water and Related Water Management gave a new thrust to the Rural Water Supply Programme. Safe and adequate drinking water is to be provided to the entire rural population by the end of the Seventh Five-Year Plan.

The impact of the poverty alleviation programmes coupled with the development in various sectors reduced the rural population below the poverty line to 37 per cent by the beginning of the Seventh Plan. The target is to bring this down to 28 per cent by the end of the Seventh Plan Period.

Agriculture and allied fields provide the largest sector for women's employment. It largely determines the rural women's socio-economic status. This is the sector where women's role as unpaid labour in productive activities is most prominent and is responsible for conferring women a non-working status. In case of both agriculture and animal husbandry, development strategies have provided very little attention to women in comparison to their active involvement in both the sectors. Some training is imparted to women in agriculture and animal husbandry under the programmes for Farmer's Training and Krishi Vigyan Kendras. But the Farmers Training Programme has lost much of its importance after the introduction of the new extension system of Training and Visit (T&V). Though women constitute a major work force in agriculture which with regional variation is estimated to be around 60 per cent, they are invisible in the T&V system. Currently there is one major extension programme for women in Karnataka and 2-3 such programmes on the anvil in other states. There is an in-built resistance observed in them in viewing women within their home making role. Even the visual presentations (slides, filmstrips and films) which are used for the orientation of the functionaries, often depict the women in the field and the extension agent talking to the contact farmer on the same field, fail to project the full dimension of women's role.

While rural women have become marginally visible in the anti-poverty programmes, they have not been adequately recognized in agricultural development, land reform, or rural industrialization. Non-recognition of women in agriculture has many implications. Intensive agriculture and the green revolution have reduced women's participation in farm activities but the work load related to the home based farm activities has increased considerably. That has only reduced them from the 'working' to a 'non-working' status. Limited employment opportunities created by technology resulting in the means of production being concentrated in the hands of a few, and increased landlessness for the poor led to men replacing women in many of their traditional areas of employment. But women have had to work and survive. They are thus found to be gradually moving to the non-traditional sectors seeking employment for survival.

Following the Sixth and Seventh Plans, the Department of Rural Development issued directives to the State Governments to give priority to women headed households, enhance the share of women under the anti-poverty programme (IRDP), and the programme of Training for Self-Employment (TRYSEM). Guidelines for NREP and RLEGP envisage increasing participation of women in wage employment and creation of assets specific to the needs of women's groups. At present the share of employment generated under NREP for women is approximately 20 per cent. A special programme for women entitled DWCRA was also introduced in 1982, as a sub-component of IRDP to accelerate the process of integration of women in the rural development programmes. Up to 1987, there were 11,553 groups which were reported to have been organized in 106 districts under this scheme.

The Integrated Rural Development Programme meant for the poorest in the rural areas has been formulated for creating assets with a view to increasing the productivity and income generation abilities of the beneficiaries. Efforts have been made under this programme to select female headed households. The scheme of DWCRA could be strengthened and modified in order to ensure that the benefits reach more target groups. The National Rural Employment Programme (NREP) and Rural Landless Employment Guarantee Programme (RLEGP) would generate additional employment to women in the lean season. Under Training of Rural Youth in Self-Employment (TRYSEM), one-third of the beneficiaries were expected to be women and special attention was to be given to improve existing skills of women and imparting to them new skills under the programmes of farmers training, fodder production, post harvest technology, application of pesticide, budding and grafting, training in horticulture, fisheries, poultry, dairy and social forestry, etc. The training of women under TRYSEM exceeded the target to 44 per cent in January 1988. Out of a total of 37.23 lakh families which received benefits under the IRDP during 1986-87, the number of women headed families was 5.67 lakh which amounts to only 15.23 per cent as against the target of 30 per cent. On assessment of the programmes, it is observed that considerable efforts are required to elicit the participation of women in these activities. The training provided under TRYSEM and DWCRA is not always viable and there is a tendency to limit to a few traditional crafts, though the Department of Rural Development is laying greater stress on taking up innovative activities too. Therefore, a fresh look is needed to be given to identification of trades and activities which may gainfully be taken up by women. Many income generating programmes have not succeeded due to full thought not being given to the input availability, training and marketing of products.

Special development projects linked to certain ongoing activities need to be taken up on a project basis to improve the effectiveness of the programmes related to women. Specific projects such as sericulture for tribals in certain states like Bihar and Orissa, development of dairy units linked to Operation Flood areas, fruits and vegetables cultivation linked to marketing through Mother dairy, prawn farming and fishing in the coastal region were commended. Agro-based industry schemes, etc., are essential.

The scheme of Training of Rural Youth for Self-Employment (TRYSEM) should be revamped with a view to organizing training in trades with assured employment potential to women in rural areas, as well as for wage employment in peripheral metropolitan and urban areas. State Emporia, marketing channels of KVXIC, etc., should be tapped to ensure elimination of middlemen and better prices.

The Accelerated Rural Water Supply Programme (ARWSP) and the Minimum Needs Programme (MNP) are of special significance to rural women who are the victims of drudgery, such as fetching water from distant locations. The Technology Mission on Drinking Water and Related Water Management lays emphasis on purification of water to make it potable, training in the use of water and maintenance of water sources. Women are the target of the awareness creation programmes as well as agents for creating awareness in conservation of water and maintenance of water sources. The low cost sanitation programme is also of great importance to women, who are otherwise subjected to a lot of privation due to lack of appropriate sanitation facilities. Rural Technologies and innovation promoted by CAPART aim at relieving the drudgery to women in several areas of their households and economic activities. They include the improved varieties of stone grinder, wheel barrow, ball-bearing pulley, groundnut shelter and smokeless chulhas.

The limited performance of the programmes introduced to achieve the integration of women in the development process suggests that only policy directives do not achieve the desired objectives. Programmes do not get implemented due to the lack of comprehension of the relevance of women's contribution to national development. Although a concern for development of women is well articulated at the central policy making level, an ambivalence is observed at the implementation level. The policy directives issued by the Government of India for the increased share for women in the development programmes and the promotion of a participatory approach, do not provide for corresponding development in the infrastructure, extension, training information support and a strong monitoring system which is particularly lacking at the State level. The programmes for rural women still continue as a separate exercise within the sectoral programmes with marginal attention, resources and inadequate monitoring.

The major shortcomings noticed in the implementation of the programmes for women with development objectives are:

(i) Perpetuation of the concept that women need only welfare services;

(ii) That the developmental benefits will automatically accrue to the women as a result of economic development of the family;

(iii) Inadequate knowledge and skills for designing socioeconomic activities for women and in group organizations; and

(iv) Lack of supportive services such as credit, childcare, marketing, training and technology for reducing the drudgery.

The approaches used for integrating women in the mainstream of development have raised some methodological issues. These relate particularly to the organization of groups, involvement of the voluntary sector, and the household approach in development programmes for rural women.

The organization of women's groups is considered to be one of the most effective tools for integrating women in the development process. Yet it has raised several issues which are not fully resolved. Some of the questions which are being asked repeatedly are:

(i) Who will organize the groups (the role of intermediaries)?

(ii) What will be the size, structure and status of groups formal or informal?

(iii) Should the groups be organized first and the choice of activities to be undertaken by the groups come next?

(iv) Should women be assisted individually under the IRDP, etc. or be formed into groups.

Apart from these unresolved issues, there are problems in selecting and working out economically viable group projects. Women activists argue against giving individual projects to be carried out within the household as it would only perpetuate their subordination in the household hierarchy. They claim that assistance to the voluntary agencies, which was expected to provide grass-roots structural support in this regard, is either not forthcoming or has not been sought.

It is logical that the size of the group to be mobilized should be such as to enable close interaction amongst the members which is only possible when they come from the same background and from one cluster of villages. It is also evident that poor women acquire confidence when they get organized. The delivery system will respond positively even if they are informally grouped. But in the interest of economic viability, and to strengthen their earning capacity, it is desirable for the group to be formalized. It is however, impossible or advisable to suggest one organizational model for all situations. The experience by and large is that the organization based on personal interface and on localized issues is more effective, more flexible and functional than the highly structured and impersonal form of organization.

Some of the processes under IRDP, such as identification of beneficiaries/ productive activities, preparation of loan applications, sanction of the same and procurement of assets have not been given much attention in terms of proper planning, particularly of the linkage required after the asset is given, to make the same optimally productive. Such linkages include most critically the supply of raw materials and facilities for marketing. These processes and linkages are more effective when implemented through the group approach.

The crucial question in the field of land reforms is how rural poor women should get land and have access to land. Power structures in the villages are dominated by the relatively better off classes. Considering that implementation of land reforms measures leaves much to be desired, there is an urgent need for people's participation more specifically of the women, by promoting their groups organizations and through Panchayati Raj institutions. Each village should have a village plan which should include cultivable lands, *gochar* lands and forest lands with clearly demarcated boundaries.

The involvement of intermediaries in development programmes for rural women has been considered vital, particularly in demonstrating and promoting the participatory model and to provide support to the grass-root structure. Here too, there are basic issues which need to be carefully resolved. Among others, it is queried whether the role of the intermediary organizations has been understood by the Government, or whether it is feasible for the voluntary organizations to function in partnership with the government, given the differences in approach.

There is no uniform understanding and acceptance of the role of the voluntary agencies in the States. In some cases, there is a complete lack of rapport between the Government and voluntary agencies. In others, there is the tendency of associating the women's programmes entirely with voluntary action, showing a lack of initiative on the part of the, Government. There is little doubt that the voluntary agencies are committed to the cause of women and have expressed a real concern for the enhancement of women's status. They have also demonstrated skills for mobilizing women, and in trying innovative projects. In view of this, the association of the voluntary agencies with the programmes is bound to enrich the programmes as well as the delivery mechanisms. Yet, they cannot be a substitute for Governmental action. To end women's isolation from rural development, the Government must work in partnership with voluntary agencies.

Currently debated issues in the context of women in rural development and in the anti-poverty programmes, is the household versus group approach; some argue in favour of ensuring a share of developmental resources and benefits to women in all sectoral programmes, while others argue in favour of having separate investments for women.

In India, the family is hierarchical, traditional and the status in the family is determined by sex and age. In the patriarchal society, it is the man who holds the position of the head of the family and the bread-winner. Therefore, it is the man who gets attention in the investment of developmental resources, training, extension and other supports. Women's contribution to the family's earnings goes unrecognized. This bias, in fact, is responsible for the earlier programmes not taking note of women headed households whose number is currently estimated at 30-35 per cent of all rural households. With mounting pressure on the government to give priority to this group, it has been convincingly argued that an improvement in the income of the household does not necessarily mean development for women. The household approach instead of creating equitable conditions, perpetuates the subordination of women and limits their opportunities for self-growth and self-expansion.

Having a special component within sectoral plans can stimulate action for women provided the components are monitored separately. The introduction of the scheme of DWCRA within the programme of IRDP was aimed at stimulating the response of the State Governments to integrating women into anti-poverty programmes. Therefore, in case of women, it can be contended that a combined approach is desirable. This would allow women to be adopted as a target in all sectoral programmes, with earmarked resources along with special component plans aimed exclusively at women. Such dual approaches can be continued until women acquire sufficient power to articulate their needs and demands, and until such time as women's concerns get to be internalized in the planning and administrative structures.

Share in Family Property

In the economic sphere and in particular in the rural sector, the empowerment of women relates mainly to their access to means of production and control over the fruits of their labour. The access to the means of production implies ownership of land, other productive assets, access to capital and access to technology and acquisition of various skills required to make labour power more productive.

The aspect of ownership of land relates to rights of inheritance which are governed by personal laws of different communities. These personal laws at present are discriminatory against women and have a bias in favour of the male heirs. The State Governments of Kerala and Andhra Pradesh have sought to remove some of these discriminations with a view to give daughters in the family, coparcenary ownership in the family property on the same level as the sons. But even these changes do not go far enough and still discriminate against a married daughter and a widow and do not apply equally to the separate properties of the father in the Hindu Customary Law. There is discrimination against women of different types in the personal laws of other communities also. In the customary law of certain tribes, only male agnates in the male line are recognized as valid heirs and an unmarried daughter is only entitled to usufructuary maintenance. It would be necessary to introduce correctives to overcome the discrimination, in order that the gap between the State's proclamation to achieve equality of the sexes and its laws which deny it, is bridged. Women's undiluted access to land, the most productive resource, would undoubtedly bestow on her necessary economic independence and power and would improve her social position in the family as well.

Regarding access of women to land, the land records do not incorporate the rights of women in the landed property shown in the name of the husband or the father. Only where a woman is a widow and happens to be the 'karta' of the family, her name may figure in the record of rights as the owner of property.

Co-ownership of property by women, should not merely be confined to land but also to other productive assets like house, family wealth, shops, factory or any other income generating establishment or asset. This would provide sufficient conditions for women to participate in and influence the decision concerning the use and disposal of such properties..

As regards access to capital, there is a general reluctance on the part of the public financial institutions to extend credit to women independently of the male head or guardian of the family.

The existing land ownership pattern in India is largely male oriented except in some areas of the North-east and a few other places where matrilineal system is in operation and inheritance of property passes through the institution of the mother. The land records, to the extent they reflect the ownership and other interests in land, only record the names of men. Similarly, where shareholders of such lands are recorded, it is usually the male shareholder who finds mention in the land records. The processes of preparation of land records, i.e., the survey and recording of rights also deal with such male holders of interests in land. The only exception would be in such cases where a widow with no other male person, manages the land. Her name is recorded as the owner and manager of land. Land reform measures have also not taken into cognizance interests of women as co-owners or cultivators of land, and to this extent land reform measures seem to have bypassed the women. The most prominent example where this inherent discrimination in land reforms has been noticed is the case of ceiling laws where most State laws have provided for a separate unit of ceiling for major sons in the family but not major daughters married or unmarried. Although from the point of view of implementation of such ceiling laws, addition of yet another unit in the name of major daughters would have further defeated its objectives, nonetheless, the discrimination cannot be denied. Further, in the matter of distribution and allotment of various lands, it is usually the male head of the family who gets the 'patta' in his name. Recently, of course instructions have been issued to give joint 'patta' on the name of both husband and wife while allotting land and house-sites. Similarly, in the matter of collection of minor forest produce and enjoyment of rights over common property resources, the rights of women are not focused, even though it is the women, who have to collect fuel-wood and fodder and minor forest produce from such lands.

Tribal social structures are more egalitarian and open and less stratified than social structures of larger and more advanced communities in India. The status and position enjoyed by tribal women in society is, therefore, in certain tribes, much better than their counterparts in other communities. This is on account of many reasons. Tribal society has a tradition of both men and women working on an equal footing whether in agriculture or in other vocations. Thus tribal women have access to income and are therefore, economically independent. There are also no restrictions on women going out for work independent of men, and not necessarily along with them. Usually tribal women go out for work in large groups. In social matters and family life also tribal women are far more emancipated. They have a much greater say in the decision making in family and community matters and are not subjected to the same degree of social control by male members of the family as women in other communities are.

Despite this, in matters of inheritance of father's/husband's property and in access to land, there is a certain built-in discrimination against women in some tribal communities. The customary law of some tribal communities excludes women from inheritance rights, such inheritance rights being restricted to "male heirs in the male line". These customs are even enshrined in tenancy laws wherever enacted and applicable to these communities. This discrimination against women has a harmful effect on their lives, rendering them economically and socially powerless and driving large numbers of them into destitution. Infact, in certain tribal communities, for example, the Ho Tribe in Singhbhum district of Bihar, a large number of women remain unmarried so as to ensure to themselves usufructuary rights available to them as unmarried daughters. Many of them are harassed by their husband's and father's male agnates who wish to deprive them even of this usufructuary right. A number of women are forced to migrate in order to earn their livelihood, since their hold over the family land is so insecure and dependent on the attitude of their male relatives even though these women do the bulk of agricultural work. Sometimes, the women are declared witches, the concealed motive being to drive them out of the village or even to kill them in order to usurp the family property.

The married women also enjoy limited usufructuary rights in the deceased husband's property. Even these usufructuary rights cannot be freely exercised by them since the husband's male agnates often harass them and try to get rid of them in the hope of asserting their inheritance claims to the land. If the married woman has a son, he inherits the land from his father, and she has no legal claim to it. If the husband has one or two or more wives, the sons of other wives have inheritance rights to the land, and she is dependent on them for maintenance. In case, the marriage breaks up, or a man remarries or deserts his first wife, the woman is absolutely without land rights, since she has, by marriage, lost the usufructuary rights in her father's house, and she is also deprived of rights in her matrimonial home. Since tribal communities have their customary laws, the Hindu Succession Act, the Indian Succession Act, or any other succession Act do not apply to them.

The discrimination against women in the customary law of tribal communities, historically speaking, may have evolved with a view to preserve the integrity of the tribe and to prevent land passing from the tribal to persons outside the tribe which would have the effect of disintegrating the tribal society. While, it is necessary to preserve the integrity of the tribe and to protect the interest of the tribals in land against any encroachment by non-tribals, it is also necessary to protect the interest of tribal women in land by giving them rights to inheritance in father's and husband's property. But safeguards will have to be provided in the event of marriages outside the tribe.

Therefore, provision in law and customary practices which discriminate against women in matters of inheritance of property and restrict such inheritance to male agnates in male line should be changed, while at the same time preserving alienation of tribal land to non-tribals.

Women, especially tribals, migrate in search of work. They are employed in large numbers in the unorganized sector like brick-kiln, road construction, irrigation works, agricultural operations, forestry operations, stonecutting, domestic labour, etc. They are subjected to brutal exploitation at places of work by contractors and the middlemen, who recruit them. The exploitation is not merely confined to payment of low wages, long hours of arduous work and other dismal working conditions. They are also subjected to sexual exploitation. It is necessary, that for each category of employment in the unorganized sector, specific institutional mechanism be built-in to protect women's interests.

3

Family Setup

The Indian woman's life revolves around her dual roles of wife and mother. She lives to serve her husband and to give birth to his children. Her upbringing activities and aspirations are all tied to these two roles. Therefore, the marriage is her major goal and purpose in her life. Since she desires children, sex is necessary, but her own enjoyment is secondary to that of her husband. She may enjoy sex but any overt expression of this enjoyment is unacceptable. She is faithful to her husband and serves him with her body, mind and spirit. Pre-marital, extramarital and sex after widowhood are despised and disapproved by the society.

Self-denial and Sacrifice

Love to the Indian woman means self-denial and sacrifice for her husband and children. She seldom reflects on her own needs or interests. She merges herself so completely in her dual roles as extensions of her husband and children that she exists as a body without a soul, without a "being" aspect. The Indian culture has propagated this unselfish ideal. However, the points worth pondering over are: Do women really enjoy self-denial? Does the Indian culture really desire that women should be simply the mothers with no individuality of their own? Are women only suited for these two roles of wife and mother? A "yes" response to all these questions may come because of centuries of socialisation, which has controlled the fabric of women's lives. But in case we take the outlook of the modern women into consideration the answer to all these questions would be a clear-cut "no".

Marriage among Hindus is a sacrament and is expected to last whole of the lifetime of the couple. Most of the women belonging to the middle and upper classes live up to this ideal. Among the lower classes where marriage traditionally has not been considered so tie-binding mores are changing. A tendency towards more permanency in marriage is being observed. Generally lower class women are more liberated concerning marriage and divorce customs even though they are often victims of act of sadism committed by their husbands and other males.

Matrilineal and Patrilineal Descents

Although the two descent systems in India, i.e., matrilineal and patrilineal, differ in some respects, men have recognised authority over women in both the systems. In the matrilineal system, the power rests with the men in wife's family. Men have authority but the lineage is counted through women. A husband does not become a member of his wife's family and his rights over his wife and children are minimal. The wife's brothers, father or uncle's control property. Even though the women enjoy more rights and privileges than in the patrilineal system men still make the major decisions regarding her life. The current changes in society are affecting the matrilineal system because men who move from their homes to other parts of the country take their wives and children with them and they, therefore, exercise more power over them. New legislation on marriage, inheritance and dowries is also making this system as redundant.

The majority of the Indian population is patrilineal in its mode of descent. The male is the perpetuator of the lineage and family name. The daughter in this system is ordained to belong to her husband's family rather than the one in which she was born. In either her own or her husband's family, she is subordinate and gains recognition only through her father or husband. Marriage is a religious rite, and the girl's father has a duty to find a husband for her. Among Hindus, marriage is performed by the Vedic rites. In other religious groups, it is conducted according to the marriage rites of those religions. Marriages are also performed by civil code. In civil marriages, very small amount of money is spent and the ceremony is very simple. In religious ceremonies, money is lavishly spent and the festivities last for a whole day or for a number of days.

Symbol of Union

In Hindu marriages, the symbol of union is seven steps taken by the couple around the sacrificial fire in the presence of the priest who at the same time chants the sacred verses. The Hindus have classified marriage into eight types. Each kind is different from the others on the basis of the ceremonies performed. Only four of the eight are approved, and one, the Brahma, is most widely accepted by the upper classes. Most of the high caste Hindus offer dowries to their daughters' husbands at the time of marriage. Many Muslims and Christians of India have adopted this custom but it is not universally acceptable and is considered as an evil by majority of them. The dowry may be labelled as a form of bridegroom purchase.

Dowry System

Whatever might have been the origin of the dowry system in India, it has now become a social evil. The Dowry Act of 1961 failed to introduce any worthwhile measures for the abolition of this evil. Various State Governments have enacted stricter legislation for penalising those that give or receive dowries. The Indian Penal Code makes this practice a penal offence. The social reformers try their best to discourage parents of the girls to offer any dowry. The mass media also makes efforts to shape public opinion against this evil custom. In spite of all these efforts the dowry system has taken so firm roots in the social milieu that it is still a widely prevalent practice.

One of the reasons for the prevalence of the dowry system is the greed of the parents of the bridegroom. They know that the girl's parents are keen to marry her at the earliest and so they demand their price. A spinster in the Indian society is looked down upon. The parents of every girl want that their daughter may get a suitable husband as soon as she is of marriageable age. When the girl is of marriageable age and they select an eligible mate for her they try to fulfil the monetary and other demands of the boy's parents. In choosing the husband for their daughter the parents confine their search to their own caste and religious groups. Mostly their choice of a suitable match for their daughter is confined to a very small segment of their community. Since the choice is limited and the number of eligible bachelors for their daughters is quite limited, there is usually a competition among the parents of the girls in roping the boy into matrimony with their daughters. The dowry is the bait, which the parents throw. Because of such conditions existing in the marriage market the abolition of the dowry system has become extremely difficult. The only remedy lies in educating our girls so that they achieve economic independence and assert their free will. They should no more remain a liability for their parents.

Desire for a Male Child

The desire for a male child is very deep-rooted in the psyche of Indian people. Pinkharn quotes an ancient text in the following words: "Vouchsafe blessings upon the wombs that bring male children forth". The Hindu religious literature also stresses this aspect. The literature emphasises that the couple should be in the proper frame of mind for sexual union in order to produce male offspring. Certain ceremonies are prescribed for the couple before the sexual intercourse. The couple is to dispel all lascivious thoughts and animal desires. The husband and wife both are asked to consciously and deliberately will that progeny shall be spiritual and preferably male. Sex is not considered to be an enjoyable passionate experience. Sexual act is to be performed only for the purpose of propagation. Since the parents in India live with the son, preferential treatment to the son is a normal practice. The economic factor is the main motivation for the aspiration to bear sons. This factor is interwoven with the religious faith that the male and female both believe that for them there is no salvation unless they produce sons in legitimate wedlock.

In spite of the religious down-playing of sex for enjoyment, various erotic texts like the Kama Sutra of Vatsyana or Pandit Koka's Rangmala and paintings and sculptures on temple walls express sexual interest and enjoyment for its own sake rather than for producing offspring. But this open display of sexual act on the walls of the temples, etc. does not mean that sexual act was an open affair in India at any time of her history. Sexual intercourse has always been a very private affair in India. Recently, however, some studies have indicated that Indian women are expressing an interest in sensitive sex. Promilla Kapur found in her study of the "working women" that sexual maladjustment, irrespective of whether it was the cause or effect of sexual dissatisfaction, was found to be present in nearly ninety-five per cent of the cases of marital maladjusted working women. Many of these women described their husbands as rude, sexually impotent or very direct or brutal in their sexual act. In some cases women reported being turned off sexually when the husband spoke obscenities during sex. Marital adjusted women made no mention of vulgar language. It seems that women do not like being coarsely handled and wanted their husband to treat them with consideration during sexual act.

The practice of child marriages also inhibits the women's sexual responses. In spite of laws against such marriages, they still are prevalent particularly in Rajasthan, Haryana and some other backward states. The origin of child marriages is traced to a myth woven around a Vedic mantra. According to this mantra, the husband says to his bride:

"First, Soma had thee, Gandharva had the next; Agni became thy third lord; the fourth (lord) is 1, born of man. Soma gave thee to the Gandharva; the Gandharva gave thee to Agni; then thee to me has Agni given with the capacity to bring forth wealth and progeny".

This led to the belief that it would be the best to marry a girl before Soma and the other gods have enjoyed her. Recent legislation along with better enforcement has reduced the molestation of the adolescent girls and the number of child marriages. Hate's survey published in 1969 had reported that nearly one-fifth of the girls in the age group from ten to fourteen were married. Many of these girls were from rural areas. Since the rural areas are still tradition-bound the situation regarding child marriages might have only marginally changed for the better. According to the survey the average age of marriage in the urban areas was twenty-three. Hate felt that the considerations of caste, status and dowry were the obstacles, which were being overcome as the marriage age was rising.

Since the parents arrange most marriages the mutual physical attraction which is an important aspect of sexual enjoyment does not form the criterion for making the choice of the life partner. Arranged marriages have many features, which highlight the unequal status of women with men. A very common practice is that the girl is presented before the boy with whom there is a proposal of her marriage. She is shown as a commodity, which is being sold in the market. The psychological impact on the girl of such a practice is usually very bad especially when the boy or his parents reject her. Some girls who are rejected again and again suffer severe mental tensions so much so that they either commit suicide or reach up to the stage of taking such an extreme step.

The marriage contracts of the Muslims give unequal rights to the men and women. It permits unilateral right of divorce and polygamy to the husband. The bride's consent to marriage is a mere formality. The institution of marriage places her in a subordinate position. Muslim women get some security against the possibility of divorce by Mehar (dower), but very few women are able to assert this claim. While Islam recognises women's right to inherit property, in practice this right is rarely upheld. The Muslim man can divorce his wife at any time with only an obligation to pay the dower, a sum fixed at the time of marriage. The Muslim woman is, however, free to remarry as soon as her period of Iddat is over. This period of Iddat is prescribed to avoid confusion over parentage in case of pregnancy.

In Hate's study, Muslim maidens were asked if they would put down any conditions for marriage. All replied that they had no say at all in the choice of mate or marriage arrangements which were all taken care of by the elders. When Margaret Cormack questioned Indian informants who were female graduate students at Columbia University, she was told that they were surprised that the Western marriage vows use the word "Obey". They disapprove the legal enforcement of obedience. This might be due to their exposure to the freedom enjoyed by the women in the United States at that time and to the movements for women liberation at the time of the study conducted by Cormack. Abolishing of such a vow would be unthinkable in a Hindu marriage ceremony. Obedience to husbands is part of the socialisation process in India and needs no legal reinforcement.

In the opinion of Jamila Brij Bhushan: "Muslim women can have a position of economic and personal independence that could be the envy of women in all but the most liberal countries." She believes that the Muslim women do not exercise their rights in India. She opines that "Call it masochism, call it the culture or whatever you like but the fact remains that the majority of them will not reach out to grasp something that is theirs by right and can, under no circumstances be denied to them". No doubt the Muslim women in India are as weak-willed as other women belonging to other religious groups. They are just as dependent upon their men for guidance and support as others. Modesty, decorum and chastity are the virtues that are inculcated in them since early childhood. Muslim law has at least endeavoured to provide economic security to women for whole of their lives but the women largely ignore these provisions. In those cases where the women take initiative to assert their rights the male ego comes forward to interpret the law in such a manner that the women are further humiliated. Jamila observes that "no respectable woman would dream of claiming her dower money".

Muslim law considers marriage as a contract but in modern Muslim life, especially among the higher echelon of society, it is considered as sacrosanct for women. This may be due to the cultural configuration as well as the Muslim male's urge to dominate and usurp many rights of the women so that they remain dependent and ignorant. The main reason for placing men in authority over women, however, is the frequently cited verse in the holy Quran:

> "Men are the managers of the affairs of women.
> For that God has preferred in bounty
> One of them over another, and for that
> They have expanded of their property
> Righteous women are therefore obedient...

Gail Minaulet writes:

> "In the matter of court witness, where two women's testimony equal to that of one man, Mumtaz Ali points out that the verse in Quran refers specifically to business matters, in which women may have less experience. But their lack of experience is a product of social conditions, not an inherent defect."

Among Christians, the biblical image of woman as temptress and seductress has strengthened the husband's right to control his wife and her property. Even though the taboos on women's freedom are less evident among Christians, women are considered subordinate to men. Among Christians incest, adultery, bigamy with adultery, rape, sodomy, bestiality, or the husband's apostasy from Christianity coupled with marriage to another woman all give the wife the grounds for divorce. But according to this religion, "woman is the unclean one, the seducer, who brought sin into the world and caused the fall of man. Consequently all apostles and fathers of Church have regarded marriage as an inevitable evil, just as prostitution is regarded today". Peter tells women emphatically: "Be obedient unto your husbands". Paul also raises his influential voice against the higher education and culture of women, when he says:

> "Let the woman learn in silence with all subjection, but I suffer not a woman to teach, nor to usurp authority over the man, but to bear in silence".

Augest Bebel emphasises.

> "At the creation woman is commanded to be subject unto man. The ten commandments of the Old Testament are as a matter of fact addressed only to man, for the tenth commandment names woman along with the servant and the domestic animals. In truth, woman was a piece of property, which man obtained for a price for a corresponding service on his part".

Raman Lal Mehta wrote in 1933 that the failure of marriages in Hindu society was a comment on the sacred concept of these marriages. The woman was forced to submit to her husband's every whim and to calmly endure crude habits without any recourse to dissolve the union. He believed that in itself was enough to call for an immediate change, in the Hindu system and marriage concept.

The Marriage Act of 1955 introduced a number of reforms in Hindu women's legal rights. It disallows bigamy, which is punishable as a crime. Relief by way of judicial separation, declaration of nullity of marriage and divorce are permissible under this Act. It permits women divorce on the grounds of adultery, change in religion, insanity, leprosy or venereal disease, renouncement of the world to become ascetic and desertion for seven years. Divorce is also allowed if their husbands are guilty of rape, sodomy, or bestiality. Desertion and cruelty are grounds for legal separation and eventual divorce if continued over a long period of time.

The Special Marriage Act of 1954 gave sanction to people of different faith to marry each other. Any male over twenty-one years and any female over eighteen years can marry under the provisions of this Act. This form of marriage can also be, dissolved by divorce.

Another Act which has helped provide equality is the Hindu Succession Act of 1956. Previously a Hindu woman could not own any other property except her streedharan or those valuables offered to her at the time of her marriage. According to this Act the widow and mother are now entitled to inherit the property of the deceased husband or son. Hindu women now have the right to hold, sell, mortgage or donate property if they so wish.

Two other Acts have also greatly helped the women. The Hindu Adoption and Maintenance Act of 1956 allow a son or daughter for adoption by the husband with the consent of the wife. Previously, there was no provision for adoption of the daughter. A wife is also allowed to claim maintenance even if she is living separately from her husband, provided he is proved to be a guilty party. The Medical Termination of Pregnancy Act of 1971 aimed to reduce the incidence of criminal abortions. This Act allows termination of pregnancy on therapeutic grounds, eugenic grounds, humanitarian grounds or social grounds.

These and some other recent legislations have been enacted in an attempt to allow women to attain higher status and equality of rights with men. Many other measures have also been taken to give women a place of dignity in the society. They are in the process of being given 30 per cent reservations in the Parliament and State Assemblies and also in the Government jobs. But unfortunately these laws and measures have little meaning to the majority of Indian women. The main reasons for this state of affairs are two overlapping factors. The majority of women, belonging to the poorer and backward sections of the society are illiterate and ignorant, and secondly, the myths woven around their obligations for serving their male relations are much more powerful than any law or reformists' words.

In our country widows outnumber widowers about four to one who have not remarried. This indicates that deterrents to remarriage of widows are still highly activated in spite of the Hindu Widows Remarriage Act, 1956 that legalised the remarriage of Hindu widows. One major reason for this state of affairs seems to be the absence of a mass movement by the women to achieve their legal and human rights. The high-class society women mostly dominate the women organisations, which are working in the direction of empowerment of the women. Their efforts are confined to the educated women only. Their impact on the rural or slum area women is almost negligible so also on the orthodox and traditionally-oriented women. The male members also look their efforts with suspicion. It may be this factor that the reservation bill in our Parliament is finding much opposition from a section of the parliamentarians who are asking for the reservations within 30 per cent for the women of the minority communities and backward classes.

Why have the majority of the Indian women not revolted against the tyranny of centuries of subordination? Pondering over this question gives an interesting insight into the psyche of the Indian women. In the next chapter, the Indian woman's motivations and aspirations are being discussed in an attempt to find out an answer to this question. The educated women are also not very clear about their roles in the households. They wish to assert their independence but do not have much courage to do so because they are afraid of the social sanctions. They typify a real predicament. They desire to be more liberal but when the problem of training of their own daughters comes up they become quite conservative. They wish to inculcate such values in their daughters as self-sacrifice, self-effacement, modesty and reserve and when daughters do not accept these values they are very much agitated. These women know that the old values are difficult to inculcate but they are also not prepared to accept the new values that are based on the modern western values of complete liberalisation.

This dilemma is universal in India today. The parents are in confusion. They continue to idealise Indian traditions that they know cannot continue to exist. The younger generation drifts because of this indecision on the part of their parents. The task of education then becomes to steer a clear path out of the confusion between the old and new. The present generation can neither ignore the Indian ideals nor can remain completely insulated from the modern outlook which emphasises the women's complete freedom of will, and action. What is best for the Indian girls must be propagated by the Indian educational system. The educationists must try to evolve out from the good ideals prevalent in India for centuries the modern outlook. 'Ibis' means that the Indian girls should have freedom of will but do not turn away from their domestic duties. They must learn to understand that absolute freedom is neither feasible nor desirable but a life of subordination and denial of will is also not to be tolerated.

A Different Order

Modes of descent, types of family organisation, and the nature of the institution of marriage provide the major contours of the socio-cultural setting in which women are born, brought up and live their lives. These features of social organisation are related to the economy in such a way that while their roots often appear to lie in the economic system, even large-scale changes in the latter are not able to carry along with them parallel changes in these areas. The lag between the two is a matter of serious concern. These institutions in the Indian society, have implications for the status of women.

From Mother's Side

India has only a limited number of matrilineal communities which are concentrated in the south-western and the north-eastern regions of the country. Kerala has been the stronghold of matrilineal culture. The Nayars and Aiyars; of North Kerala, and several temple servant castes, occupational castes, and some forest tribes have followed this mode of descent which governs group placement, property rights and successions of authority. Matriliny is found in parts of Karnataka and Tamil Nadu also. The legal systems of these communities have undergone drastic changes since the close of the last century. Muslims following matriliny are Moplahs of northern parts of Kerala and the inhabitants of the Union Territory of Lakshadweep. The. latter are classified as Scheduled Tribes. They have all along Rowed their customary laws for inheritance of matrilineal property and present an example of a rare kind of organisation which is characterized by absence of the institutionalization of the unit of husband, wife and children as an independent entity or as one embedded in larger entity, and which has struck a remarkable compromise with Islam. Of all the matrilineal systems in India, the one found in Lakshadweep islands is so far the least affected by the processes of change.

In the north-east, the matrilineal pattern is represented mainly by the Garo, the Khasi, and the Pnar in the States of Meghalaya and Assam. At least 44% of the Khasi and 30% of the Garo population is Christian, but adoption of a new religion has not drastically affected their patterns of kinship and marriage.

Since the last few decades of the nineteenth century the matrilineal cultures in both the corners of the sub-continent have been exposed to processes of change brought about by introduction of market economy, opportunities for education and mobility, diversification of occupational structure, and changes in the legal framework. They have introduced differences in pattern, of marital residence and composition of operative units, bases of economy, constituents of property, rules of inheritance, and authority structure.

Thus, the Nayars have functioned as an integral part of the larger caste system of Kerala and have mostly been landlords or non-cultivating tenants in the feudal system. The main occupation of men was military service while the women were bound to home and hearth. Cultivation was supervised by the elder among the males. Through hypergamous marriage, women were perhaps helpful in establishing favourable political connections for their own kin-groups. The traditional residential unit was groups of matrilineal kin in which the husbands were outsiders. Whereas among the Nayars and Tiyyars of North Kerala, the woman customarily went to live with the husband, and through her also her children, retained her right in the natal property.

The Moplahs have been principally traders and have tended to accommodate the sons-in-law as resident members. The Khasis and the Garos have flourished in a hoe culture in which actual use of land and not absolute ownership has relevance. In the traditional land tenure system clans or matrilineages have commanded certain territories to be taken under cultivation by their members. Marital residence is predominantly uxorilocal in which the husband comes to live with the wife's people or in the wife's land.

Such differences notwithstanding, it is possible to view these matrilineal systems in relation to the status that they accord to their women. This is only to bring into relief the institutions and groupings based on patrilineal descent ideology which tends to view women in a different way. There is also another valid reason for their consideration. It is the opinion of many scholars that matriliny was widespread in India in pre-Aryan days, on which the Aryan patriarchal culture was superimposed. The ambivalence in attitudes to women, a manifestation of which may be seen in the low status of women in the same community which also worship the goddess mother in various forms as a benevolent matriarch, a destroyer of demons, as an indignant goddess demanding attention and respect, is attributed to the matrilineal base of Indian culture.

In a matrilineal system the genetic line is continued through women, but power does not usually vest in women. For this reason we should not confuse matrilineal systems with matriarchal systems. In the matrilineal systems political power, including social control and decision making in matters of land and other property, vests in men; in matriarchy this power should vest in women. Matriliny has been associated with such economic systems in which women are not really dependent on men and can manage most of the business of living themselves. Men render some help; they engage in hunting, fishing, trading and warfare. Simple agriculture, without the use of the plough, is suited to matriliny. The Garos have taken to plough cultivation only in the past few decades. The matrilineal communities in the south-west – the land-owning Nayars in particular are an exception, for their women do not engage in any productive work but they still enjoy full property rights and serve as links for inheritance and succession.

In matrilineal systems the woman is the perpetuator of the line. Children owe to the mother their social placement and it is through the mother that they acquire their right in movable as well as immovable property, and men succeed to positions of authority. It may, however, be noted that the status of a woman does not depend on her proved fertility. As fertility is not subservient to the continuity of a male line, she does not have to prove her worth by giving birth to children or by producing children of one particular sex. She is a full member of her matrilineal group and cannot be alienated from the natal group on marriage. Among the Khasis the youngest daughter gets the major share of the ancestral property; for she is responsible for the rituals of the house, death rites, propitiation of ancestors, and care of the aged parents. The Garo parents select one of the daughters to be the heiress. The Nayar girls are co-sharers of property with the male members.

Among these groups there is no premium on the birth of a male child. In fact among the Garos the birth of a daughter is more welcome for among them there prevails a feeling that a son brought up only to work in the fields of his in-laws and not of his parents.

Where there is a greater concern with the maintenance of group boundaries and the retention of the status of the group, we find greater constraints on women because of her biological function of child bearing. For example, the Nayars living in the complex caste society would not allow their women to contract unions with men of groups lower than their own. Proper paternity used to be ensured by men of the lineage by having a control over the marital unions of the women and by the requirement of the payment of delivery expenses by the father of the newborn. In contrast, in this respect there appears to be much less rigidity among the Khasis. The children of informal unions with outsiders do not have a problem of group placement. The Garo women operate under greater restrictions as compared to the Khasis. This is because among the Garos the household-based on the bond between husband and wife is the unit through which relationship between two lineages continued over generations and the husband has full managerial powers over the property of the wife. Among the Khasis and the Nayars, however, the maternal uncle or elder brother is the manager of ancestral property.

The degree of freedom of movement and operations is also directly related to the contribution of women to the economy. The Khasis, the Garos, and the Lakshadweep islanders stand in a better position compared to the Nayars. However, in all these communities division of labour between the sexes emphasizes differential rights and expectation. A Khasi proverb says, "war and politics are for men, while property and children are for women". Modesty is a female virtue. Muscular strength of men is recognized. As noted earlier, political organisation is in the hands of men. Rulers, chiefs, and elders are all men. Managers of property too are men-either matrilineal kin or in some cases, husbands. Only for some matrilineages in Kerala and Karnataka women were entitled to headship. In the pattern of family living of the Garos and the Khasis, each generation sees the establishment of separate households of non-heiresses in which the women can hold considerable initiative and authority.

Women in matrilineal systems seem to fare better as members of kin groups and in dyadic (interpersonal) relationships. Husband's position vis-a-vis the wife is considerably different from that prevailing in the patrilineal systems. He is not her supporter, nor does she gain her status through him. She can, therefore, hold her own in this intimate relationship. She does not lose her children on divorce. The mother commands genuine respect from the son. Among the Nayars, the mother's curse is believed to be very powerful. Between brothers and sisters, age is important for guiding their behaviour, but there is a feeling of awe and sacredness about the sister. The mother's brother is an authority figure, but on the whole, woman is fairly secure in her natal home. Her rights give her a certain dignity; her consent is necessary for property transactions. She cannot, therefore, be ignored.

A comparative status evaluation of women in matrilineal communities with the help of indicators like economic power, religious responsibilities, degree of constraint at home and outside, and decisiveness and value of female roles shows that where a woman has an active role in the economy and besides subsistence, production also participates in handicrafts and marketing outside, and she enjoys better status and greater influence.

Matriliny is not a mirror image of patriliny. There is a certain inherent conflict in this system that authority is in male hands while group placement is in female hands. A husband is not incorporated in the wife's group; he is still needed in his mother's group for positions of authority and for taking decisions about the lineage land and other property. He is insecure because of minimum rights over his wife, hardly any rights over his children, and only right of use in the ancestral property. There is much suppression of fatherly inclination in a matrilineal system. It is based on the principle of the unity of matrikin and their collective control which cannot be sustained under the processes of change. With opportunities for education, new avenues of livelihood, and geographical mobility, a man can gain some control over his wife and children but this certainly disrupts the matrilineal system as such.

The disintegration of Nayar Taravads has come about because of political and economic changes and passing of new laws, which changed the implications of marriage and conferred on individual members the right of demanding their shares. The

Taravad still continues in its name, which is used by its members for identification and in rituals. Within smaller kinship and domestic units, the matrilineal ideology still persists. The Nayar woman was home-bound and did not contribute to the economy, but as a property holder and as a perpetuator of the line, she has enjoyed respect. The study of Taravads over generations tells us that Nayar girls used to receive education at home at the hands of a teacher. They are now taking advantage of educational opportunities offered to them. Old values and norms and their share in property help them to enjoy some status even in the new kind of family husband, wife, and children which is becoming common because of diversifications of occupations and spatial mobility. However, to the detriment of women's status, the Nayars have also moved towards Sanskritic rituals like those associated with marriage and are already settling marriages with the help of dowry.

From Father's Side

The overwhelming majority of the Indian population follows the patrilineal systems of descent. Though the influence of this system on institutions of family, marriage, or the place and role of women vary between religions, regions, castes and socio-economical levels, there are some common underlying principles and patterns.

Patriliny is used for the formation and continuation of discrete kin groups, for example, clans which are often based on putative kinship and lineages of different orders. These have an important role to play in occupation of territories, use of ownership of land and other economic resources, and political and religious organisation of a community. Innumerable tribal groups of India and caste groups like the Jat and the Rajput may be mentioned here. Even where there are no corporate kin groups with a depth of a number of generations, recognition of patriliny variously known as 'Vansha', 'Kula', 'Khandan' is most common. Patriliny is emphasized with the help of a common name, a common place of origin, ancestor worship, common deity and rituals, pollution observed on death of patrikin, and such other means. Family in India is embedded in this patrilineal setting for patriliny is used as the framework for family grouping, big or small.

This has direct relevance to the place of woman in society. A boy is the perpetuator of the patriline; he will continue the family name. By contrast, a girl is of no use in this respect. Her contribution in this sphere will have to be made in some other house. "A bird of passage," "another's property", "a guest in parents' house", "a thing to be preserved for an outsider", or "a thing which has to be given away" are some of the common descriptions of a daughter. Such notions may be overtly expressed or covertly held. In the urban areas even those parents who do not think in this manner are made aware of it on various occasions. Educated girls revolt against this notion, but most of them have to remain reconciled to it.

This transferability of the girl from the parents' house to the husband's house is a poignant reality of Indian society. Bidai, Rukshati, and Doli signify a sorrowful goodbye to the daughter after her marriage. We would like to emphasize that this cannot be dismissed as a mere stereotype for it seriously affects the daughter's jural rights and her socialization and training. There was no tradition of daughters having a right of inheritance from the father except among the Muslims. There is ample evidence to show that among the Muslims, daughter's rights have often been ignored. This is true to tribal India also. An Angami Naga may give his daughter fields to use during her life-time after which they have to be returned to the patrilineal kin. A Mizo daughter gets her mother's weaving apparatus. Such examples can be multiplied but they only indicate inferior rights of daughters. Besides her right of maintenance as an unmarried girl and the right of being married off in an appropriate manner, a daughter basically has only a moral right to be invited to the natal house periodically and to receive gifts. By way of residual, contingent rights in her parental house she is customarily entitled to return there and seek support in the event of desertion, divorce and widowhood.

But essentially this also is only a moral right, which is being eroded through the process of socio-economic change. Many widowed and deserted women whom we met during our tours told us that they could expect support and shelter from their family only as long as their father was alive.

The custom of retaining a daughter in the house by a son-less father by having a resident son-in-law, who should look after the property and would provide male progeny to be the rightful heirs of the maternal grandfather, does not alter the situation regarding daughters in general. Even today the provision of the daughter's share in her father's property in Hindu law is not fully implemented. Many daughters give up their rights of their own accord or may not fight for it. A common argument is that such insistence is likely to destroy the affection of brothers who at present feel morally bound to make appropriate contribution for her marriage and to give, gifts to the sister and her children on various occasions such as festivals, weddings, child birth, etc.

In the patrilineal and patrilocal kinship system, a son is looked upon as the father's natural apprentice and successor and supporter of the parents in old age. Sons are supposed to build up family prestige and prosperity. A father believes that he will continue to live in this world through the son. All this imparts a special value to the son.

A son is necessary for performing the prescribed rituals of his parents when they die. Even in domestic rituals a daughter cannot take the place of a son. Although ritual considerations are less compelling among the lower castes, the relative importance of the son has become generalized throughout Hindu society.

A daughter cannot effectively take the place of a son. Her loyalties change at marriage. As a popular saying in Telugu puts it, "Bringing up a daughter is like manuring and watering a plant in someone else's courtyards", for her services and affections are to go to others. A daughter is an easy source of disrepute for the family, particularly before marriage and also after marriage for she is always referred to as the daughter of such and such family. Since marriage of a daughter is a matter of anxiety and expenditure, daughters mostly are not welcome. People complain that daughters have to be educated as well as married off. This puts a double burden on parents.

According to our survey, 44.57% of the respondents said that people react differently to the birth of a girl and a boy, whereas only 35.41% said that they do not react differently. It is commonly seen that in hospitals the menial staff asks for a larger tip at the birth of a son. In villages and towns the midwife expects twice as much gift at the birth of a son than at the birth of daughter. At the birth of her first baby, the mother gets better gifts from elders if the new-born is a male. A first son, whether born as a first child or later, invariably gets a warm welcome. It is no wonder that while striving to get a son, a family may come to have a number of daughters.

Reaction to the birth of a particular girl depends on the socio-economic culture of the family and her place in the sibling group. The act of "giving away" a daughter is believed to earn special merit; her contribution in terms of domestic work and affection is also valued. Without a daughter a household is not really complete. And yet it is often remarked that whereas a couple miss something if they do not have a daughter, they are also saved from much worry and trouble.

Discrimination between sexes in the allocation of scarce sources in various fields such as nutrition, medical care, and education is directly related to the greater desirability of the son and transferability of the daughter. In most families girls are taught to see that brothers get more and better food. This attitude is internalized by girls often without being conscious of it; but a conscious effort is also made, so that the girls inculcate the cultural norms which legitimize a differential treatment between girls and boys. In educated families we may not find so much of discrimination. Among tribal and other groups for whom a girl is an asset, as a help in domestic and productive activities and as a bringer of gifts and cash by way of bride-wealth, such discrimination is somewhat less. But discrimination in giving modern education at all levels is certainly related to the distinction between the rules of male and female children. According to conventional thinking, parents cannot expect economic support from the daughter, once she is married. Many still considered it improper to accept such support, even if it were offered. While the process of economic and social change is driving many families out of this pattern of thinking, the resistance of the in-laws still prevents many daughters from giving such support to parents, even when it is needed.

In her husband's house also a woman does not acquire rights comparable to those of the male members. Though ceremonially welcomed there with symbolic expressions of her future role as a contributor of prosperity and fertility, she is an inferior partner, and has to make a place for herself by establishing a relationship with the husband's kin, by learning the traditions of the family, and by producing progeny. The degree of incorporation expected of a woman in her husband's group differs in different communities and socio-economic levels.

Even in tribal and rural areas her rights to property are extremely limited. Men are the possessors and inheritors of land and its resources. In the cognitive map of the people the wife works on her husband's fields and lives in her husband's house. Where divorce or separation are permitted she may have to leave if she does not satisfy and she may leave if she is not satisfied. Wife beating, which is still prevalent in our society, cannot be explained only by the superior physical strength of the husband. The notion of the wife being a possession of the man is also responsible for it. Whether a widow has a right of usufruct on husband's land or whether she can inherit his land and other property, these rights are subject to her not remarrying. Children do not belong to the mother. In the event of divorce or separation small children may accompany the mother to be returned to the husband when they grow up. Even in those areas where a woman's contribution to the economy is substantial and she has considerable leeway, the cultural notion that her role is only supportive has to be traced to patrilineal descent and patrilocal residence.

However, it is not the fact of patriliny by itself but its association with joint property, and joint family household and certain rules and patterns of marriage which lead to greater constraints over women and affect their position in an adverse way.

The Structure

Family in India largely exists in the framework of patrilineal descent, but differences in its form, function, and process are crucial to the position of women. A common image of the Indian patrilineal, patrilocal family is that of three generational, commensal and co-residential group formed by close male patrikin with their wives and unmarried daughters. This group has a common budget, common residence, and common hearth. Joint landed property, a family business or family craft are conducive to this type of family as they require pooling of their skill, labour and resources.

In common parlance such a family has been described as "joint family". While the fundamental feature of a joint family according to Mitakshara law, is a corporate group of companies parceners i.e., patrilineally related males who have a joint right to property for our purpose of examining the role and status of women, co-residence and commonality are immediately identifiable characteristics of a joint family household. Such a consideration would also accommodate family patterns of those areas which have followed Dayabhaga law and of Muslims and other communities. It would also accommodate family which hardly have anything by way of ancestral or immovable property but which may comprise more than one couple related through patrilineal links, i.e., father and sons along with wives and children, or brothers and their wives and children. This type of joint living is observed in all parts of the country, though its incidence is variable, depending on:

(a) the culturally patterned time of break-up which differs across caste, community and area;

(b) on demographic profiles based on such factors as average life expectancy, average age of effective marriage, average number of children born per couple, age of father at the birth of various children, etc.; and

(c) on influence of education, spatial mobility and diversification of occupation.

The findings of anthropologists and sociologists about the familial patterns in India tell us that among the tribal groups of India, nuclear household is the most common and culturally approved form of domestic group. It is common for sons to have separate hearths as they get married or as they come to have one or two children. But the sons tend to have their houses close to their father's residence. In terms of locality the marital residence is largely patri-virilocal viz., where on marriage, a woman comes to live in the house or in the locality of her husband's father. Moreover, at any point of time, there may be some family units of husband, wife, and children with additional members like an aged parent of the husband or his unmarried brothers and sisters. In some tribes like the Bhils in Rajasthan at least one of the sons is expected to live with parents. Only a few tribal groups like the Tharu, the Rabha, and some Gonds have joint family living during the lifetime of the father as the cultural norm. We would thus like to conclude that by and large, family organization among the Indian tribes does not impose as much constraint on the women as amongst non-tribal groups particularly the upper and middle strata. Joint family living appears to be more characteristic of land-owning and trading classes and of upper castes in general, though Brahmins are not at the top in this respect. It is least characteristic of Scheduled Castes. There are also regional differences, the Gangetic plains show higher incidence of joint families. One significant finding is that although the majority of households are nuclear, majority of people may live in joint and supplemented nuclear families. There is something like patterned rearrangements of family structure through time. There are definite group and regional differences in the customary time of break-up of the joint family and these differences appear to correlate with the incidence of joint families at any point of time.

Indian patri-virilocal family has to be viewed in terms of its developmental cycle. It develops into a joint family after the marriage of a son and coming of a daughter-in-law. After the death of the father, brothers generally separate. In the villages of Andhra Pradesh for example, sons are expected to stay together along with the parents till all of them are married, after which they tend to separate, the parents generally choosing to live with one of the sons. Thus, joint family is broken into one relatively smaller joint family household and perhaps a few simple households. It is common to find an aged parent and dependent siblings living with a man and his wife and children. The role configuration of such households is undoubtedly different from that of a simple family. This type of household is found also in urban areas, though it is being subject to severe strains. Lack of adequate housing facilities sometimes leads to a break-up, or it may, contrarily, compel a family to remain joint. Changing attitudes, aspirations and norms of different generations, however, imposes a constant strain on joint families and often results in a break-up. Occupational mobility of individual members have contributed to this process, and break-ups in such cases take place without any serious overt tensions in the family.

An understanding of this family organisation entails recognition of degrees of jointness such as (a) jointness of property, income or production and domestic grouping (b) jointness of property and income or production but not of domestic groupings and (c) jointness of property alone.

Another feature of Indian family organisation is the recognition of a kind of oneness between the father's and the son's households, or between the brothers' households. A son's family is in a sense an extension of the father's family. In fact they are one 'family'. It is in this 'family' that the incoming wife has to be incorporated. There is always the contingency of younger siblings or aged parents of the man coming to live with his simple family household. Parents may divide their time between various sons. Vicinage and common business or property interests are conducive to the continuation of this sense of unity. Formal obligations towards relations by marriage and towards the daughters of the house are expected to be shared by this 'family'. Each generation experiences weakening of the ties between brothers, usually after the death of parents, and a growth of their own respective branches.

There is great emphasis on adjustability in the socialization of girls. In their training for sex-linked roles, they are made aware that they are girls and constantly reminded of the pitfalls they must avoid and of the uncertainties they must face. In urban educated families, there may be little discrimination between boys and girls in regard to food, medical attention and even education, but notions about the appropriate spheres of men and women are implicit in the general distribution of household work and in the concessions and freedom of behaviour permitted to the boys. In middle-class families girls receiving education does not undermine their femininity. Even for young boys and girls of urban areas socialized in the sixties and seventies, the need for reallocation of work and responsibility within the family is not emphasized. In joint living, discrimination tends to be more pronounced. Even where girls are exempted from onerous tasks and a rigid routine, it is often with an expression of the feeling that since they will have to do all this after marriage, they should at least have some comfort and freedom in the parent's house.

Very few women start their married life independently in a simple household. Even when the husband is working away from his parents, a girl 'enters' as daughter-in-law in the house of the parent-in-law or husband's elder brother. In the first few years of married life her behaviour is to be governed by the norms of a subordinate and submissive role appropriate for a daughter-in-law. She has very little hand in any kind of decision making, and has to start her new life under severe restrictions.

These are more onerous in certain regions and in the well-to-do and middle classes than in poorer sections. Norms of segregation and seclusion of women, marriage rules, degree of distinction between bride givers and bride-takers, as well as the extent of contribution of the woman to family earning are responsible for these differences.

Among the Muslims, the prevalence of marriages between close kin, including children of two brothers, does not allow a sharp distinction between bride-givers and bride-takers, and where such marriages have taken place, rules of avoidance between a woman and her husband's kin may not be as rigid as among the Hindus of North India. But by and large similar rules of avoidance operate in Muslim families of particular regions and socio-economic levels. A distinct notion about women's subordinate role, general segregation and seclusion of women, and conception of patrilineal and patrilocal family have their effect on the status of the Muslim women in general.

In the authority pattern of a joint family the daughter-in-law is directly subordinate to the mother-in-law. According to a Telugu proverb, 'good and bad scorpions both have their sting; the difference is that one uses it more than the other'. A woman is at the peak of her life when her daughters-in-law are young and her husband is an active provider. It is only gradually that a daughter-in-law's position in her husband's family improves. In the words of Mandelbaum, "A young wife, of any jati or region, usually has the lowest status in the family and is given the more onerous chores. Whatever goes away, she is apt to be called the culprit. Whenever the finger of blame is pointed, it somehow swings to her."

With a long standing in their husband's family and as mothers, old and experienced women in the middle-classes enjoy considerable authority and respect in the family and have a say in the decision making. They may even be consulted by men in matters of land, property and business.

Our survey however reveals that the women members of the family as a whole have a marginal role to play in decision-making. The only decision in which the woman takes an active part is in buying the foodstuffs. Male dominance in decision making is more pronounced in rural areas and among lower caste groups.

Decisions such as those about educational career to be pursued, about jobs and marriage, are collectively taken by the family, as revealed by low percentage of respondents saying that the children take these decisions 'himself/herself'. A higher percentage of respondents said that the 'sons' take their own decisions about the job they want to take and educational career. Though the overall percentage of female participation in such family decisions is lower it is slightly higher for decisions affecting the daughters, whereas the male members of the family were instrumental in deciding about the sons. On these issues again the major part in decision-making is that of the male members. Decisions about marriage of sons and daughters are mostly collective in nature.

A woman's authority is reflected directly in her control over the daughter-in-law, but it would be a mistake to view the position of a mother-in-law as indicative of the status of women in general. For, the same woman's status may decline with old age, widowhood, and with the daughter-in-law's coming into importance as mother and as the wife of the principal provider.

Besides her kinship status, a woman's status in the family is also influenced by her husband's social position and his contribution to the family economy. Thus, her own efforts by themselves may often not be able to bring her status. In middle and upper classes, the amount of dowry a daughter-in-law has brought and the gifts that her parents send also contribute to her status in the family. With greater diversification of occupations in urban areas, the husband's status becomes more relevant for the woman's status.

With the authority of the mother-in-law or elder sister-in-law, little contact with the husband, and a general expectation of subordination, a woman's position in a joint family can be miserable. In this social milieu, it is difficult for a woman to evoke a balanced relationship with the husband and have a role in decision-making. Many of the critical decisions of her life remain beyond her control, such as planning one's family, further training or education, taking up or continuing a job.

Our survey attempted to obtain first-hand data on the observance of rules of avoidance with the husband's kin by asking whether purdah was observed in the presence of the father-in-law, mother-in-law, husband's elder brother and husband's elder sister. The findings reveal that in the presence of the father-in-law purdah is observed in the case of 44.04% Sikhs, 40% Muslims, 39.19% Jains and 32.08% Hindus. Distribution by States reveals that such avoidance is highest in the Northern States in the following order: Haryana (72.61%); Rajasthan (62.18%); Delhi (60.78%); Himachal Pradesh (51.19%); Uttar Pradesh, M.R and Gujarat follow. Manipur also has a high incidence of avoidance. Figures for purdah in the presence of father-in-law are as follows : Kerala (4.29%), Tamil Nadu (4.93%), Mysore (5.44%) and Andhra Pradesh (9.40%). Maharashtra has a little higher incidence. In Goa, purdah is wholly absent. Obviously this is a cultural difference, and indicates a major area of constraints for women in North India.

A simple family allows a greater scope for a woman to have less restricted roles and greater part in management and policy decisions. As has often been pointed out, in a simple family a woman is subordinate to no other woman. The husband is dependent upon her for running the house, rearing of children, and management of social relations. Depending on the personalities of the couple and personal equation, a woman can truly be the mistress of the house. If she is educated and enlightened, she acquires a personality and a dignity of her own.

Thus situated a woman has much greater initiative to have sustained contacts with her own kin, not only as prescribed by custom (and mainly on formal occassions) but on a basis of equality in which both mother as well as father are equally relevant for reckoning kinship ties. It has been found that those away from the patrilocal village and settled in urban areas have greater freedom to choose their contacts.

With the absence of large-scale joint family, greater freedom of association and movement, and economic contribution of both husband and wife towards living, a woman gets a better status in the family. This is largely true of small-scale agriculturists and artisans, but it is the women of the lowest category who seem to be more equal to their husbands: "In certain senses women whose fortune it was to be poor enjoyed higher status than those who were rich". Participation in extra-domestic economic activities does not give these women status in the larger context because the work they do is of low prestige.

4

Marriage as Institution

Many problems of major importance for women are linked with marriage. Various issues like age at marriage, procedures for contacting and executing marriage, customs of dowry and bride wealth, patterns of presentations between the wife's and the husband's kin groups, multiplicity of spouses, divorce and separation, widowhood and remarriage are vitally relevant for assessing women's status.

In a patrilineal society, marriage signifies a transfer of the woman from her natal group to her husband's group. This is associated also with the notions of male superiority and secondary importance of the female in the continuity of the line. The 'seed', people believe, is more important than the 'field'. Concern with paternity tends to become stronger in a patrilineal system, and paternity can be approximately assured only by controlling women's sexuality. Another way adopted by some tribal groups is to establish definite rules for assigning the children born to an unmarried girl.

By and large insistence on low age of marriage for girls is related to avoidance of unclaimed progency. Notions of vulnerable purity of women, value of virginity for girls at marriage, and a clear differentiation between primary marriage and secondary marriage for women, in castes which have the institutions of divorce and remarriage also follow from this. Widespread prevalence of child marriages in the country has its roots in this feature of human biology coupled to a concern for ascertaining paternity. The custom of mock marriage, in which a girl is ritually married to some object like a spear, an arrow, a pestle or Mahua tree, before she attains puberty also reflects the group's concern for the purity of women.

Existence of caste in Hindu society which traditionally limits marriage contacts within certain groups, rules against marrying within gotra, clan and lineage. Regulations about not marrying certain types of close blood relations, and customs which enjoin or indicate reference for marriage between certain types of relatives or groups, make arranged marriage the most desirable form of marriage. Among Muslims and other religious groups, also there are either certain socio-economic categories or groups and sections within which marriage is restricted. Where inter-group marriages are approved, they are mostly on hypergamous basis, daughters being accepted from lower groups. The concept of purity of blood among Muslims seems to be responsible for preference for marriage between close relatives, particularly between children of siblings and for exchange marriages. Many Muslim groups in North and Western India, consider marriage between the children of two brothers as most desirable. A common explanation for this preference is offered in terms of the desire to keep the property within the family since, according to, Islamic law, girl is also entitled to a share in her parental property.

In the south there has been a preference for marriage of a girl with her father's sister's son, and less generally with her mother's brother's son or with her mother's younger brother. Some castes practice direct exchange also. In the matrilineal communities marriage with mother's brother who belongs to the same lineage as the sister's daughter is unthinkable.

Marriage cannot be left to the young if these restrictions and preferences are to work. The institution of arranged marriage thus fits well with the social structure. Only in subsequent marriages one's own choice can be exercised.

In urban areas there is a trend towards ignoring for the sake of marital relations, the differences between caste groups which belong to the same generic category or are closely situated in hierarchical grading. Education, travel and liberalization of ideas have contributed to this trend. In the salaried sections economic considerations and status also play an important part in ignoring these distinction.

Patterns of selection of marriage partner have become varied, particularly in urban areas. Between one's own choice at one end and the selection by parents without any consultation with the marriageable son/daughter at the other end, we find self-choice with parent's consent and parent's choice but with the approval of the marrying parties. Another intermediate pattern is one in which boy's wishes are given weight but it is not considered necessary to consult the girl with any seriousness. The position in which the elders alone decide is more prevalent among those who have little or no education.

However, the young who want to take their own decision in this area of life are not many. Respect for parents and desire to avoid uncertainties are behind this attitude. In many surveys of the attitude of college girls towards marriage, an interesting combination of approval of greater mixing between boys and girls and preference for arranged marriages under parental guidance has been revealed.

The studies made in the pre-Independence phase and those made in the post-Independence period highlight certain interesting points in selection of partners. Merchant, who had made his study when romanticism was emerging in the young boys and girls found that 79.2% of his respondents opted for self-choice of the partner. This romantic approach to marriage does not last long and in G.B. Desai's period i.e., 1945, more respondents (68.2%) favour marriages arranged by parents. Perhaps in absence of any opportunity for free-mixing, the younger generation might be finding it very difficult to make independent choice, and hence basks under parental security. It is for this reason that we find Raj Mohini, Kaker and Ramanamma's data indicate younger generation in favour of arranged marriages. The major change noticeable is that with the impact of urbanization and education, individuals would like themselves to be consulted before the match is finalized.

Another aspect of arranged marriage, is the humiliation that a girl has to face when she is obliged to present herself repeatedly before marriageable boys and their relations and friends. In a few sophisticated families the two parties may be treated on an equal footing as genuinely trying to assess each other's suitability. But in the middle-class families, by and large this situation is most humiliating for a girl. Inter-caste marriages today are not common and inter-religious marriages are even rarer. The freedom movement which also included a rejection of social taboos, propagated inter-caste as well as inter-religious marriages. At that stage such marriages were regarded as not only progressive but also as patriotic. But the momentum of this ideology seems to have receded in the years since Independence.

In a study done in 1969, only 24 out of 1036 i.e., 2.31% women had been married in castes other than their own. In the survey of affinal and consanguineous marriages conducted in 569 villages during 1961 Census operation, only 966 of 1,33,775 marriages i.e., 72% have been reported to be across castes. The percentage of such marriages is 0.82 among the Hindus and only 0.01 among the Muslims. In another study made in 1972, it was found that 60% of respondents did not approve of inter-caste marriages.

In the actual rituals and ceremonies of marriage the unequal status of man and woman becomes apparent. In a Christian marriage the bride has to be ceremonially given over to the bridegroom and the bride is exhorted to promise that she will love and obey her husband. In a Muslim marriage, the parties to the contract are in a sense the husband and the bride's 'wali', though with her formal consent. In many parts of India, a Muslim bride duly decorated and sitting with a modest demeanour is actually lifted by the bridegroom and put in the vehicle which is to carry her to his home.

Like language forms, rituals and ceremonies not only reflect the unequal treatment accorded to the sexes in a social system but by repetition emphasize and perpetuate the same inequality of status. Marriage is essentially a social affair and therefore succeeds in indoctrinating coming generations in the ideology implicit in it. It is because of this conservative attitude, particularly among women that in order to enjoy the rights given by the Constitution or law, women have to assert themselves. It is women who exercise the greatest vigilance over the members of their own sex regarding the observance of norms rooted in tradition.

The rites of Hindu marriage stress male primacy and superiority. Kanyadan is a gift of the virgin daughter for purposes of Dharma, Artha and Kama. The parties to the transaction are father of the girl (accompanied by his wife) who is the giver and the bridegroom who is the receiver. When the bridegroom accepts the bride he tells her that union with him is bringing her prosperity, cultivation, and auspiciousness. In fact marriage is the first major Sanskara for a Hindu woman. Promises made by the two during the rites like circumambulation of fire, walking seven steps, or the bride's changing over from the right to the left side of the groom are also worth noting. While emphasizing life, friendship and partnership for the two, they exhort the bride to follow the husband, to act according to his wishes, to remain steadfast in the loyalty and love. The bridegroom promises to protect and support the bride. He asks her to serve the elders of his family, be affectionate to the young, and not to be lazy. There is a special significance of the rite of showing the polar star (or Sun or Atar of Arundhoti) to the bride and of making her stand on a stone. She is to be steadfast like a stone and the polar star, not deviating from the right path and be calm and ready to suffer in silence.

The basic rituals of Hindu marriage are not confined to the so-called twice-born castes but are enacted with some variation among other castes also. The process of acculturation has resulted in the lower groups inviting the Brahmin priest who recites the "mantras" and helps his clients to enact the Sanskritic rituals. The lowest groups in the Hindu hierarchy, who operate without a Brahmin priest and also very many tribes, are seen to imitate some of these rituals – Kanyadan being the most popular among them. It is perfectly congruent with their notion of transfer of the bride.

While it is true that kanyadan relegates the status of the woman, in accepting the bride, the bridegroom has to make the following promise to the bride's father – Dharme arthe Ca kame Ca naticarami (i.e. I will not transgress in the attainment of duty, wealth and desire). There is also no doubt that the bride is given a warm welcome in the husband's house and is referred to as Laxmi (Goddess of prosperity). Her future role as home-maker is associated with great prestige. She is one who will give him progeny to continue the line, to free himself of his debt to ancestors, and to support him in old age. However, a close examination reveals that the rites of Hindu marriage stress male primacy and superiority. It is worth noting, that the Brahmo Samaj had made special efforts to rationalize the ceremony of marriage and to drop those rites, which perpetuated low status of women; the content analysis of Bengali and Marathi magazines and newspapers in the thirties and the forties of the present century show that there were strong reactions against these rites and "mantras" in some regional languages like Marathi and Bengali.

One important aspect of marital alliance in Hindu society, except in some parts of South India, is the unequal status of bride-givers and bride-takers. Just as woman is inferior to man, and bride is inferior to bridegroom, bride-givers are inferior to bride-takers. The son-in-law and his kinds are to be respected. Marriage automatically establishes the lower status of the bride-givers. This distinction between bride-givers and bride-takers is far more pronounced in the northern States, but it is also very much there in central and western India. In the south because of common patterns of marriage among close kin which involves direct exchange or delayed exchange, systematic differences in the status of givers and takers do not emerge. In the context of a particular marriage because of the symmetrical relation between husband and wife, slight distinction of status between wife's kin and husband's kin may be there; this is particularly so among the Brahmins with their emphasis on Sanskritic rituals. But the overall pattern creates an ethos of near-equality between bride-givers and bride-takers. Marriages in the south tend to be contracted within a limited group and thus the girl is not thrown in with strangers. There is a regular to and fro movement and contact between the wife's family and the husband's family so that the girl is not left alone to face a hostile environment. Rules of behaviour are not as stringent for a daughter-in-law in the south as they are in the north where the contrasting norms of behaviour for the daughter and the daughter-in-law tend to make the life of woman alternate between freedom and restrictions, between harsh and soft treatment, and certain restrictions which do not allow her to become a freer person. She has roles but no personality. It is well-known that in western U.P., where marriages are arranged outside the village, daughters-in-law were not sent to the literacy classes while the daughters of the village could go in groups for election campaigning but the daughters-in-law were not permitted to do so.

The distinction between bride-givers and bride-takers is made harsher by the pattern of unilateral gift-giving. The son-in-law, and his parents are entitled to receive gifts from the girl's parents on different occasions but the latter are not even supposed to accept any food at the son-in-law's house. Common people in the north observe this rule strictly. These differential norms of behaviour are likely to be more pronounced in rural areas where the village is a kind of in-law village, or paternal village, and particularly in such castes and communities whose women do not work outside the home. These norms of behaviour operate in urban areas too. It is not uncommon to encounter a girl in her parents' house in a modern outfit and the same girl in her in-laws house in traditional clothes, partially veiled.

Different Types

Practice of hypergamy, i.e., marriage between man of higher and woman of lower groups, brings down the position of women. Within a caste, groups are ranked as the relatively high or low status. Practice of hypergamy is found among such groups as the Rajput and the Jat of North India, Anavil Brahmin and Patidar of Gujarat, Maithil Brahmin of Bihar, and among the Kanyakubj Brahmin and Sarayupari Brahmin to some extent. In hypergamy, clans and lineages are of unequal status; gotra and families among the Brahmin may also be of unequal status. As women in hypergamous marriages are treated as of inferior status, their incorporation in the husband's family is a painful process. Female infanticide among the Jat and the Rajput was partly a consequence of hypergamy, for the girls of the highest groups had very little choice for marriage as boys of these groups could marry lower down. Dowry is generally high in hypergamous communities.

Both the variants of polygamy, viz. Polygyny (plurality of wives) and polyandry (plurality of husbands) are found in India.

Polyandry is confined to tribes like the Toda in the Nilgiri, groups, like the Khasa in the Jaunsar Bawar area of U.P. and the people of Kinnaur and Lahul and Spiti in Himachal Pradesh. Some of these, like the Khasa, belong to the Hindu fold and are divided into castes. But today all these polyandrous groups of the Himalayan region are declared as Scheduled Tribes, and hence do not come under the limitations imposed by Hindu Law regarding monogamy. They practise fraternal polyandry. This group is numerically insignificant. But among the higher castes of Jaunsar Bawar there is now a tendency of taking as many wives as there are brothers but there appears to have grown a vested interest in polyandry, particularly since they have been declared as a Scheduled Tribe with all its privileges. However, from the point of view of women's status it is worth noting that these are patrilineal and patrilocal groups and a woman has absolutely no right over her children and property. Polyandry in patrilineal setting far from being a privilege, is an obligation for a woman to allow sexual access to the rightful share.

Social reaction against polygyny as an indignity offensive to the status of women was one of the most marked features of the 19th Century Reform Movement. While the acceptance of monogamy as a necessary principle for civilized living became widely prevalent among the educated classes, there was a difference of opinion regarding the action necessary for eradication of this practice. While leaders like Iswar Chandra Vidya Sagar and the Brahmo Samaj and Christian Missionaries wanted legislative action to prohibit the practice, others believed that it would die a natural death with the spread of education. Partly as a result of this social reaction and partly due to declining material prosperity, among the classes which had earlier practised polygyny, the prevalence of this practice declined considerably over the last hundred years. The demand for legislative action against polygyny gained momentum under the influence of Gandhiji and made women's organisations increasingly vocal, resulting in legislative measures in different provinces and in the princely States even in the pre-Independence period. The Hindu Marriage Act introduced the principle of monogamy in 1955. As already mentioned, it is only in Muslim Law that plurality of wives is still permitted.

A study undertaken by the Census of India in 1961, however, found polygyny to be still prevalent among most communities to a certain extent, though its incidence had declined over the decades. The survey was based on a total sample of nearly 1 lakh marriages. 5,911 marriages in the sample were found to be polygynous. If the time when these marriages had taken place is ignored, then the incidence was found to be the highest among the tribal communities (15.25%), Buddhists 7.0%, Jains 6.72%, Hindus 5.8% and Muslims 5.7%. As, however, the marriages covered were not selected on random sampling basis, the Census authorities observed that it would be risky to draw any quantitative generalization from this data. But at the same time, it has to be kept in view that the size of the sample is fairly large and hence until more valid quantitative data are available, one would be justified to question the validity of the prevailing notions in this matter. The most interesting finding of the Survey was regarding the trend of change in incidence.

According to the data, the highest incidence, (7.15%) in the Hindu Community was found for marriages performed between 1941 to 1950, after which it declined to 5.06% in 1951-60 and the frequency declined steadily. Among Muslims, the highest incidence was found between 1931-1940 (7.29%) after which it declined steadily coming to 4.31% in 1951-60. Among the Jains, the highest incidence was recorded between 1931-40(13.63%). As for Buddhists, the highest incidence (10.93%) is recorded between 1911 and 20. Incidence during 1951-60 was 8.13%. Amongst the tribal community, however, the trend has been markedly different. The lowest incidence 0.68% was between 1921-30 and the highest 17.98% during 1951-60.

Most tribal groups in India permit polygyny. Those not permitting it are very few; most of them either follow matriliny or recognize both the mother's and the father's line. The most important culturally accepted motivations for polygyny are barrenness of the wife, economic advantages accruing from plural marriages, and gain in prestige. Entanglements culminating in bringing another wife are also accepted by the society. Tribal groups like the Bhil in Rajasthan, the Bagata, the Raj Gond, and the Birdugond, see economic advantage in polygyny in two ways. Wives can contribute to the agricultural and other economic activities by their own labour and by producing sons who would supply the needed labour for working in the fields, tending cattle, and building houses. In a patrilineal setting where land and other economic resources belong to the men and where women's contribution to the economy is substantial, this can prove to be a strong incentive. Another incentive is that of prestige. Where bride price is high, it needs resources to obtain more than one wife and having more wives adds to one's prestige. The chiefs and village headmen, as also such other important men prefer to have more than one wife. During our tour of Arunachal Pradesh, we were informed by many that polygyny was mainly practised by chiefs or headmen. Similar was the case in Nagaland. It is interesting to note that such marriages among Christian Nagas still receive customary sanction though they are not permitted by the Church.

Even though a particular society permits polygyny, it is only a few people who can take advantage of it, and it is seen that only men of some means and power can avail of it. In many tribes it is feared that the coming of a second wife would lead to clashes among the wives and the first wife might leave and go to some other man that acts as a deterrent. A temporary phase of polygyny is also not uncommon.

Among the essential social reasons, the most important are infertility of the wife, her prolonged sickness and the lack of a son. In some communities, the custom of marrying one's elder brother's widow, sometimes results in polygyny. Another social reason, which has become increasingly important in recent years, is the cultural and communication gap that often results when the wife is illiterate and uneducated and the husband receives modern education. Most of these cases result from child marriages. With the changing aspiration, pattern of social needs of the educated husband, finding their first wife a social handicap they turn to a second marriage in many cases. Many of them do this not without serious misgivings. In some of these cases their offers of divorce to the first wife are rejected by the latter, who finds herself unable to face the consequences of a divorce, because the status of a deserted wife is better than that of a divorcee. Married status gives them certain rights in their in-laws' home which would be denied to them, if they were divorced. In most of these cases their reluctance for divorce lies in their social and economic dependence and absence of the necessary equipment for earning. Resistance from their family may also be an added reason for their preparedness to put up with the indignity and unhappiness rather than seeking a divorce.

An important motivation of polygyny, however, is economic gain. Where women are not a burden but are self-supporting and contribute substantially to productive activity like cultivation and handicraft, they are real assets and a man can gain by having more than one wife. (Its long term implication that more hands will be available for work also has its temptations for some). Thus polygyny in Manipur dearly indicates that sometimes women's worth as productive workers may become a hindrance to their unopposed status in the family. Economic motivation for polygyny also operates among artisan groups, both Muslim as well as Hindu. Religious allowance for a man to marry as many as four wives at a time proves useful for the Muslim inhabitants of a district in Karnataka engaged in lacquer work, for what they gain by having extra hands to work is much more than what they have to spend on their keep. This, certainly, is a form of exploitation of women.

While the census study indicates that the incidence of polygyny among Muslims is not as high as it is believed to be, there is no doubt that the prevalence of legal sanction for polygyny caused widespread resentment among the women of this community. During our tours, we met many groups of Muslim women in different parts of the country, who expressed their unhappiness and resentment at the continuation of this situation. We met many such women who had been abandoned by their husbands as a consequence of a second marriage. Still many others had to acquiesce to the second marriage because of their economic dependence. They also expressed a view that a protest against this institution from them had invariably resulted in acute oppression against which they obtained no protection from society. While it is a fact that changes in law alone cannot eradicate the prevalence of this practice, it is our view that continuing sanction by the law in a way perpetuates it. The role of law in such social matters in our country has usually acted as a norm in order to arouse the public conscience. We cannot appreciate the denial of similar support to Muslim women in their struggle against this social injustice.

Even though it is nearly 20 years since the law was passed banning polygyny for Hindus and making it a criminal offence, we regret to admit that the practice has not been eradicated altogether. Apart from the findings of the census study in 1961, the committee, during its tours, heard large number of complaints from women that their husbands had married again. Their lack of knowledge about their legal rights and social acceptance of the situation make the position of these women deplorable. In Andhra Pradesh, the Committee was told about the prevalent practice of wives being compelled to sign a document giving their permission to the remarriage to their husbands. Dependence on their husbands, both socially and economically and inadequate social condemnation of their deeds are the causes of the wives' acquiescence. Most of them believe that signing such a document deprives them of their legal right of redress. Education, economic independence and fuller knowledge of their legal rights can ultimately free society from the stranglehold of these traditions. We feel strongly that women's voluntary agencies should launch a campaign against this type of marriage by ostracising the men who commit bigamy and by mobilizing public opinion, particularly among women, to resist this practice.

As a Commodity

Solemnization of marriage is a social occasion. In the Indian context it signifies the creation of a bond between two individuals and also between their families. It involves, with a few exceptions, the transfer of the wife to the husband's family. Two major types of transfers of material wealth accompany marriage: in one the wealth travels in the opposite direction of the bride and in another it travels along with the bride in the same direction. The former is bride-price; the latter is dowry. These need to be considered as components of marriage because of their implication on the status of women.

The patrilineal tribal groups of the Indian subcontinent customarily pay bride-price. The form and amount of bride-price vary from region to region and from tribe to tribe. Some pay only in cash, while others make the payment in kind, and still others pay the bride-price in both cash and kind. The second category, i.e., payment in kind, includes a wide range of subjects such as clothes and ornaments, tools and implements, liquor and grain, and cattle and goats. The Uraon of Chhotanagpur take sets of clothes for the bride's relatives, while the Ho and Munda concentrate on heads of cattle; so also in Arunachal Pradesh where mithun is the customary bride-price. The Ao Naga give baskets of paddy and an indigenous dagger. Bhumias of Orissa have to offer some cash, five to six sarees, and three goats as bride-price. Bargaining for bride-price is common. A survey of recent information indicates that in many tribes bride-price has increased manifold.

Many castes on the lower rungs of the hierarchy and some on the middle rungs also have a tradition of bride-price. As they come under the influence of Sanskritic values they tend to give up their custom and instead adopt the custom of dowry.

Analytically speaking, payment in cash and kind to the bride's father by the bridegroom's father is made in exchange for the authority over the bride which passes from her kin group to the bridegroom's kin group. The idea of compensation for the loss of a productive worker is also implicit in it. This lends some status to a daughter. Data show that so far as the girls' status in her natal group is concerned, in the communities which follow the custom of bride-price, a daughter is not regarded as a burden, and parents do not have to dread the time when she will have to be married. At her departure a daughter is likely to bring some material wealth. Birth of a daughter is, therefore, not regarded as some kind of a calamity. However, there is a custom of buying a wife in the transaction of bride-price. The fact that wealth has been spent to bring her home is not easily forgotten. When a woman leaves her husband and goes to another man, in the settlement of the amount of compensation to be paid by the latter, a reference to the amount of bride-price paid by the former husband comes into the picture too. This certainly speaks for the relatively low status of the woman vis-a-vis man. In. spite of it, in these societies the woman has some bargaining power in regard to her relationship in the husband's house. The man cannot drive her too hard or else she will leave and he will have to pay bride-price to bring another wife. The compensation that he will get for her will not be the same as the bride-price that he will have to pay.

Among the underprivileged sections, the custom of bride price often places a man and his family in debt. It has been responsible for pushing many tribal and caste groups into the clutches of moneylenders. It is well known that in South India the landless farm labourers owed their almost permanent servitude to particular landowning families for generations because of debts incurred during marriage and death. It is reported that among some Scheduled Castes of Uttarkashi region a wife may be sent for prostitution to clear the debt incurred in her own marriage.

Both from the point of view of improvement in the condition of life of the people and for changing the conception of woman as someone's possession, the custom of bride-price needs to be eradicated. In fact the law aimed at prohibition of dowry is directed against bride-price also.

With a raise in social status by economic prosperity or regular wage earning and under the influence of the high prestige groups who practise dowry, many castes of the lower and middle rungs and even some tribal groups are shifting towards dowry. When it is adopted by the well-to-do families in the caste, the poorer ones also succumb to this change for it becomes a trend in the marriage market. The peasants of the village in Karnataka have changed over from bride-wealth to dowry over the last fifteen years or so. In Andhra Pradesh, the Golla or the caste of cowherds, and nomadic Larnbadas have been gradually changing to dowry. This was also confirmed by our tour of the Himachal Pradesh. Various villages studied by individual scholars and the Socio-Economic Survey Division of the Census of India have reported this trend. Whereas the people changing over to the form of dowry consider this a matter of prestige, the result of it is to make the daughter a liability. A girl's value to her husband and the in-laws is enhanced when she is accompanied by a substantial dowry. Epstein's study of the social life of peasants of Karnataka clearly shows that withdrawal of women from productive activities along with absence of training of girls in agricultural work is one of the potent factors contributing towards a change over from bridewealth to dowry.

Technically, dowry is what is given to the son-in-law or to his parents on demand either in cash or in kind. There are baffling regional variations in people's understanding of dowry. From the point of view of women's status the custom of dowry has to be looked at as constituting (1) what is given to the bride, and often settled beforehand and announced openly or discreetly. The gift, though given to the bride, may not be regarded exclusively as her property; (2) what is given to the bridegroom before and at marriage; and (3) what is presented to the in-laws of the girl. The settlement often includes the enormous expenses incurred on travel and entertainment of the bridegroom's party.

In the continued relationship between the two families, gift giving characterizes the occasions of visits, fasts and festivals, and ceremonies like those associated with marriage, childbirth, initiation, etc., particularly in the first few years of marriage. It is a matter of general observation and experience that in such gift giving, the bride's family is under compulsion and heavy pressure. These subsequent expenses are often regarded as making up for the deficiencies in the dowry and can cause severe hardship to the girl's parents. In the first few years of marriage, the girl's treatment in her husband's house is linked to these gifts. Thus according to Goody and Tambia in Dowry and Bridewealth: "Dowry is not one isolated payment but one array of gifts given over time. But it is also clear that amongst the ways of payment that constitute dowry, that given at the time of marriage is most important and conspicuous."

Dowry is linked with a number of social and cultural elements which sanction, justify or explain the practice. It has been viewed as a kind of pre-mortem inheritance of the daughter who has to leave her natal family to join another but has some rights over the former. Dowry thus stresses the notion of female property and female right to property.

Both among the Hindu and the Muslim communities, this notion of dowry as the realization that daughter's right is prevalent. It is commonly expressed that claim to dowry takes care of a daughter's right to inheritance given by Islam. In Hindu law, a daughter's claim to maintenance in the joint property included her marriage portion with the help of which she could be married property. An important ingredient of stridhan are the gifts given to her by the bride's relatives during and after marriage. In many communities in the South and Maharashtra, such as Mangalorean Christians, Tamil Brahmins, Deshasth Brahmins, the bridegroom's parents customarily buy the ornaments to be given to the new daughter-in-law out of cash received from her father.

A daughter should have something to fall back upon in times of crises, and also for setting up her house. This aspect is so deep-rooted in the minds of the people that ornaments, particularly of gold are regarded as "security". Ornaments impart to a girl a special position in the in-law's house. The bride's parents associate their own prestige with these valuables. In the upper castes of Tamil Nadu and Karnataka, diamond eartops constitute the most prestigious item of jewellery to be given along with a pair of gold bracelets and maybe a gold necklace.

It is not considered odd for the bridegroom's mother or other relatives to examine the jewellery on the person of the bride and comment on it. All over India, jewellery (gems, gold and silver) is given importance. There is a new trend in more sophisticated urban families to give cash or savings certificates, but jewellery remains the most accepted form of security, since it also has an exhibitive value.

Among the landowning castes of Andhra Pradesh like the Reddy and the Kamma, or the Paganeri, and the Ambalakkareu of Tamil Nadu, a father may give to the daughter land and jewellery. The cash has to be given to the bridegroom's father or the bridegroom himself, but land is registered in the name of the daughter. During our tour of Andhra Pradesh, we received two points of view. One group supported the practice on the ground that while cash or movables can be disposed of by the in-laws, land remains as secure property of the woman. The other group felt that as the land was looked after by the father or the brother, the income from it that reaches the woman depends on the whims of the former. This often reduces the woman's share, particularly after the father's death.

Pots and pans and cots and beddings are important items included in bridal gifts. These are mostly regarded as belonging to the couple. In the matter of utensils, however, customs differ.

In North India, where there has been a tradition of large utensils being given at the time of marriage to the daughter, they are generally in the control of the in-laws.

Living in the social milieu of inequality there is a genuine desire on the part of parents to see their children well-placed. "It was a matter of preserving the status of a daughter as well as the son. Sons might inherit all the productive capacity but the daughters had to be assured of marriage that would provide them with the same (or better) standard of life to which they were accustomed". The daughters thus have to be endowed with some property, generally movables. Transfer of wealth at the time of marriage enables a girl to enter into a desirable match. Hypergamy is based on consideration of status by birth. We find that caste groups following hypergamy have had a high incidence of dowry.

In the past few decades there has been a diversification of occupations within endogamous groups, and a sharp rise in economic and social inequality between their members. This has been one of the most important inducements for dowry, and operates at all level of the society. The amount of wealth that is involved may range from a few hundreds to lakhs of rupees but its weight on the persons is not substantially different. This motive is often expressed in the form of a fond desire of the parents to see that their daughter is not placed in conditions to which she is not accustomed. Whether it is about working in the fields and carrying water, cooking and washing clothes, or being accustomed to the use of a refrigerator, car, and air-conditioner, similar arguments operate. Desire for special mobility for the daughter and indirectly for the parental family is also very strong.

The most common rite associated with Hindu marriage is kanyadan. It is recommended in the Shastras that she be duly adorned with jewellery and then gifted. This is related to the desire to obtain security and good status for the daughter. Increasing the value of the girl with jewellery and household goods is especially prevalent in these sections of Indian society. Irrespective of religion, in which women are homebound and do not contribute to the economy of the family in terms of gainful work.

According to Hindu Shastras, the meritorious act of *Dana* or ritual gift remains incomplete till the receiver is given a *Dakshina*. So, whenever a bride is given over to the bridegroom, he has to be given something in cash or kind. This *Vardakshina* has assumed enormous proportions. The bridegroom and his kin group are believed to have done a favour by accepting the girl in their fold, for marriage with an appropriate person in the path of honour for a girl. They, therefore, deserve to be honoured with gifts. They are higher in status by virtue of their being bride-takers. In the south of India and in Maharashtra, there is some exchange of gifts between the two parties. In Bengal, close women relatives of the girl are honoured with some presents. But nowhere are the parties equal, the proportion of the gifts for the bridegroom and his people being much larger. Non-Hindu communities also tend to manifest these regional variations.

In North India, what the bridegroom's parents bring for the bride is supposed to go into the bridegroom's family because the bride is joining his family. In the South, traditionally there is greater respect for *stridhan* which includes also what has been represented by the husband's family. But in groups which have the custom of divorce/separation and remarriage the general custom is to deprive the women of the valuables that she has received from her husband and his people, in case the marriage breaks up. Only if the husband is proved to have been at fault would the situation be different.

In actual practice it is difficult to locate the principles enumerated above in a reasonable form. As regards pre-mortem inheritance, in dowry there is hardly any consideration of rightful share for the girl. It is demanded and given without regard to the actual wealth of the girl's father; it is also not equal for all the daughters and its payment often plunges the girl's father and brothers into debt.

This fact was brought to our notice in practically every State. The financial burden on the family worsened, with increasing rates of interest for such loans, which ranged from 5 per cent per month with security to 10 per cent in the absence of security. In exceptional cases the rate even goes up to 18 per cent. Of the expenses incurred by the father only a small portion consists of the belongings of the girl herself. Often even her jewellery is not in her control and it does not help her in times of crises. The household goods given at the time of marriage may not belong to her. In North India they may be disposed of by the in-laws, and even where they are utilized in her home, in the event of separation, nothing appears to belong finally to the woman.

The settlement of dowry has all the characteristics of a market transaction. What was originally intended to be a token *dakshina* for the bridegroom has now assumed enormous proportions. All over India, the committee heard the complaint that prevalence dowry is on the increase, and has penetrated communities and regions which did not practice it earlier. Its extent depends on the socio-economic status of the bridegroom and differs in different regions and, in different caste groups. There are more or less well defined grades of dowry for men in different professions. For example, men in the IAS and IFS in Orissa, Bihar, Uttar Pradesh and Punjab, belonging to well-to-do communities, can easily expect to get in cash and kind, at least a lakh of rupees. Business executives rank next. Engineers and, doctors stand lower in these matters than the business executives. This class seems to expect that marriage would bring them not only a partner but also all the things needed to set up a modern household, such as a car, refrigerator, stereo system. These groups serve as pacesetters and naturally influence those below. Thus, a peon or a clerk would demand such things as a bicycle, a transistor and wrist watch. A scooter is a common item of gift to the son-in-law in the groups at the middle level. In villages too, there are similar demands.

Among Muslims of many regions the custom of giving cash to the bridegroom is prevalent. It is so in Kerala among patrilineal Muslims. In Andhra Pradesh, this money is known as "Jode Ka Paisa", i.e. cash given for the bridegroom's outfit. In ordinary middle-class families this is settled in thousands. A general understanding is that this money is to be used for the expenses of marriage on the bridegroom's side. It is customary for the bridegroom to present sets of clothes and jewellery to the bride and give at least a feast after the bride is brought home. Socioeconomic status of the families of the bride and the bridegroom and education and earning potential of the bridegroom are important determinants of the amount. In many parts of the country, the bridegroom is given cash after the 'Nikah' ceremony. This is called "Salami". The orthodox Christians of Kerala and the Catholics of Mangalore and Goa also have the custom of dowry, and expenses of marriage for both the parties are to be borne by the bride's people. The Christians of Mangalore follow their preconversion custom of Kanyadan, and their gift-giving puts heavy pressure on the bride's parents. It is reported that in Kerala the custom of dowry makes marriage near to impossible for many Christian girls belonging to large families. They may choose the ecclesiastical line or may leave the State in search of jobs, particularly opting for nursing. Many of them earn their dowry.

There is a distinct trend among middle-class girls to take up clerical or teaching jobs, nursing, or working as sales girls to earn their dowry in urban areas. The committee was told about it specifically in Kerala, Orissa, Bihar, Mumbai, UP and Delhi.

Dowry may also be demanded in the form of residential accommodation in places like Mumbai and Calcutta. Financial support for foreign education, or for setting up business is not uncommon. In a village near Delhi, we were told that motor cars were in great demand for ultimately to be put to use as taxis.

It is a disturbing trend that the girls themselves aspire to have their household set up in a grand style by the parents and to have clothes, jewellery, furniture and vehicle, etc. This is supposed to enhance the girl's status in the in-laws' family. There is some truth in it for she has to face comparisons of gifts received by the brothers of her husband on the occasion of their marriages. A daughter-in-law's treatment is also related to the amount of dowry she has brought. This trend is spreading all over even among those do not practise dowry.

Desire for ostentation and sense of prestige and status have contributed to an increase in wedding expenses incurred by the parents. This works both ways; the parents of the girl try to excel in ostentation and the boy's party also make fantastic demands. The Committee encountered a most ridiculous situation close to the capital city of India in which the bride's parents had to spend thousands of rupees to satisfy the demand of the bridegroom's party that a helicopter must be arranged for them to come to the wedding.

Both in villages as well as towns parents offer certain justifications for demanding and accepting dowry. First, since they have to give dowry for the daughters, they are, in a way, forced to ask for dowry for their sons. Second, the fathers of educated boys like to get back the amount they spent on the son's education. Some also argue that owing to changed circumstances in which a son generally has a separate establishment and has a job somewhere away from home, the parents cannot expect much help from him, and so they consider his marriage as the major occasion on which their investment in his education can be recovered.

It is disconcerting to find that education, has hardly had any liberalizing influence on the minds of the people in respect of dowry. On the contrary, education has willy-nilly increased the scourge of dowry both in rural as well as in urban areas. An educated boy, and more so, one whose education and specialised training have helped him in acquiring a lucrative source of earning in life, expects a higher amount of dowry. The girl's parents on their part want to buy a good future for their daughter. It is often possible in some of these cases to delink the boy's parents' socioeconomic status from the boy's status, and parents of girls compete among themselves for such a boy.

Education of girls also increases dowry, though indirectly. An educated girl aspires to marry someone who is better qualified; her parents also have similar aspirations. There is hesitation on the part of young men to marry better educated girls. In fact this is common expectation in an arranged marriage that a boy should be better qualified than a girl. Thus, the more educated a girl is, the more qualified a husband she needs. This necessitates greater dowry. In such situations, parents of the girls often feel almost cheated in educating their daughters. Of course, where the girl is allowed to earn and is capable of earning her own dowry, education may be an advantage, but it does not lessen the dowry. Only where a girl has taken up a career or has a permanent job will the boy's relatives be satisfied with a modest dowry. This clearly indicates the relation of dowry with economic dependence which is associated with women who are principally housewives. Dowry encourages the belief that regards the value of women's work in the home as non-productive.

Although, in the context of the family, dowry may appear to give a certain status to the woman who is fortunate enough to be able to bring more of it, the custom reflects upon and helps in, perpetuating the inferior status of women in the society. In her natal home a girl is considered a liability, and consequently a drain on the family's resources. This has its effect on the socialization of children. There is traditionally sanctioned discrimination between boys and girls in the family with respect to food, medical care, etc. The enlightened sections may find this unimaginable but its truth cannot be denied. In the sphere of education, the middle classes all over India give more importance to boys' education and whenever a choice has to be made because of scarce resources, it is the boy who is likely to win in preference to girls, irrespective of the relative capabilities of the two. Undoubtedly, dowry is a big impediment in the progress of education of girls.

The present trend which comprises all kinds of objects of utility, comfort, and luxury (and also of obvious ostentation and false prestige) in dowry, the subtle demands for cash, assurances of 'decent marriage', and ways of conveying to the boy's people the direct and indirect gains that would accrue to them through a particular match, have all a strong flavour of market transaction. It is difficult to pinpoint what is bought and sold : a secure future and leisure for the daughter? Or transfer of responsibility of the girl who was hitherto a liability to her parents? What is more than clear, however, is that girls have to face an extremely unfair competition, in which their own worth is hardly recognized. The prospects of marriage produce considerable strain on the girls during their childhood and adolescence.

It is interesting to see how the values inculcated in the society operate to perpetuate the evil. A folksong of eastern UP says, "Let my daughter be married in a family where she will be swinging on a swing all the time". A rich girl's stereotyped ambition is that after marriage she should have nothing to do but sit on a comfortable mattress and chew betel. Most certainly these ideas set standards of desirability for others. It is revealing that the committee during its tour in Rajasthan found that in a girls' college, few girls could be counted on the tips of one's fingers looked forward only to a respectable and secure marriage so that they would not need to work for a living. With progressive standardization of lifestyles and greater communication between groups and communities, the values of a high consumption society; with its false ideas of prestige are influencing other sections also.

A notable feature of our society, which is closely related to dowry, is the involvement of man's prestige in the kind of work that the women of his house are required to do. That is how the norms for women of properties and business classes and also those belonging to the official class, include them to lead an almost parasitic existence. The farmers all over the country have been known to withdraw their women from the fields as soon as they become a little prosperous. Similarly, the aspirant middle-class in urban areas are tending to withdraw their women from the area of gainful work, as soon as they have a stable source of income.

Dowry is an all-India phenomenon, but it is possible, to identify its differential impact and working. There are some communities and groups (excluding those who follow the custom of paying bride-price) who have been relatively free from the menace of this custom. To give a few examples: most Muslim communities, the non-Catholic Christian groups outside Kerala and the Parsees do not practise the custom of dowry. The Nagar Brahmins of Gujarat, the Khatris of UP and the Mathur Kayasthas did not customarily settle marriage transactions in cash or kind. Several castes in Maharashtra also fall in this category. But today people belonging to these groups are also adopting dowry. It is rampant in Punjab, UP, Bihar and Rajasthan and to a lesser degree in Bengal, Orissa, and Madhya Pradesh. Here, as mentioned earlier, the flow of gifts is almost unidirectional. Aggarwals and other Vaisya groups in the Hindi-speaking areas, the Rajputs and the Kayasthas and the landowning castes of Bihar and UP practise dowry. Among the Kanyakubja Brahmins, the Rajputs, the Padidars and Anavil Brahmins of Gujarat and other communities, hypergamy has resulted in establishing high rate of dowry. In the South, the following groups are known for demanding and giving high dowries: the Reddis, the Kammas and the Velmas as also the traders and well-to-do Brahmins of Andhra Pradesh, the Naidus, the Brahmins, the Vellalas, the Mudaliars and the Chettiars of Tamil Nadu; Brahmins, Vaisyas and some Lingayat groups in Karnataka and the various Christian groups in Kerala. In Bengal, all the upper castes practise dowry. Dowry among the Muslims previously consisted mainly of clothes, jewellery, and articles of household use of the daughter; and the other principal item of expenditure used to be entertainment of the bridgegroom's party and celebration of the wedding. In North India and in the princely States, marriage of a daughter had always involved substantial expenditure. But now, even among the Muslims dowry is demanded, though may be in a more subtle form. There is in fact no difference now in pattern and motives for conspicuous consumption and dowry, either religionwise or castewise:

Black money and unaccounted earnings have given a fillip to dowry during the post-Independence era. A new class of noveau rich has emerged that buys a daughter's future with dowry, to raise its own social status by entering into marriage alliances families of high status. These people are keen to get rid of the black money, so they spend it lavishly during the wedding. In this process the level of expectation in the marriage market has changed altogether. Men of honest means and moderate income find it extremely difficult to remain in order to compete with this class that has a free flow of black money. The committee received innumerable complaints from common people, who are fully aware of this situation and are also very bitter about it.

We would like to emphasize that the spirit of dowry and the transactions involved in it, particularly at the upper middle class and upper class levels go against the goal of a socialistic society. Such value patterns of marriage expenses tend to influence other socio-economic groups. It is an undeniable fact that excepting a few rich, almost everybody has to spend beyond his means where dowry is involved. During our visits, women all over the country complained bitterly about the increasing burden of dowry and also told us that many girls had to remain unmarried because of this evil practice. The limited means of the parents and the abnormal demands for dowry impose a great strain on the minds of some young girls. In Orissa, some doctors reported to us the increasing incidence of nervous breakdowns in this group.

Elsewhere too we even heard of some cases of suicides by young girls who were faced with this problem.

Material considerations like wealth, jobs and professional opportunities have always formed one of the important incentives for marital unions even in countries where marriage is supposed to be based on love. What is deplored in the case of dowry is its compulsive character and material transactions in actual consideration for marriage. We require some concrete measures to do away with this state of affairs. The attack on dowry has to be multipronged. Our measures, though aiming at proximate ends, should take a determined step forward towards an egalitarian society. Social consciousness needs to be aroused particularly amongst women, to enable them to understand that by encouraging dowry they are perpetuating the inequality of the sexes. Reforms in marriage customs to simplify the ceremony, increasing opportunities for employment, condemnation of the ideal of a parasitic existence for women, a reassessment of the value of household work, and home making, as socially and economically productive, and the enforcement of the Anti-dowry Act, are some of the measures necessary to fight the increasing problem of dowry.

The problem of dowry cannot be solved only by educating the young. Therefore, it is necessary to examine the present law against dowry and do away with the loopholes which have made it totally ineffective. The present law may be regarded as only proof of the growing social awareness about the evil custom of dowry. It is essential that acceptance of money, property, or goods in consideration of marriage be made a cognizable offence. It will then activate social service organisations to take up the case and pursue infringements of the law.

In banning dowry it does not seem feasible to ban gifts for the daughter herself. The present law does not ban it, nor can future law prohibit it totally. This is likely to pose a difficult problem. This issue will have to be tackled at the level of mass education and social pressure. It will be necessary to keep record of things given to the daughter so that they remain her possessions and are not appropriated by the in-laws.

If public display of gifts is banned, it may hold unhealthy competition in check. It will spare the bride's parents much humiliation. This is not a minor issue. In Gujarat it is common practice to send round invitations to women to see the gifts being given to the bride and her in-laws. In many other areas, though not mentioned in such specific terms, there are a few occasions for which invitations are sent specifically meant for displaying the dowry This must arouse strong social censure. We feel the women's organisations can play an active role here.

Ostentatious celebrations involving enormous expenditure on food, lighting and entertaining should also be banned. Viewed in terms of national interests, this is a drain on national resources and public amenities which are in short supply. Control over the expenditure on weddings should be viewed as an anti-inflationary measure. It is here that the interests of women and the nation converge.

Compulsory registration of marriage for all may gradually lead to simplification of rituals and would help eliminate occasions for gift giving. Further, it will be easier for the young to break the stranglehold of endogamy. During our tours, many persons, both men and women observed that inter-caste marriage is one of the ways to fight the evil of dowry. For this it is necessary to build up strong public opinion in favour of such marriages. This would naturally go against endogamy and hypergamy wherever it is prevalent, and would lead to raising the women's status by undermining the importance of dowry.

It is necessary to devise ways and means to make women conscious of the limitations of their self-image. Whether they are transferable assets, as in the case of bride-price, or liabilities whose value has to be enhanced so that they become acceptable, women are demeaned. It is regrettable that women not only concur with but even encourage this practice. It is imperative that programmes on adult education and mass media should be purposefully framed to make the women understand the implications of both dowry and bride-price.

There is also need for a separate machinery to enforce the proper implementation of legal measures connected with marriage and dowry.

Lonely Women

It is often mentioned that the problem of widow remarriage is the problem only of a section of society. It is necessary to ascertain how large this section is. In the absence of use of caste as a category for the collection of census data since 1941 onwards, population figures for 1931 census have been used to obtain some idea of the proportion of Hindu population which traditionally did not practise remarriage of widows. Population of these castes was added together and its percentage to the total Hindu population in 1931 was worked out. This is only an approximation. Our calculations show that at least 13.9 per cent of the Hindu population in 1931 did not customarily practise widow remarriage. This percentage is enough proof that the problem does not concern the whole of the Hindu society. But if we have a look at absolute figures (3,32,56,068) and think of the rate of population growth since 1931, it certainly does not appear to be an insignificant problem.

Furthermore, it is these groups who have served as reference groups for society, and have also been instrumental in bringing about legal reforms which are to affect the whole society. One example should suffice to bring this point home. There is enough evidence to tell us that only an infinitesimal number of widows in the general population were immolating themselves, that outside ruling and priestly families, the custom did not have a wide appeal. But in certain parts of the country reverence is shown for women who committed sati in the past. Commemoration stones of these acts can still be found in some regions. Newly married couples are sometimes taken to sati stone to show reverence and obtain blessings.

Even among those who allow widow remarriage, many groups do not look upon it favourably At the most, it is accepted as a solution of the problem of maintenance of a widow. Among 'high class' Muslims too widow remarriage is frowned upon.

According to 1951 census, there were 22 million widows i.e., 123 widows per 1000 females. According to 1961 census 10.8 per cent of total female population consisted of widows as opposed to 3.70 per cent widowers. The census of 1971 recorded 8 million widowers as against 23 million widows.

This proportion has not changed drastically in the 1971 census. Presence of children is a positive deterrent to remarriage of mothers, particularly after they have crossed the age of 35 or 40 years. The fear of losing the children and not being able to have them with her is very real for a woman, and this applies to all women except those in matrilineal communities.

The condition of widows in our country may be examined from two angles: social and economic. These two are interrelated and are often indistinguishable from one another. Social attitude towards widows differs at different socio-economic levels with regard to details.

A change in the lifestyle of women after they are widowed is characteristic of Indian society, though there are regional and group variations at different socio-economic levels. Restrictions imposed on Hindu widows have been mentioned earlier. It should be emphasized here that with the conception of man as the breadwinner and the woman as his dependent, the married state for a woman is considered fortunate and conversely widowhood is associated with great misfortune. Lifelong mounting is imposed on them. The signs of the married state have to be removed from the person of the widow. In many communities this process is made specially painful. It emphasizes that her existence has been rendered worthless by the death of the husband. The Muslims of respectable families also follow regional practices of making a widow distinguishable. Other religious groups follow this behaviour pattern in varying degrees.

An important purpose of these restrictions on a widow is to make her unattractive. Reactions of the respondents in our survey to a question as to whether a young widow should be required to change her mode of dress are revealing. Combining partial and full approval we find that 59.52 per cent Hindus approve of such a change, whereas 61.49 per cent of Muslims, 62.16 per cent Jains and 52.94 per cent Parsees fall in this category. Though low in comparison to the above groups, the percentage of Christians (44.21 per cent) approving of such a change is not negligible. Only 30 per cent of the Sikhs expressed the same opinion. This low percentage among Sikhs may be due to the fact that most respondents belonged to Chandigarh which is a modern city. The lowest percentage is among the tribals, 27.78 per cent. Even today the social norm is that a widow should look different from a married woman in every manner. Even in educated circles deviation from this norm on the part of a widow is commented upon.

Association of inauspiciousness with widowhood still continues. Widows themselves avoid taking an active part in ceremonial occasions. For instance, among the Bohras, a widowed mother would not break the coconut for her son's birthday. Responses to our question indicate that there is some disapproval on the widow's participation in auspicious ceremonies. As many as 23.41 per cent Hindus disapprove of such participation while 10.14 per cent do so only partially. Over 22 per cent Jains, 13.13 per cent Muslims and 16.33 per cent Christians disapprove of widows participation, As against 58.87 per cent Hindus who approve, there are 71.94 per cent Muslims, 71.88 per cent

Christians and 88.24 per cent Parsees who approve such participation.

A very interesting pattern is seen in the response according to caste groups: the percentage of upper caste Hindus approving of widows participation is the highest (63.45 per cent), next comes the middle caste Hindu (60.43 per cent), then the lower caste Hindu (58.28 per cent) and last came the Scheduled Castes (50.66 per cent).

Thus, it appears that the distinction between a married and a widowed woman is kept more alive at the lower social levels; in fact there are definite ritual occasions in which widowed women are debarred from participating. However, these women, if young, are expected to remarry. Among Muslims if a son dies during the lifetime of his father, then his widow does not get any share of the property.

It is regrettable that though the condition of widows in our society caused such serious concern to the social reformers, and the Widow Remarriage Act was passed as early as 1856, societal attitude to this unfortunate group has not registered any appreciable change in all these decades. Immolation may have stopped, and cases of remarriage of child widows may have increased, but by and large, the condition of widows continues to be a blot on our society. The large group of widows, of all ages, whom we met in Varanasi, were in a state of destitution. Many of them had children. Only a few had any visible means of economic support. Allowances from the family were either negligible or non-existent. In the absence of any employable skills, most of them were depending on petty trades like making paper bags, packets of incense, selling pakoras, etc., earning an average income of Rs.15 to 20 per month. Some joined 'bhajan mandalies' and earned about 37 paise in an evening and even that was not a regular income. Some were reduced to absolute penury.

The widows' scheme, adopted by the UP State Government, provides a small pension. According to the District Officer, only about 10 per cent of the recommended cases have received this pension. In their discussion with us, these women stated that though their lives were finished, neither they nor society had provided any protection or security for their children, whose future looked no less bleak than at present. We were informed by a member of the Gandhian Institute of Studies, that some teenage daughters of these widows were employed as compositors by some of the small presses in Varanasi. They were mostly illiterate, and had to do their work by recognizing letters without being able to read which imposed tremendous strain on their eyes. He described their expressions as 'sightless' and 'vacant'.

Many of these widows had been sent by their families but family ties with brothers, sons or in-laws had gradually become tenuous. Some even said that they had run away to escape from ill-treatment by relatives. The older ones, no longer able to look after themselves, were prey to cheats. When they fell sick, the only care they could get was from some neighbours belonging to the same group who are in no position to look after others. Some of the worst cases are left before the Ramakrishna Mission Old People's Home. The latter, being already fully occupied, has stopped further admissions, hence even this avenue for care of these old and destitute women is now restricted.

According to the Gandhian Institute, which conducted a small investigation, there are approximately 5000 destitute or semi-destitute widows in the city of Varanasi. Majority of them come from Bengal but some were also from South India and Maharashtra. We have recorded our impression of this group as a symbol of the status that our society allots to widows.

For those who have any property, however, legal reform securing the right of widows to a share of the husband's property has improved the condition considerably. The decision of the government to provide family pensions to widows of government servants during their lifetime, with additional allowances for children during their minority has also guaranteed a modicum of security.

The Age Factor

Although the past few decades record a distinct rise in the mean age of marriage for women in India, the problem continues to be serious as is evident from the percentage of married persons (which would also include widowed persons) even in the age groups 10-14 and 15-19. Table 4.7 gives the percentage distribution of ever married persons according to sex and age during 1961 and 1971.

In rural areas in the 10-14 age-group, 13.79 per cent girls are already married, while in the 15-19 age group, 63.9 per cent are married. In Urban areas this percentage is much less: 4.21 per cent in the age group 10-14 and 36.24 per cent in the 15-19 age group. According to another source, in the 12.5-17.5 age group, 45.21 per cent girls are married as compared to 13.29 per cent boys.

One redeeming feature of child marriage in India is that customarily the consummation of marriage takes place after the girl reaches puberty. It may be noted, however, that this age does not necessarily tally with the legal minimum age of marriage. The magnitude of this phenomenon is not easy to measure for the simple reason that people are not able to report their correct age in the census.

Low age of marriage is related with the near-universality of marriage in India. In a sense marriage is not an individual decision but a cultural one. Only 0.5 per cent of women never marry. Since all girls have to be married off, the thought of their marriage has to be entertained from their birth or early childhood. Early marriage is accompanied by seemingly easy solutions for a number of problems. Rules of endogamy prescribe that marriage should be arranged within a certain group and other norms of prescription, preference and proscription (such as close kin marriages, *gotra*, clan and village exogamy, and marriage within one's class) are best taken care of in the case of early marriage. Leaving the girl to decide when to marry may also mean her deciding whom to marry and her choice may not conform to the traditional norms and rules. Betrothals; end early marriages are encouraged towards this end.

Closely connected with the concern for maintenance of group boundaries, is the desire to preserve the purity of women. The biological facts of gestation and lactation make repudiation of motherhood next to impossible. The emphasis on the purity of women springs from this. Chastity gets strong emphasis among Muslims also and with emphasis on purity of blood, early marriage appears to be the best solution, particularly for those who do not keep their women secluded. This concern for the purity of women was reflected in the compulsion of pre-puberty marriage among the Brahmins; for whom its violation results in ostracism. A father who could not get his daughter married before puberty was believed to commit a grave sin. In spite of strong opposition to early marriage from the reformers, it remained popular till the decade of twenty of the present century. Because of the ban on widow remarriage among the upper groups, early marriage was nothing less than a curse. Although not as low as among the Brahmins, age of marriage among the Kshatriya castes and trading castes was also fairly low.

It is striking to note that among the Brahmin and the Scheduled Castes, the age of marriage was the lowest. As pointed out earlier, since 1931, there has been a gradual but distinct rise in the age of marriage, especially among middle and upper classes in the urban areas but the rise is not so noticeable among the Scheduled Castes.

Census has stopped collecting data for marital status of girls below the age of 10. Therefore, it is not possible to know the incidents of child marriage between the ages of 0 to 10 years. But in our tours, we came across a number of children below the age of 10, who were already married. We were also informed of marriages where the bride had to be placed on a *thali*. In a village in Darbhanga, we saw a girl of three in a Balwadi, wearing sindur mark. (In a factory in Indore that we visited, a baby of 18 months in a creche was already married).

One of the important factors connected with early marriage is that onset of puberty is regarded as the right age of marriage, as the girl is considered ready for maternity. The notion that a girl can be married with proper rites only when she is a virgin is also an important factor accounting for early marriage. Thus, for those, whose girls cannot be confined to the house as they have to share in the work outside, early marriage is necessary in order to ensure their reputation and protect them from motherhood before marriage. This association between relatively free movement of girls, and early marriage is fairly clear. Some social scientists have related the continuance of the custom of early marriage among Scheduled Castes with their helplessness in protecting their women from the lust of men of upper groups who have economic power over them.

Scarce resources also constitute an important reason for early marriage. Since the girls do not support the family, the responsibility in respect of them is transferred to another family as early as possible. Another reason given for early marriage is to enable the proper adjustment of girls in their conjugal family.

Though not the only factor, low age of marriage is responsible for population growth, low standard of health of women, and high mortality in the child-bearing age. It is essential to take strong action in this regard. Compulsory registration of marriage would never help to curb the evil of child marriages.

Early marriage and lack of education constitute a vicious circle. A determined effort will have to be made to educate the girls in rural areas, and those from lower socio-economic groups in urban areas, if the age of marriage of girls is to be raised. Education of both boys and girls will inevitably contribute to raising the age of marriage. An important measure will be to educate the people so that they learn to de-link onset of puberty with preparedness for maternity.

In urban areas and for the well-to-do in rural areas, education and the need for employment of boys has raised the age of marriage and this has contributed substantially to the raising of age of marriage for girls. Thus, education of girls is both a cause and an effect of raising of age of marriage.

In studies of attitudes regarding age of marriage which were conducted mainly in educated urban middle and upper classes, the desirable age suggested for the marriage of girls broadly ranges from 16 to 24.

Child marriages do not pose such a problem among the tribes. Among the hill tribes, few girls are married before 15. Only a few tribes like the Bhumia, Mahalis, Omnatya, Bajuras, Tharuas, some Koyas and some sections of Gonds practise child marriage. Banjaras hold the betrothal early but do not marry their girls before the age of thirteen, which is the age allowed by their panchayat. Marriage immediately after puberty is fairly common and among many tribes of Central and Western India, in fact the onset of puberty is associated with maturity.

The Tradition

Customary marriages are normally coterminous with easy forms of divorce, and secondary marriages. Secondary marriage of a widow or a separated or divorced woman is accompanied by a nominal ceremony, mostly signifying the renewal of the "married" state for the woman. Depending on the region, the gifts by the man consist of things like glass bangles, vermillion, nose ring, etc. A feast announces and accords social approval to the union. But often the union may start with the man bringing the woman to live with him or the woman entering his house and starting to live with him. Feast and ceremony would follow much later.

While marriages among the dominant higher castes are performed by ritual ceremonies, since marriage is recognized as a sacrament, there have also been various forms of customary marriages practised by other castes, which do not involve any rituals, but are based on simple practices. These marriages are fully accepted by the community. Throughout the Himalayan tracts, Jhajra, which means putting a ring in the bride's nose is the customary form of marriage. In the trans-Giri territory of Simur, regular marriage is termed Jhajrath. Earlier, marriage according to Hindu rites was unknown but now the well-to-do and respectable Kanet and Bhat families have adopted them. In Maharashtra, the poor people practise Mohutur, which is shortened form of marriage, not as sacred but a completely legal union. In some parts of Madhya Pradesh, if an unmarried girl elopes she may be married only by a simple ceremony, which is used for secondary marriages. In Manipur, however, cases of elopement, which are then followed by a proper ceremonial marriage, are of frequent occurrence, and not disapproved by the community. These are only illustrations of various forms of customary marriage.

Where a woman leaves one man and goes to another, payment of compensation to the previous husband may be said to be characteristic of the majority of those castes, among whom secondary union is permitted. In many areas there is no formal divorce; when a woman goes to live with another man, who is willing to pay compensation for her to the previous husband, with a fine and feast to the caste or village, the union is recognized.

It has been brought to our notice that in some of these cases, where a compensation has to be paid by the new husband, the woman's decision is not always voluntary. We were told in Himachal Pradesh that in the Reet form of marriage while the former husband must consent to the remarriage of his wife to another man, the wife's consent to this exchange is not essential. There have been cases where she is compelled to it by the former husband or by her father as the case may be. The women who met us, both in urban and rural areas, were outspoken in their criticism of this practice. Similar cases of compulsion have been reported from Madhya Pradesh.

The tribals are governed by the customs of marriage and divorce of their respective tribes. In the case of primary marriages most tribes have a preference for marriage by negotiation, but there are also provision to accommodate unions which are established by elopement. We were told by members of the Wanchoo tribe in Arunachal Pradesh that though negotiation is preferred, if a girl is emphatic in her refusal to accept the groom chosen by her family, then her decision is accepted. We believe this is common among most tribes.

A popular custom in the tribes of the plains is to get a boy to serve and help the girl's household for a few years to earn his bride. It is in the subsequent unions that individual choice gets exercised. Going to live with another man, who pays a compensation, to the previous husband, is equivalent to divorce and remarriage. There is considerable variation in customs regarding marriage and divorce among the tribals, but an examination clearly indicates that the two partners are not at par with each other. There is compensation for the loss of woman, and the mother has to leave her children behind. There is, however, no stigma on divorce and remarriage. The average age of marriage is also higher among tribals, and no marriage takes place before puberty.

5

Dissolution of Marriage

The concept of 'union for life' or the sacramental nature of the marriage which renders the marriage indissoluble has gradually been eroded and through legislation the right of divorce has been introduced in all legal systems in India, but the same variations and unequal treatment of sexes characterizes this branch of law also. A monogamous marriage without the right of divorce would cause great hardship to both parties to the marriage.

According to the Census of 1971, the total number of divorced or separated women in the country is estimated to be 8,70,700 ; of which 7,43,200 are in the rural areas and 1,27,500 in urban areas. The ratio of divorced or separated women is 1630 per thousand males. The table 3.3 indicates the relative percentage of divorced or separated men and women to the total male and female population in 1961 and 1971. It is dear that the proportion of women who remain in this state is higher than men, in both rural and urban areas.

A survey undertaken by the Census in 1961 in 587 selected villages with a sample of 1,33,775 marriages covering a period of 50 years, had indicated a wide acceptance of divorce by the village community and some variations of incidence among the religious communities. Incidence of divorce was highest among the Muslims (6.06%), followed by Hindus (3.21%). Among the Buddhists it was 3.7 per cent, among the Jains 1.68 per cent and among Sikhs 0.91 per cent. The incidence of divorce among Christians, was considerably lower (0.41%). The causes for divorce show that adultery and barrenness are the commonest grounds for divorce in most of the villages studied. Extreme poverty is also found to be cause for divorce. In Rajasthan, sexual incompatibility and incapacity are recognized as grounds for divorce.

Laws for Separation

According to traditionalists, divorce was unknown in Hindu law. Even today, divorce is not a socially accepted norm among many sections.

We can take judicial notice of the fact that even today considerable sections of the Hindu society look with disfavour on the idea of dissolving a marriage.

Polygamy, without the right of divorce, caused tremendous hardship, in many cases.

Contrary to the general notion regarding the indissolubility of Hindu marriage, a large section of Hindus among the lower castes have traditionally practised divorce. These customary forms of divorce were recognized, both socially and judicially. The usual customary forms are:

(a) by mutual consent;

(b) unilaterally—at the pleasure of the husband or by the abandonment of the wife;

(c) by deed of divorce (char-chitti);

The custom of obtaining divorce by mutual consent is prevalent among certain castes in Mumbai, Madras, Mysore and Kerala. In Madhya Pradesh, it has been held that divorce by mutual consent is a valid custom among the Patwas of that State. A customary form of divorce by agreement (chuttam-chutta) amongst the Barai Chaurasiyas of UP has been declared valid by the Allahabad High Court. These are only a few illustrations to indicate the existence of divorce by mutual consent.

According to the custom prevailing in Manipur (Khaniaba), it has been stated that a husband can dissolve the marriage without any reason or at his pleasure. Among the Rajput Gujaratis in Khandesh, and in the Pakhali Community, marriages dissolved if the husband abandons or deserts the wife. Among the Vaisyas of Gorakhpur in Uttar Pradesh, a husband may abandon or desert his wife, and dissolution takes place even without reference to the caste tribunal.

This form is prevalent among certain castes in South India, also in Himachal Pradesh and the Jat community. Recently the Supreme Court has upheld a deed executed by the husband divorcing his wife.

Usually customary divorces are implemented through the intervention of the traditional Panchayats or caste tribunals. Therefore, in States where this has not been customary, the courts have not permitted Panchayats to take upon themselves the right to dissolve a marriage. Once the custom is proved, however, the courts will not interfere.

The courts have exercised a lot of judicial scrutiny and discretion in upholding or rejecting such customary divorce practices. In doing so, they have applied the strict test for the validity of such customs. In cases where the existence of a custom was not proved, or where the custom could be regarded as running counter to the spirit of Hindu law, or was against public policy or morality, courts have declared such customary forms of divorce as invalid.

Under customary law, there is no waiting period after divorce to remarry. But if divorce is obtained under the Hindu Marriage Act, then either party to the marriage can lawfully remarry only after a lapse of one year after the decree of divorce (Sec. 15). Retention of customary forms of divorce under the Hindu Marriage Act is advantageous because this process of dissolving the marriage saves time and money in litigations. The only difficulty that may arise is if the divorce according to customary law is brought at some stage to the notice of the court, and the latter decrees that particular form of divorce to be against public policy or morality. If one or both parties have remarried, such a marriage will be void and the status of the children will be affected. To minimize this, it has been suggested that the Ministry of Law should prepare an exhaustive record of customs relating to divorce found in different States and set up a panel of socio-legal experts to determine if any of these customs are invalid. Copies of the record should be made freely and easily available to the people and the Panchayats.

With the enactment of the Hindu Marriage Act of 1955, divorce became a part of the law governing all Hindus. The ground for this had been already prepared by the passing of the Hindu Women's Right to Separate Residence and Maintenance Act in 1946, which inter alia, permitted the wife to separate from her husband on the ground that he had married again. Following this, some of the States took the initiative and as with monogamy, legislated to permit divorce for Hindus.

The various grounds on which a husband or a wife can obtain divorce are (a) living in adultery, (b) conversion to other religion, (c) insanity, (d) incurable form of leprosy, (e) venereal disease, (f) renunciation, (g) where the respondent has not been heard of as being alive for a period of seven years or more by persons who would naturally have heard of it, (h) failure to resume cohabitation for a period of 2 years after the decree of judicial separation, and (i) failure to comply with a decree for restitution of conjugal rights. Two additional grounds have been given to the wife to obtain a divorce: (i) if the husband has more than one wife living, and (ii) if he has been guilty of rape, sodomy or bestiality. The former has a retrospective effect in the sense that when the marriages took place (i.e. before the Act), polygamy was legally permissible. This right can be exercised by either of the wives, and has obviously been provided to strengthen the social policy of monogamy. From the cases reported, it appears that many women have benefited from this provision.

An Offence ?

Since adultery is a very grave matrimonial offence, a very high degree or standard of proof is required. The courts have insisted that the offence of adultery should be proved beyond reasonable doubt. A husband or wife can ask for divorce only if at the time of filing the suit, the other party 'is living in adultery'. A single act of extramarital intercourse is not sufficient to dissolve the marriage, though it is sufficient for a decree of judicial separation. The Bombay Ḥigh Court, therefore, rejected the petition of a husband as at the time of the petition there was no evidence that the wife was leading an adulterous life, though there was evidence that she had done so earlier.

Another provision of Act which is often taken advantage of is non-compliance with a decree restituting conjugal rights for two years or the lapse of the same period after a decree of judicial separation. One of the grounds for judicial separation is desertion, provided it is 'without reasonable cause.' It is in interpreting, reasonable cause, the judiciary has often exhibited their inability to appreciate the socioeconomic changes and the Constitutional right to equality.

Whenever conjugal rights have come into open conflict with the woman's right of equal opportunity in education or employment, the attitude of the judiciary has often been rather ambiguous. Instead of guiding the conflicting parties towards a rational adjustment to the process of social change, the judiciary has either evaded the issue or thrown its weight on the side of the traditional view of the husband's authority. Two illustrations will suffice to demonstrate this tendency:

(a) A husband's demand for his wife to resign her job as a teacher in city away from his place of employment, to join him, was upheld by the Punjab High Court, which ruled that it was the duty of the wife to remain under the 'roof and protection and submit obediently' to the authority of the husband.

(b) In a similar case, the Allahabad High Court took a step forward by opining that the concepts of protection and society are "inelastic and rigid rules which cannot be interpreted in the context of present day conditions and needs of society. In view of the altered social and economic conditions, both husband and wife may think it necessary to work and contribute to the family chest."

The Court, therefore, conceded the right of deciding the question to the wife where "in cases of economic stress for the sake of the family and children" the wife genuinely thinks it is necessary for her to work. The judgement, while conceding the right in cases of genuine economic necessity, totally evades the issue of the individual woman's right to decide whether to work or not.

We are of the opinion that difference in the place of work should not be regarded as a ground for a case of desertion or restitution of conjugal rights.

Cruelty and desertion have not been made grounds for divorce though they are recognized as grounds for a judicial separation. It, therefore, follows that in these cases the innocent party to the marriage, against whom there has been cruelty, or who has been deserted, has to wait for two years before he or she can get a divorce. Uttar Pradesh has given the lead in this and amended their law to make these grounds for divorce. In our opinion these should be added as grounds for divorce in the Hindu Marriage Act so that persons are not compelled to follow the present circuitous route and undergo the expense of going to court twice.

A Different Law

Under Muslim law a husband has an absolute and unlimited right to repudiate the marriage at his will. This is known as Talaq. A Muslim wife had no such right to dissolve her marriage. Unwritten and traditional law tried to ameliorate her position by permitting her to seek dissolution under the following forms:

(a) Talaqi Tafwid. This is a form of delegated divorce. According to this, the husband delegates his right of divorce in a marriage contract which may stipulate that inter-alia on his taking another wife the first wife has the right to divorce him. The courts have upheld these pre-nuptial and post-nuptial agreements as not opposed to public policy nor against the spirit of Muslim law. The Assam High Court has strengthened this right by declaring that such a power of Talaq given to the wife is irrevocable.

(b) Khul: This is a dissolution by an agreement between the parties to the marriage, on the wife's giving some consideration to the husband for her release from the marriage tie. The terms are a matter of bargain and usually takes the form of the wife giving up her dower.

(c) Mubarrat: This is divorce by mutual consent.

According to Hanafi law, the inability of the husband to maintain his wife does not give her the right to dissolve the marriage. Following the Hanafi law the courts in India had refused the wife the right to dissolve her marriage on the ground of non-payment of maintenance. The Shafi and the Maliki laws, however, allowed the wife to obtain divorce on this ground.

This Act took advantage of the law as enunciated by the Maliki and Shafi Schools and recognized the right of a wife to dissolve the marriage on the following grounds:

(i) that the whereabouts of the husband have not been known for a period of four years;

(ii) that the husband has neglected or has failed to provide for her maintenance for a period of two years;

(iii) that the husband has been sentenced to imprisonment for a period of seven years or upwards;

(iv) that the husband has failed to perform without reasonable cause, his marital obligations for a period of three years;

(v) that the husband was impotent at the time of marriage and continues to be so;

(vi) that the husband has been insane for a period of two years or is suffering from leprosy or a virulent venereal disease;

(vii) that she, having been given in marriage by her father or other guardian before she attained the age of fifteen years, repudiated the marriage before attaining the age of eighteen years; provided that marriage has not been consummated;

(viii) that the husband treats her with cruelty;

(ix) on any other ground which is recognized as valid for the dissolution of marriage under Muslim Law.

Muslim women have been benefited by the Act. The provision that have been resorted to most frequently are the 'option of puberty' and failure to provide maintenance by the husband.

According to traditional Muslim Law, when a minor girl had been given in marriage by the father or the father's father, the marriage was valid. She could, however, repudiate the marriage if she could show that the guardian had acted negligently or fraudulently. But if the minor had been given in marriage by any other guardian, she had the right to repudiate the marriage on attaining puberty. The present Act has modified the traditional law permitting her to exercise the right irrespective of who was the guardian who gave her in marriage. The courts in India have interpreted this right very liberally, often invoking the principles of equity and justice in favour of the girl. They have not rigidly applied the letter of the law in regard to the time when this right could be exercised. It has been held that a minor wife did not lose her right to repudiate the marriage within a reasonable time after she came to know of her right and not necessarily when she attained puberty. In such cases they have even waived the condition of non-consummation when such consummation was by force or before she attained the age of 15.

Women's Right

This right has been interpreted in two ways. One group of decisions, basing itself on the traditional 'fault theory', has denied the right to a wife to divorce where her conduct was such as to absolve the husband from his duty to provide maintenance. The other group has tended to uphold the right, irrespective of the wife's conduct.

These two groups of decisions clearly indicate that legislation alone cannot eliminate right traditionalism, with its desire to preserve the status quo. Without supporting judicial interpretation, even the policy of the law is negated. The decision of Justice Krishna Iyer is, therefore, significant as he has focused his observations on the right of the Muslim wife to divorce when her husband has failed to provide her maintenance for two years. He has used his erudition to support the theory of dissolution when the marriage has broken down, irrespective of the relative faults of the parties :

> There is no merit in preserving intact the tie of marriage when the parties are not able to and fail to live within the bonds of Allah, that is to fulfil their mutual marital obligations and there is no desecration involved in dissolving a marriage which has failed. The entire emphasis is on making the marital union a reality and when this is not possible..., the Quran enjoins a dissolution... This secular and pragmatic approach on Muslim law of divorce happily harmonizes with contemporary concepts in advanced countries.

We recommend that the right of the wife to divorce, on the failure of the husband to maintain her, irrespective of her conduct which may be the main or contributory course, should be clearly spelt out.

Muslim Law had always recognized that in some cases the wife may be able to get a divorce. To the uncodified law the Dissolution of Muslim Marriages Act, 1939 has added further grounds. But the power of the husband to pronounce talaq unilaterally remains, and has in no way been curtailed either judicially or through legislation. As long as this absolute and unlimited right remains, the position of the Muslim wife will remain insecure and her status cannot be raised. We totally disagree with the view that with justice Krishna Iyer's judgement and her right to obtain divorce by 'Khul', a Muslim woman's rights "are brought into approximation with those of the man." While the judgement is undoubtedly a great step forward, it has to be remembered that she still has to wait for two years will out maintenance before getting her release. Also, a right to buy her release, as provided in the Koran can hardly be regarded as approximating the unilateral right of the man.

Legislation is the only instrument which can bring the Muslim divorce law into line with not only the needs of society but with the prevailing law in other Muslim countries. Turkey and Cyprus have completely prohibited unilateral divorce, while in Tunisia, Algeria, Iraq and Iran the husband has to apply to a court. In Pakistan, Legislation has restrained the freedom of the husband to divorce his wife. He has to inform the Arbitration Council which will try and bring about a reconciliation. The husband's pronouncement of 'talaq' without informing the Arbitration Council has been declared to be an offence.

We recommend immediate legislation to eliminate the unilateral right of divorce and to introduce parity of rights for both partners regarding grounds for seeking dissolution of a marriage.

Other Laws

All Christians are governed by the Indian Divorce Act, 1869. Under the Act, both husband and wife can obtain a divorce, but there is a great difference between the rights of the husband and the wife. The husband can obtain a divorce if the wife has committed adultery. The wife can seek a divorce on the following grounds:

(a) husband's conversion from Christianity and marriage with another woman;

(b) incestuous adultery;

(c) bigamy with adultery;

(d) marriage with another woman with adultery;

(e) rape, sodomy or bestiality;

(f) adultery with cruelty;

(g) adultery with desertion.

Thus, the wife has to prove two offences by the husband before she can obtain a divorce.

The law is so outdated that a need for revision has been felt for quite some time. The Government, realizing the need for reform, referred the matter to the Law Commission in 1960. The Commission prepared a Draft Bill. The Christian Marriage and Matrimonial Causes Bill, 1960, contains almost all the grounds included for divorce under the Special Marriage Act, 1954, such as desertion, cruelty, adultery, leprosy, venereal disease, conversion to another religion, and wilful refusal to consummate the marriage. Further, either party to a marriage can also obtain a decree of judicial separation on any of the grounds mentioned for divorce.

We regret that in spite of these preparatory steps, no action to enact this measure has been taken by the Government so far and recommended no further time be lost to reform and amend this law on the lines suggested by the Law Commission.

The Parsees are governed by the Parsee Marriage and Divorce Act, 1936. Both the parties to the marriage can initiate divorce proceedings on the following grounds:

(a) continuous absence for 7 years without information to those persons who would naturally have heard of him or her;

(b) non-consummation;

(c) insanity;

(d) adultery, bigamy, rape or an unnatural offence;

(e) causing grievous hurt or venereal disease;

(f) imprisonment for 7 years or more;

(g) desertion for three years;

(h) non-resumption of cohabitation following a decree of judicial separation or restitution of conjugal rights;

(i) conversion

In addition to these common grounds, the wife can obtain a divorce if she has been compelled by her husband to prostitution. The husband has the right to dissolve the marriage if the wife was pregnant by some other person at the time of marriage.

The Jews in India are not governed by statutory law but by their customary law. Originally, the ghet was the only form of divorce. In India, however, dissolution of the marriage can be done through the court on grounds of adultery or cruelty. The marriages are generally monogamous excepting in certain specified cases. Because they are a small minority, no effort has been made to codify or reform this law. We feel that this should be undertaken now and the principle of monogamy as well as the normal grounds for divorce as provided in the Special Marriage Act should be adopted for this community also.

This Act provides for a secular form of marriage which can be taken advantage of by all persons in India irrespective of their religious faith. Persons who marry under this Act will be governed by the provisions of the Act and not by their own personal law, with respect to their matrimonial rights and remedies.

The grounds on which divorce can be obtained by either party to marriage are adultery, desertion for a period of three years, cruelty, unsound mind for 3 years, leprosy, venereal disease, continuous absence for 7 years without information to those persons who would naturally have heard of him or her, non-resumption of cohabitation for 1 year following a decree of judicial separation or restitution of conjugal rights. In addition to these, the wife can obtain divorce on the ground of rape, sodomy or bestiality. A special feature of this Act is that the parties can also dissolve the marriage by mutual consent. All that the parties need do in order to opt for divorce under this provision is, to present a petition to the court that they have been living separately for a period of one year or more, and that they have not been able to live together having mutually agreed to dissolve the marriage.

In the field of personal law and particularly in divorce, the existence of various legal systems create a peculiar situation. The Constitution recognizes the right freely to profess, practise and propagate religion. Conversion, therefore, from one faith to another is an individual's right and the motive for the conversion is or should be beyond judicial scrutiny. But, when such conversion impinges on the right of another person, the question poses a problem. In India today as a legacy of the multiple systems, a person by his or her conversion also acquires the right to be governed by a different set of laws. Even after the Constitution, the codified Hindu Marriage Act has mentioned conversion as a ground for divorce. Is conversion then to be treated as a matrimonial wrong?

Under statutory Muslim law, a woman converted to a faith other than Islam or renouncing Islam has only the right to divorce if the husband has committed a matrimonial wrong— Conversion per se does not affect the validity of the marriage and is in no way a bar to its continuance. On the other hand, a man converted to Islam from another religion has the right to be governed by his new personal law, including the right to marry more than once. This is so even when his first marriage was a monogamous marriage. He is also entitled to claim that his new faith does not permit him to remain married to a Hindu and he can, therefore, proceed to divorce her by uttering 'talaq' three times. The Indian Divorce Act does not recognize conversion as affecting the validity of the marriage unless it is followed by the marriage of the husband to another woman. The Converts' Dissolution Act permits the convert to Christianity to dissolve the marriage provided the marriage has in effect broken down as a result of the conversion.

It requires to be proved clearly that cohabitation has been discontinued because of the conversion. Under the Parsee law, conversion is ground for divorce provided the suit is brought within 2 years. This thorny question is dealt with in many ways, but the problem remains of reconciling the right to freedom of religion with the possible impact of conversion on marriages. It has been suggested that the question of marital rights on conversion should be governed by principles of equity, justice and good conscience. The other is that non-converted person can, for a period of two years at least, be able to affect any marital rights by resorting to the new religion. While the second suggestion has the merit of deterring people from easy conversion to solve their matrimonial problems, in our opinion conversion should not be a ground for divorce as it offers an easy way of evading matrimonial obligations.

Our review of the different laws governing divorce indicates that both customary laws and the secular law, i.e. the

Special Marriage Act, 1954 recognize mutual consent as a ground for divorce, but this is conspicuous by its absence in any of the statutory laws governing different communities. On the other hand, the religious laws and judicial interpretations of them have generally tended to emphasize the fault theory, being particular to prevent the party of a matrimonial wrong from obtaining a dissolution of the marriage. This leads often to the use of perjured evidence. There is even today an indirect way of getting divorce by mutual consent, by registering one's marriage under the Special Marriage Act. It is thus recommended that after celebration according to religious rites the marriage should be registered and this ground should be recognized in all the personal laws so that two adults whose marriage has, in fact, broken down can get it dissolved honourably.

The provision in the Parsee Marriage and Divorce Act, 1936 which enables a wife to obtain a divorce if her husband has compelled her to prostitution, in our view, is a very desirable protection. We recommend inclusion of this provision in all other Personal laws.

As a general principle, we recommend parity of rights regarding grounds for both husband and wife. This already exists in some of the personal laws, and in our view is essential to guarantee equality of status for both partners. It may be noted that the findings of our survey on this question shows an overwhelming opinion in favour of parity. There are on an average 74 per cent of the respondents (72.9 per cent of males and 74.37 per cent of females) who have stated that the grounds for divorce should be the same for both husband and wife.

Owning a Child

"Adoption is the institutionalized practice through which an individual belonging by birth to one kinship group acquires new kinship ties that are socially defined as equivalent to the congenital ties. These new ties supersede the old ones either wholly or in part". It is the act of a person who takes upon himself the position of a parent to a child who in law is not his own child.

The origin of the custom of adoption is lost in antiquity. It has, however, been recognized in India for centuries and is also recognized in other South Asian countries, such as Burma and Thailand. Adoption forms the subject matter of personal law. In India the only personal law which recognizes adoption in the true sense of the term is Hindu Law which regarded adoption as the 'taking of a son as a substitute' in case there is no male issue.

Even though Muslim law does not recognize adoption, in India previously the law had permitted this right to Hindu converts to Islam, who had enjoyed this right prior to their conversion. This customary right was, however, partially abrogated by the Shariat Act under which a Muslim could make a declaration that he and his sons would in future give up all customary rights including that of adoption and be governed by the Act.

But the custom of adopting sons was in vogue in Arabia at the time of the Prophet Mohammad. The word *adia* used in the Holy Quran means adopted sons justice Ameer Ali held that a family Waqf could be made not only for the benefit of descendants of the founder but also of dependants, which would include an adopted child who has resided with the settler as a dependent relation. The Lahore High Court held the word 'family' to include an adopted child who had resided with the settler as a dependent relation. All these clearly indicate that adoption was not unknown among Indian Muslims.

Islam never gave any special significance to an adopted son, as it does not to a natural son. Islamic religion, unlike the Hindu one, does not associate a son, or any other relative, with the performance of the last rites of a deceased Muslim whether male or female. It, therefore, does not recommend adoption of son or a daughter for a person dying issueless, nor does it absolutely prohibit it. The Quranic verses having a bearing on adoption did not lay down a specific negative rule.

For the Parsees, there is no law of adoption as such or adoption recognized by custom. However, the widow of a Parsee dying issueless can adopt a Palak on the 4th day of the deceased's death, for the adhoc purpose of performing certain religious rites for the deceased. This adoption is only for a limited purpose and does not confer any proprietary rights on the Palak.

The institution of adoption is not known in Christian Law in India. If Christian parents have no issue and desire that some child takes that place, the only way open for them is to approach the Court under the Guardian and Wards Act and be appointed a legal guardian. This is the procedure being followed today also by foreigners who want to adopt Indian children. In such cases if the Court has given permission for the child to be taken out of the country, adoption according to foreign law (i.e. law of the guardian) takes place outside the country.

The law relating to adoption has been amended and codified and brought in line with the principles of social justice. Previously, the object of adoption was to ensure spiritual benefit by performing the last religious rites and also to continue the line. The devolution of property was regarded as of secondary importance. It was because of this basic approach to adoption that Hindu Law did not recognize the right of a Hindu to adopt girls as she could neither ensure spiritual benefit nor continue the line of her father.

With the passing of the Hindu Adoption and Maintenance Art 1956, the whole basis of adoption has been changed. The Act makes three clear departures from the previous law of adoption:

(a) A Hindu can now adopt either a son or a daughter, since the religious purpose has given place to the secular idea of parents wanting a child.

(b) The husband can no longer give or take in adoption without the consent of the wife. In the case of an existing marriage, however, the primary right continues to be of the husband. The wife's right being confined to consent only is in a sense, continuation of the 'Superior' right of a man which has been the running theme in Hindu Law.

(c) A woman can now adopt, if she is unmarried, widowed or divorced. Similar right is conferred on a married woman if her husband has completely and finally renounced the world, has ceased to be a Hindu, or has been declared by a Court to be of unsound mind.

The uncodified law did not recognize the right of a woman to adopt and even in the case of a widow, who adopted as the agent of her late husband, the rules differed and some schools prohibited it altogether.

The fundamental departure that the new Act has made, is in recognizing the right of a woman to adopt in her own right and no longer as the agent of her husband (dead or alive).

While the Act has certainly improved the status of women, we recommend that the right of adoption should be equal for husband and wife, with the consent of the other spouse.

We welcome the step taken by the Government in introducing a uniform and secular law of adoption – The Adoption of Children Bill 1972 – which is now before Parliament, since this would benefit the entire community.

The statement of objects of the Bill reads:

> In India there is no general law of adoption though it is permitted by statute among Hindus and by custom amongst a few numerically insignificant categories of persons. In recent years there has been a growing demand for a general law of adoption in India.

The growing demand was noticed by the Committee during its tours as a large number of women expressed their approval of right to adoption being extended to all.

We recommend the early enactment of the Bill as it will extend the right of adoption equally to men and women of all communities, and will be a step towards a uniform secular law.

6

Various Allowances

Expenses Paid

The obligation of the husband to maintain his wife arises not out of any contract, express or implied, but of the status of the marriage. As in other branches of law, the right to maintenance forms a part of the personal law and therefore is not uniform.

Apart from the right given in the personal laws the Criminal Procedure Code, enacted in 1898, provided for right of maintenance. The right of the wife and dependent children to move the court for relief against the husband or the father who neglects or refuses to maintain his dependent family members is thus not confined to any particular religion but is given to all wives and children irrespective of their personal laws. In this aspect uniformity had been achieved in at least one sphere of family law. Considering the date of this law, the obligation was, understandably, confined to only the husband or the father, with no corresponding obligation being placed on the wife or the mother.

The Code has, however, been repealed recently and we are today governed by the New Criminal Procedure Code of

1974. In spite of the passage of 76 years, the new Code continues to reflect the old attitude to women. With some modifications like extending the right to demand maintenance to indigent parents and to divorced wives, the obligation to maintain continues to be that of the man. In the changed social context and particularly in view of our firm declaration of equality, it is irrational to place the obligation only on the man. However small the number may be, today there are economically independent women who can not only look after themselves but also their husbands and children. Similarly the duty to look after indigent parents cannot be restricted only to sons. As a matter of fact the exclusion of daughters from the obligation may be used as an argument to deprive them of their share in the father's property.

As we believe in equal status of husband and wife and of son and daughter, we recommend amendment of the law to provide for obligations expected of the economically independent woman:

(a) to maintain her dependent husband;

(b) to share with him the duty to maintain their children;

(c) to share with her brothers the duty to maintain their dependent parents.

The inclusion of the right of maintenance in the Criminal Procedure Code has the great advantage of making the remedy both speedy and cheap. The underlying principle of this is to prevent starvation and vagrancy, which usually leads to the commission of crimes. From this point of view, it seems unjustified to limit the total amount of maintenance for all dependent persons to Rs 500.

We welcome the extension of this right to divorced wives as earlier the implied financial deprivation in case of divorce was the only obstacle to a woman wishing to free herself from an unhappy marriage. But in extending this right to divorced wives uniformity has been sacrificed and no longer can all women claim to be governed by the same law which they had been governed by since 1898. An exception has been introduced, to deny maintenance to those divorced wives who have received a 'sum of money payable under customary or personal law'. This clearly excludes Muslim women who may have got the dower at the time of the dissolution. There is no scope even for judicial scrutiny to examine whether the amount paid as dower is adequate for maintenance or not. This exclusion of all divorced Muslim women defeats the purpose of the section to provide a speedy remedy to indigent women.

We, therefore, recommend that the ceiling placed on the maximum amount payable as maintenance should be removed and the term 'wife' to include divorced wife be made applicable to all women without any exception.

Various Regulations

Unlike the right given under criminal law, where the claim of the wife depends on the husband having 'sufficient means', under Hindu Law her right is absolute and the husband cannot claim inadequate means to deny maintaining her. Even a previous order of the criminal court will not bar her right to seek further relief in a civil court. But she loses her right if she deviates from the path of chastity. Even a single lapse from chastity may alter her right detrimentally. Under criminal law, however, the right will be affected only if the wife is living in adultery at the time of her claim. Her past adultery will not affect her right but may be a factor in fixing the amount of maintenance.

The exacting standards are perhaps explained by the fact that both under the uncodified Hindu law as well as under the present law, the Hindu Adoption and Maintenance Act 1956, she gets a real maintenance. According to judicial opinion "just an adequate fare with nothing for clothing, residence as also for medical attendance and treatment falls short of maintenance: and these are "minimal in a civilised society. " While assessing the amount of maintenance, the court takes into account various factors like the position and status of the parties, the reasonable wants of the claimant and the obligations and liabilities of the husband. It also judges whether the wife is justified in leaving the husband. The justifiable reasons are spelt out in the Act.

The lacuna in limiting the obligation of maintenance to the man only has been remedied by the codified Hindu Law. Maintenance pendente lite (pending the suit) and even the expenses of a matrimonial suit will be borne by either husband or the wife if the other spouse has no independent income for his/ or her support. The same principle will also govern the payment of permanent maintenance and the court will fix the amount taking the needs of the applicant into account. If necessary, the Court may secure the payment of this amount to the applicant, by securing a charge on the immovable property of the respondent. Such a right will continue as long as the applicant for maintenance remains unmarried.

It is strange that while the question of maintenance as a real need and responsibility of either spouse was recognized on the one hand by the Hindu Marriage Act as early as 1955, the Criminal Procedure Code passed in 1974 should on the other hand have reverted again to the 19th century concept which regards woman as only a dependent.

Maintenance of the wife is a precept in the Quran and the highest obligation of the husband. Maintenance (nafaqa) includes food, clothing and lodging irrespective of husband's means or on the wife's lack of possession of an independent income. She has, however, to be accessible to the husband and obey his reasonable commands. The Muslim wife also has the right to sue her husband under the Criminal Procedure Code, but under that law the sum ordered can never exceed Rs 500. Under the personal law, the court while fixing the amount considers the rank and the circumstances of both the spouses. As already discussed failure of the husband to maintain his wife for two years entitles her to get a divorce. Her right to maintenance lasts only as long as she remains a wife. If she is divorced, she loses her right of maintenance and is only entitled to it for three months (the period of *iddat*). After this period she has no further claim and it is this which has created a discrimination between the Muslims and other Indian women. We recommend the removal of this discrimination and extension of right of maintenance to divorced wives.

The Parsee Marriage and Divorce Act 1936, being a pre-Independence legislation recognizes only the right of the wife to maintenance – both alimony pendente lite as well as permanent alimony. The maximum amount that can be decreed by the court as alimony during the time a matrimonial suit is pending in court is 1/5th the husband's net income. In fixing the quantum as permanent maintenance, the court will determine what is just, bearing in mind the ability of the husband to pay the wife's own assets and the conduct of the parties. The order will remain in force as long as the wife remains chaste and unmarried. The right of the wife to be maintained by the husband has been regarded as being an inherent right. Therefore any contract by her giving up future rights of alimony has been regarded as contrary to public policy.

The maintenance rights of a Christian wife are governed by the Indian Divorce Act, 1869. The provisions are the same as those under the Parsee Law, and the same considerations are applied in granting maintenance both alimony pendente lite as well as permanent maintenance. Apart from similar provisions in the Parsee Act, there are two sections in the Indian Divorce Act which reinforce the guilt theory on which the Act is based which indirectly affect maintenance rights. The first provides that if a divorce or judicial separation is obtained by the husband on the ground of the wife's adultery and the court finds that the wife is entitled to some property, it may on its discretion order that the whole or part of the property should be settled for the benefit of the husband or the children. Conversely, the second provides that where the court has decreed damages to the husband against adultery, the court may while fixing damages make an order that the whole or part of the amount recovered should be settled for the benefit of the children, or used as a provision for the maintenance of the wife.

While the right of maintenance is recognized in all the different laws, the common problem faced by most women even amongst the very few who know of their rights, is the expense and delay in first getting an order from court. Often a counter claim is made by the husband for restitution of conjugal rights in order to defeat or at least delay her right. Even when the order for maintenance is made, the husband very often fails to pay after a few months and this entails the wife's repeated visits to court and undergoing tremendous delay and expense. The arrears of maintenance are treated as a debt whose recovery is by the ordinary procedure on a par as laid down for all other debts. This is very often expensive and time consuming.

In order to minimize the hardship caused by nonpayment of maintenance, and to ensure certainty of payment, we recommend that all maintenance orders should be deducted at the source by the employer (as done in the case of income-tax). Where it is not possible to deduct at the source, as in the case of a businessman or a self-employed person, the arrears of maintenance should be recovered as 'arrears of land revenue or by distress'.

As this procedure has been adopted in the recovery of income tax, extension of it in the field for recovery of a maintenance order should not pose any undue difficulty. An additional mode of execution of the maintenance decree may be, to adopt the same procedure as is done in the case of fines under the Criminal Procedure. This has the advantage of making the recovery both cheap and speedy.

The ultimate and the best solution however, lies in leaving a specialized court like the Family Court to deal with the entire question of maintenance. Apart from matters like the income of the respective spouses or the degree of financial dependence, a Family Court would be able to approach the question taking an overall view. The matters for consideration would be : (a) the husband's obligation to his divorced wife, as well as obligations incurred by him by a subsequent marriage; and (b) the divorcee's degree of dependence on the maintenance order and her efforts to become financially independent. A continuing process of assessment is necessary and only a specialized court (which will be free of the tremendous pressure of work and time an ordinary civil court has today) can exercise this vigilance.

Right to Property

As far back as 1925, the existence of a large number of statutes dealing with succession led the government to pass the Indian Succession Act. The object of the Act was to consolidate the large number of laws which were in existence and not to unify them. The laws governing succession of Muslims and Hindus were excluded from the purview of this Act. In the process of consolidating, two clear schemes were adopted – one dealing with the succession rights of persons like Indian Christians, Jews and the marriage under the Special Marriage Act (1955) and one for succession rights of Parsees.

In the first scheme, (persons who were not Parsees), when an intestate died leaving a widow and a lineal descendant, she would be entitled to a fixed share of one third of the property and the children irrespective of their sex would share equally. This law was amended with the object of improving the rights of the widow and it was provided that where the intestate died leaving a widow and no lineal descendant and the net value of the estate did not exceed Rs. 5,000 she would be entitled to the whole of his property. Where the net value of the estate exceeded rupees five thousand, she was entitled to a charge of a sum of rupees five thousand (with interest at four per cent till payment) and out of the balance she was entitled to her intestate share. The section applied only in cases where the deceased had died intestate in respect of all the properties.

But inexplicably even this benefit has been denied to the following categories of persons:

(1) Indian Christians;

(2) Any child or grandchild of any male person who is or was at the time an Indian Christian; or

(3) Any Hindu, Buddhist, or Jain, succession to whose property is governed by the Indian Succession Act.

Since this provision seeks to give better rights to a widow without lineal descendants, the denial of the benefit to the above mentioned groups can not be justified on the grounds of policy.

But the Act confers no restriction on the power of a person to will away his property. Therefore the protection enjoyed by a Muslim widow to a share of the estate and by the Hindu widow to being maintained, is denied to other widows under this law. There is, therefore, a need to incorporate some restrictions, similar to that prevailing under Muslim law to prevent a widow from being left completely destitute.

To add to the diversity of laws, the Travancore High Court held that the Indian Succession Act did not apply to the Christians of the State. The result of the decision was that Christians in Kerala and those outside are governed by different laws. The decision includes the multiplicity of laws which govern Christians within the State. The Travancore Christian Succession Act governs the succession rights of Christians in Travancore but the Act exempts those following the "Marumakkavazhi System" of inheritance. To add to this, certain sections of the Act are not applicable to certain classes of the Roman Catholic Christians of the Latin Rite and to Protestant Christians living in the five taluks mentioned therein among whom male and female heirs of the intestate share equally. The Cochin Christians Succession Act, generally governs the succession to the properties of Christians in the, former territory of the Cochin State. The Cochin Act exempts members belonging to the European, Anglo-Indian and Parangi communities, and the Tamil Christians of the Chittur Taluk who follow the Hindu law.

A characteristic feature of the Travancore and Cochin Christian Succession legislations is that they are based on the former notions of the Hindu Law of Inheritance which discriminated against women. Therefore, a widow or mother inheriting immovable property takes only a life-interest terminable on death or remarriage. A daughter's right is limited to Streedhanam. Even in cases where she is entitled to succeed she takes a much lesser share.

Under the Travancore Act if the intestate has died leaving a widow and lineal descendants, the widow is entitled to a share equal to that of a son. If on the other hand, the intestate dies leaving a widow and daughters (or the descendants of a daughter) her share will be equal to that of a daughter. The nature of her interest (i.e. life interest) is the same when she takes the property in the absence of any lineal descendants. The widow's share is half when the intestate dies without leaving any lineal descendant but has left behind his father or mother.

According to the Cochin Act when there is a son or the lineal descendants of a son, the share of a widow is equal to two-thirds that of a son. If the intestate has left no son or the lineal descendant of a son, she is entitled to a share equal to that of a daughter.

Even though she is mentioned as an heir along with a son in Group I of Section 25 of the Travancore Christian Succession Act, a daughter is entitled to "Streedhanam" only. The Streedhanam of a daughter, for the purpose of the Act, is fixed at one-fourth the value of the share of a son or Rs. 5,000 whichever is less.

The Cochin Act provides that where an intestate has left sons and daughters, each daughter shall take one-third share of a son. But like the Travancore Act, an important limitation in regard to a daughter's share is laid down in Section 22 of the Cochin Christian Succession Act. This in effect makes the right of a daughter to receive Streedhanam only. But the Cochin Act, does not specify a limit on the amount of Streedhanam. Both legislations, however, provide that Streedhanam which has been paid, but promised by the intestate, will be a charge on his estate.

It is, therefore, apparent that the rights of inheritance of Christian women under the Travancore and Cochin Acts are meagre. Even these rights may be defeated as the testator has the absolute power of willing away his entire property.

We recommend that immediate legislative measures be taken to bring Christian women of Kerala under the Indian Succession Act as a first step to unify the law and as suggested above restrictive power be placed on the unfettered right of a person to will away his entire property.

The Christians of Goa were governed by the Portuguese Civil Code and continue to be so even today. The result is not only an addition, to the multiplicity of laws but the prevalence of a legal system which is totally different from the ones prevailing in the rest of the country.

While the Portuguese Civil Code makes no differentiation on the basis of sex, it relegates the widow to a very low position. The order of the legal heirs of a person are first sons and daughters who get the property in equal shares, failing them the parents inherit, followed by the brother and his descendants. The widow will inherit only if there is no heir in the above classes. But the widow will become the owner of "the agricultural commodities and fruits, called or pending, meant and necessary for the consumption of the conjugal couple". She will however lose even this right if she is divorced or separated from her husband.

Unlike the Christians in other parts of India, a person cannot will or gift away his entire property to the exclusion of his legal heirs. The portion over which a person has no control is known as 'legitim' and usually consists of half the property. But even this legitim can be denied to an heir under certain conditions, for example, if a child lodges a complaint against his parents for an offence which is not against his person or against his spouse.

But even a disinherited heir is entitled to maintenance. The recognition of equal rights for sons and daughters is undoubtedly to be welcomed but to relegate the widow to the fourth position and leave her with only the fruits and agricultural commodities needs to be remedied immediately.

The legal system for Christians prevailing in Pondicherry is extremely anomalous. During the French rule both Hindus and Indian Christians were governed by the Hindu law. After Pondicherry became a part of India, the Hindu Succession Act was extended to the State but as that Act only applies to certain categories of persons who come under the term 'Hindu', the Indian Christians in Pondicherry can no longer be governed by it. The Indian Succession Act has not been extended to the State, so the Christians there continue to be governed by the precodified Hindu Law, which relegates a woman to an inferior position and does not even regard her as being full owner even in the few cases where she can inherit property. The resultant position is anachronistic and should be remedied immediately. (We recommend extension of the Indian Succession Act to Goa and Pondicherry).

Different Laws

A feature of the rules governing the Parsee intestates is, that like the Hindu law and unlike the Muslim law, there are separate rules for the devolution of the property of male and female Parsee intestates. The rules relating to the intestate succession of males have the characteristic of Muslim law, namely, the share of a male heir is double that of a female heir of the same degree. For example, if a male Parsee dies leaving a widow and children, the property will be divided so that the share of each son and widow will be double the share of each daughter. Further, if a male Parsee dies leaving one or both parents, in addition to a widow and children, the property will be divided so that the father shall receive a share equal to half the share of a son and the mother will receive a share equal to half the share of a daughter. The inferior position of a mother in the scheme of succession thus becomes evident and the position is radically different from that which prevails under the Hindu Succession Act, 1956.

The above position may be contrasted with the rules applicable to the succession of a female Parsee intestate. If she dies leaving a widower and children, the property will be divided equally among them and if she dies leaving children only, among the children equally. Thus, while a son is entitled to an equal share in the mother's property along with the daughter, the daughter is not entitled to the same right when she inherits the property of the father along with the son.

It should be pointed out that the above provisions were enacted in 1939. At the time these rules conferred better rights on women than the then existing Hindu and Muslim laws. But with the passage of time, these rules have become out of step with the progressive trends in the society. The Parsee daughter's share remains half of that of a son as in Muslim law, but she is denied protection against disinheritance which is the beneficial feature of Muslim law.

Further, it is extremely doubtful whether Sections 5 to 56 of the Indian Succession Act govern the devolution of agricultural properties, as the Central Legislature was not competent to enact legislation relating to agricultural lands, in 1939. Therefore, it would seem that agricultural lands will devolve according to the rules in force prior to the amendment, according to which the son's share will be four times that of a daughter, the widow's share will be double that of a daughter; and father and mother are not entitled to any share.

The problem of succession cannot be understood without reference to the law of joint family. Under the Mitakshara law, the law of succession is intimately connected with the special incidence of co-parcenary properties. In co-parcenary properties a son, son's son and a son's grandson acquire a right by birth. Thus only males can be coparceners.

The salient feature of a Mitakshara coparcenary is the existence of community of interest, unity of possession and the right of survivorship among the coparceners. So long as the family is undivided, no individual coparcener can claim that he is entitled to a specific share of the joint estate. His share is liable for increase by deaths and decrease by births. The properties are managed by the Karta who is usually the eldest among the coparceners. The share of a coparcener is ascertained only by partition.

Though the institution of joint family was common in most parts of India, there were two major systems prevailing in the country—Mitakshara and Dayabhaga—which dealt differently with the property rights. Added to these two systems was the matriarchal system which prevailed in some southern states. Pre-Independence India, therefore, had a number of different systems of succession among Hindus and in most of them, the position of the woman was one of dependence with barely any proprietary rights. Even where they enjoyed some rights, they had only a life interest and did not enjoy full ownership. While earlier this may have been socially acceptable, with socioeconomic changes brought about in the 20th century this inferior position was no longer tenable. As discussed earlier, the rigidity that had crept into the law because of the British policy of non-intervention had made it impossible to adopt the legal systems to changes. The position, therefore, could only be remedied by legislation which would reflect the socioeconomic changes since our independence and at the same time fulfil the promise of non-discrimination guaranteed in the Constitution.

With the object of bringing in uniformity and in conformity with the norms of the post-Constitution period, the Hindu Succession Act was passed in 1956 though after stiff resistance from the traditionalists.

The Act brought in some radical and fundamental changes, the most important of which was to introduce equal rights of succession between male and female heirs, in the same category, like brother and sister, son and daughter. It also simplified the law by abolishing the different systems prevailing under the Mitakshara and Dayabhaga Schools. The Act also extended to persons in south India previously governed by the Marumakkattayarn law also. It recognized, however, that there had to be some differences in a system which was found in matriarchy. The hold of tradition, however, was so strong that even while introducing sweeping changes, the legislators compromised and retained in some respects the inferior position of the women. By yielding to pressure, it sacrificed the uniformity which had been one of the major aims in introducing this law. A close study of the Act discloses that there are still a number of different systems governing succession.

The most remarkable features of the Act, however, are the recognition of the right of women to inherit equally with men and the abolition of the life estate of female heirs. The Class I heirs of a man today are widow, mother, son, daughter, widow of a predeceased son, and sons and daughters of predeceased sons or daughters. These heirs take the property in equal shares and as absolute owners.

The one major factor which has attributed to the inequality between sons and daughters is the retention of the Mitakshara coparcenary. As mentioned earlier, membership of it is confined only to male members. No stranger can be introduced even by agreement of all the members and no female can be a member of a coparcenary. There are no succession rights in a coparcenary but the interest of a coparcener on his death goes to the remaining members. A number of decisions, as also legislation in the 20th century, like the Hindu Women's Right to Property Act, have made inroads in the concept of the coparcenary and in some ways it had really lost some of its important features. It would therefore have been quite feasible at the time of the 1956 Act to abolish it altogether. One point of view according to Mulla (1960) is that the "best solution would have been to abolish the ancient legal formula of acquisition of rights by birth and devolution by survivorship. Since the logical way was to assimilate the Mitakshara with the Dayabhaga, this could also have had the merit of equitable treatment of the nearest female heirs of a coparcener and of bringing about uniformity in the law in all parts of India." But there was strong opposition to this point of view and the institution was retained but an effort was made to make some provision for the nearest women members of a person i.e., Class I heirs.

The compromise arrived at was that if a male member of a coparcenary dies, then for the purpose of ensuring that his heirs get a share of the property, his share of the coparcenary will be demarcated, as if there had been a partition and that share will be divided among his heirs. It means that, if there is a coparcenary of a father and two sons, the share a father would have got on partition would be one-third. This will be divided among his Class I heirs. The consequence of this is that the two sons in addition to their original interest as coparceners,- will get equal shares of the father's property with the mother, grandmother and sister, etc. This naturally results in an unequal treatment between brother and sister. In a similar situation under the Dayabhaga system the daughter will get an equal share with the brothers as there is no right by birth for sons. The retention of the Mitakshara coparcenary, therefore, not only brings about inequality between the same class of heirs but also continues two different systems of inheritance.

The retention of coparcenary has also meant the continuation of two rights both of which affect the rights of female heirs detrimentally. The first is the right of a coparcener to renounce his right in the coparcenary. In order to do this, no specific formality is required beyond the expression of a clear intention. On such renunciation, the release is deemed to have separated him from the joint family though this will in no way affect the joint status of other members of the coparcenary. The result of this is that on his death, he will have no interest in the joint family which could be distributed among the Class I heirs. This deprives the female heirs of any share. A similar result can be achieved by a father who partitions joint family property during his lifetime without reserving any share for himself.

The second of such characteristics is the right to convert self acquired property to coparcenary property. The transformation of self acquisition into joint family property is frequently resorted to reduce the burden of income tax. But the effect of this is that the share of a female heir is reduced because in the self acquired property she would have had the right to inherit equally with the male members as Class I heirs.

Mitakshara coparcenary with its basic principle of right by birth of a male coparcener is the cause of unequal rights between the male and female heirs, though the Act accepted in principle the equality of the sexes. It should be noted that the Hindu Code Bill, 1948, as amended by the Select Committee, had, in fact, suggested abolition of the right by birth.

We recommend the abolition of the right by birth and the conversion of a Mitakshara coparcenary into a Dayabhaga one.

Another provision in the Act which contributes both to lack of uniformity as well as continuation of discriminatory treatment of female heirs is the provision excluding the devolution of tenancy rights under the legislation of the States, from the scope of the Act.

The apparent object is to protect the rules in State Legislations from the overriding effect of the Hindu Succession Act, which otherwise would have governed the succession to tenurial interests. The reasons behind this exemption, as they appear from the legislative debates are two-fold. First, that tenancy laws being property laws, apply to all whether a Hindu or non-Hindu. As the Hindu Succession Act is a personal law, it should not override the provisions of property law enacted in the interests of the agricultural economy. Second, that the States are responsible for agricultural laws and the Central Government is anxious not to encroach on the rights of the State Governments.

A serious objection is that the beneficial effects of the Hindu Succession Act can be denied by a resort to this provision. The bulk of the property in India is agricultural property and such an exemption detracts from the principle of uniformity. It may also be noted that the Act does not define the word "tenancy rights" nor is it defined in the General Clauses Act, 1897. Thus, on the question as to what constitutes tenancy rights, the last resort must be had to the specific legislation of the State itself, and it is quite conceivable that a State with dominant conservative groups could defeat the purpose of the Act by defining tenancy rights to include all-interests arising in or out of agricultural lands.

No particular economic justification has been made out by the States or States concerned for having separate rules for devolution of tenancies. The fact that many States do not have special provisions for succession to tenurial interests and the fact that the exception protects legislations in some States in the North, gives rise to a suspicion that it was intended as a concession to the conservative elements in these regions. The argument that the Act is a personal law and that it cannot override a property law ignores two aspects: (1) in pith and substance a law providing for devolution of tenancies is a law relating to succession, and (2) the fact that these special laws may contain features which are more discriminatory than the existing Hindu and Muslim laws.

The legislation in Uttar Pradesh (Uttar Pradesh Zamindar Abolition and Land Reforms Act, 1950), a State which comprises one-sixth of India's population, furnishes an example of this kind:

> When a bhumidar, sirdar or asami being a male dies, his interest in his holding shall devolve in accordance with the order of succession given below:
>
> (a) The male descendant in the male line of descent in equal shares per stripes.
>
> (b) Widow and widowed mother and widow of a predeceased male lineal descendant in the male line of descent, who have not remarried.

(c) Father;

(d) Unmarried daughter.

The above scheme of inheritance shows that in competition with a son the widow of a deceased is not entitled to succeed. The claims of a widow and unmarried and married daughters are preceded not only by the lineal male descendants in the line of descent, but even by their widows who have not remarried. The exclusion of the widow and the daughters cannot be justified on any principle.

The seriousness of the problem is emphasized by the fact that the Act is likely to apply to all the agricultural land in course of time, in Uttar Pradesh. The Statement of Objects and Reasons of the Uttar Pradesh Zamindari Abolition Act says : "It is expected that the vast majority of cultivators will become bhumidars. The present intermediaries in respect of their sir, khudkasht and groves will be classed as bhumidars persons paying land revenue."

In order to achieve the social equality of women as also in the interests of uniformity, we recommend the abolition of the exception provided in Section 4 (2) of the Hindu Succession Act, relating to devolution of tenancies.

Suggestions have been made to the Committee that equality of sexes could be achieved under the Hindu Succession Act, if the law was amended to permit women to become members of the coparcenary and pending further legislation to permit them to act as a karta of the joint family. We do not feel that the situation will improve by making this recommendation as the present unequal treatment will continue as far as wives or widows of coparceners are concerned, who not having been born in the family cannot become members of it.

In all other respects, uniformity has been achieved among Hindus as the Class I heirs mentioned are the same for all.

Similarly among the heirs of a female owner (with the exception of those who would have been governed by the Marumakkattayam and Aliyasantana law) uniformity as well as equality of sexes have been recognized. Sons and daughters (including the children of any predeceased son or daughter) inherit equally with the husband. A special provision however governs the property of women. In the event of her dying without leaving any children, her property does not automatically go to her husband. If the property in question has come to her from her father or mother it will go to her father's heirs, and if the property has come to her from the husband or her father-in-law it will go to her husband's heirs. For persons who were earlier governed by the Marumakkattayarn law, the property goes first to the children and to the mother, and the father and the husband inherits only if there is no heir in this category.

Another discriminatory provision in the Act is the one relating to the right of inheritance to a dwelling house. It provides that where a Hindu dies intestate and his property includes a dwelling house wholly occupied by the members of the family, then the female heirs are not entitled to claim partition of it unless the male members choose to divide their shares in the dwelling house. Female heirs are entitled to only the right of residence. Even in this there is a discrimination as this right is restricted to unmarried and widowed daughters or those deserted by or separated from their husbands. A married daughter enjoys no such right.

Obviously in enacting this provision, the legislature intended to balance the familial with individual interest. The main object of the section is unexceptionable as it asserts the primacy of the rights of the family as against the right of an individual and therefore, the restriction against partition which is against the family interest is justified, and should be retained. But nothing justifies the invidious distinction between married and other daughters. We recommend the removal of this discrimination so that all daughters enjoy the same right.

Like the Indian Succession Act, the Hindu law i.e., both Mitakshara and Dayabhaga place no restriction on the power of testation. During the debates in Lok Sabha on the bill, the fear was voiced that this may lead to the rights of a female heir being defeated. But the Law Minister had brushed aside these fears by saying, "I believe that a normal father will never do any such thing and if at all he has to do it for any reason, he will surely make a provision for his daughter when he is going to deprive her of her share by will." But this is an over simplification of the question and as was pointed out during the debate in the Constituent Assembly, "an analysis of the inmates of rescue homes in this country will prove how many of these women are those who have been turned out of the joint family." The Committee's own experience in many places, particularly in Varanasi, more than proves the point that there are many women who have been reduced to destitution and beggary because their families have deprived them of all support.

We recommend that right of testation should be limited under the Hindu Succession Act, so as not to deprive legal heirs completely.

A vast majority of Muslims in India follow the Hanafi doctrines of Sunni law and the courts presume that Muslims are governed by the Hanafi law unless it is established to the contrary. Though there are many features in common between the Shiah and the Sunni schools, there are differences in some respects. The Sunni law regards the Koranic verses on inheritance as an addendum to the pre-Islamic customary law and preserves the superior position of male agnates.

The heirs related to a deceased person by blood under the Sunni or the Koranic law are divided into three groups: (1)

Zavil-Furuz (the shares or the Koranic heirs); (2) the Asaba (agnates or "residuaries") and (3) the Zavil-Arham (uterine relations). The heirs who are neither sharers nor residuaries fall into the third category. The sharers take the estate first; the remaining estate (or the whole of the estate in the absence of heirs of the first kind) is taken by the residuaries. If there are no sharers and residuaries the estate goes to the uterine relations.

Where there are sons and daughters they inherit as residuaries. Thus, if the deceased dies leaving a widow, son and daughter, the widow takes 1/8 as a sharer, the son takes 7/12 (2/3 of 7/8) and the daughter 7/24 (1/3 of 7/8). On the other hand, a daughter in the absence of a son takes the estate as a sharer; half the share, if there is only one daughter and 2/3 if there are two or more daughters. Thus, if the deceased dies leaving father and daughter, the daughter is entitled to half the property as a sharer, the father to one-sixth as a sharer and the remaining one-third as a residuary.

One primary principle of Muslim law which grossly discriminates against women is that, under the law of inheritance, if there are male heirs and female heirs of the same degree like a son and daughter, full brother and a full sister, the share of a female member is half that of the male.

Under the Hanafi, the widow, though a sharer in every case is not entitled to take as a residuary. The share of a widow (or widows if there are more than one) is one-eighth. If the deceased dies without leaving a child, the widow's (or widows') share is one-fourth. The wife is not entitled to the radd (return). The social conditions of the present day necessitate that the measure of protection and security that a wife is entitled to, should be in no way inferior to that of any other member in the family, either during the lifetime of the husband or after his death. Therefore, a widow's position in the law of succession deserves particular attention.

Under the Shia law also, neither husband nor wife is entitled to the radd but if either of them is the sole surviving heir then they inherit the whole property.

If a Muslim dies leaving a daughter as his only close relative, she will not be allowed to take more than one half of his estate, the other half will go to some distant agnatic relative. Under the Shiah law the daughter would, in a similar situation, take one half as her share and the remaining half under the doctrine of radd.

Unlike Hindu and Christian Law, Muslim Law restricts a person's right of testation. A Muslim can bequeath only 1/3rd of his estate. The question is whether he has the power to correct any hardship that might arise under the law of intestacy in the exercise of his testamentary power (i.e. of one-third of his estate). It is beyond cavil that such hardship arises generally in the case of female heirs. But the Hanafi law appears to be particularly rigid in not permitting any device whereby the inequities of the laws of inheritance may be rectified.

A bequest to a stranger is valid without the consent of heirs, (if it does not exceed a third of the estate) but a bequest to an heir without the consent of other heirs is invalid. The consent of heirs to a bequest must be secured after the succession has opened, and any consent given to a bequest during the lifetime of the testatory can be retracted after his death. As the testamentary power exercised by a deceased in favour of an heir operates at the expense of their heirs, it is not an unnatural attitude to refuse consent to such bequests.

The Shiah law allows a Muslim the freedom of bequest within the disposable third and recent reforms in Egypt, Sudan and Iraq also permit this. If the rule is relaxed here it may be possible for a husband to make a bequest to his widow or widows which would help to make up for the inadequate share they get on intestacy.

Muslim law makes no distinction between movable and immovable property and though the right of a female heir like a widow or daughter has always been recognized and they have inherited absolutely (unlike the old Hindu law), we recommend that legislation be passed to give an equal share to the widow and the daughter along with the son as has been done in Turkey.

The medley of laws which govern the right of inheritance of not only female heirs of different communities but even of female heirs in the same community require immediate measures. Broad principles like equal rights of sons and daughters and widows, and a restriction on the power of testation, so that dependent members are not left completely destitute are needed immediately.

But legislation cannot be an end in itself. Publicity of new legislation and educating women about their rights need to go hand in hand. Otherwise, like many other social legislation, the rights remain only on paper. During its tours the Committee found a large number of women completely ignorant about their rights of inheritance. Even whey they know, they have been so conditioned that many of them oppose sisters depriving their brothers of property. Our survey report confirms this finding, as 68.16% expressed their opinion against girls having some share with their brothers in property and 57.54% were against girls and boys having equal property rights. But in the absence of social security and inadequate opportunities for employment, a woman without financial security faces destitution in our country. It is true that in a country where a large section of the people are below the poverty line, measures for ownership of property will benefit only a limited section. However, for this section, ownership of property will make women independent and they will undoubtedly gain in status. Besides, this will effectively check "the feeling that women are a burden to the family."

The various personal laws in our country are uniform in recognizing the obligations of a husband to maintain his dependent wife. The right of a wife to a moiety of the husband's property on his death is, however, not an absolute right like maintenance (except in Muslim Law), as the husband under the present system can, if he chooses, deprive his wife completely under his will. Our recommendation regarding restriction of the right of testation, if accepted, will change the moral duty into a legal one. But neither of these two rights recognize the wife's claim to be a part owner of the property acquired and enjoyed jointly by husband and wife during marriage.

In the socioeconomic situation prevailing in our country, the contribution of the wife to the family's economy is not recognized. A large number of them participate in the family's effort to earn a livelihood as unpaid family workers. Even when they do not do so, the economic value of their effort in running the house and assuming all domestic responsibilities, thus freeing the husband for his avocation is not accepted in law, either directly or indirectly. Most married women do not have any independent source of income, many even give up employment after marriage or do not take up a job for many years, in order to be able to devote their full time to family obligations, particularly in bringing up the children. They are, therefore, economically dependent on their husbands. In majority of cases, property, both movable and immovable, acquired during the marriage, is paid for out of the husband's earnings. If a matrimonial home is acquired, it will be registered in the husband's name; if things are bought for the house the legal ownership will vest in the husband, as in economic terms the wife has not contributed anything. The principle of determining ownership on the basis of financial contribution is unjust and works inequitably against women.

While our personal laws recognize the right of a woman to own and dispose of her personal property without any control from the husband, our survey discloses that only 25.74 per cent have a regular salary and 7.14 per cent occasional wages, though 79.48 per cent believe that a woman should work to supplement the family income. In case of divorce or separation, this large group of women without any earnings or savings of their own will be deprived of all property which, they acquired jointly. Even property which, she had got at the time of the marriage from the husband or his family, is denied to her in some communities. All these factors increase the dependence of the wife. The fear of both financial and social insecurity prevents her from resorting to separation or divorce even when the marriage is very unhappy.

The demand for recognition of the wife's contribution in the way of house works is growing in many countries. England has passed the Matrimonial Proceedings Act in 1970 and the judicial decisions following have emphasized the right of the wife to a share in the capital assets of the family. Lord Denning said that the wife "who looks after the home and family contributes as much to the family assets as the wife who goes out to work." He emphasized the importance of the home having been maintained by the joint efforts of both husband and wife and therefore "when the marriage breaks down it should be regarded as the joint property of both of them, no matter in whose name it stands."

It is necessary that legal recognition be given to the economic value of the contribution made by the wife through house-work for purposes of determining ownership of matrimonial property, instead of continuing the archaic test of actual financial contribution.

We therefore recommend that in the event of divorce or separation the wife should be entitled to at least one-third of the assets acquired at the time of and during marriage.

7

Outside the Household

While granting equality of rights to men and women in the Politics, Indian society implicitly accepts a sharp distinction between men's spheres and women's spheres and between masculine roles and feminine roles. Realization of true parity between the sexes granted by the Constitution will be possible only when conceptions and attitudes of the people are brought at par with it.

An overview of masculine and feminine spheres and roles in our society suggests that the inventory of activities considered proper for women and expected of them is not uniform all over India. Some basic notions about male and female roles, however, appear to be common.

Women are primarily associated with the home and man with the outside world. As home-makers women are expected to look after domestic chores, such as cooking and serving food, processing and storage of food, and cleaning the house. Woman's contribution to productive activities or to actual earnings of the family varies at different socio-economic levels and in different regions. Thus women, whether they work in the fields, factories or mines, or work at construction sites, or those who are engaged in household industries, or in white collar jobs, all of them are expected to be home-makers along with those who confine themselves exclusively to home-making activities. Housewives and mothers are the feminine roles. In the cultural understanding of the people, homemaking like child-bearing and also child-rearing cannot be distinguished from femininity. In other words these are sex-linked roles for women.

According to convention, participation in decision making for the community and the exercise of political power is regarded exclusively as the man's sphere. This is clear from the entirely male composition of the traditional Panchayats, either of villages or of caste groups including caste-like groups among Muslims.

By and large manual work for one's own house is to be done by women, as they are considered derogatory for men. They may perform them only under special circumstances, for instance, men may cook when women are disabled by illness or confinement. For community feasts cooking by men from within the group is a common feature at the lower socio-economic levels. Cooking, tailoring or sewing can be taken up as a vocation by men. Thus, suitability of women for these tasks appears to be a myth.

Broad regional patterns which show that there is no uniformity in the type and quantum of work expected of women also point towards this. What a woman does in one society or region is often dubbed as non-feminine in another. Weaving is the monopoly of woman in the North Eastern Hill areas, whereas in the lower parts of Himachal Pradesh it is a male activity. In Maharashtra and parts of South India it is done by men and women together and the woman is an indispensable assistant. Phulkari work of the Punjab is a women's craft whereas embroidery in Kashmir is done only by men.

In agricultural activities there are significant regional differences in the parts played by men and women. It is generally stated that men are supposed to do the heavier work. This is a supposition or belief which is not borne out by facts or by a cross regional survey of India. Men's tasks are not necessarily more arduous. What is more important is that men do work which is considered more prestigious. Ploughing and sowing in many parts and all the work of transportation by bullock-cart and large-scale marketing of produce are the domain of men. In the hills, women's contribution to the economy is distinctly higher than that of men, in addition to household work which is very burdensome, for example, bringing water from far-off places, keeping a vigil throughout the night to scare the wild animals away. "In Bashahr, Chamba and Mandi, women help their mates in wood-chopping. While men fell the trees women slice the timber. They carry the timber on their backs from the place where it is sawed to the place from where it is to be floated down the riven. They have been seen carrying logs weighing anywhere between 200 to 300 pounds with perfect ease and equanimity". These are the unpaid family workers of rural India.

In the middle-class (which constitutes an extremely amorphous category) the spheres of men and women are more sharply defined. Ordinarily, all the work that women do is viewed collectively as being an important component of feminine roles and it is not forgotten, that they are being performed by those, who have a certain identity in the context of the family, i.e. as mother, as wife, as sister, and so on. Since women are mostly confined to the domestic sphere, their work falls into entirely different sectors. Where the family business consists of grocery, knitwear, embroidery, snacks, and other things which can be made at home, women are the main workers behind the scene. These are the unpaid family workers who may not be returned in the census under the category of workers. Most of the work that women do in the domestic set up is semi-skilled. There is a clear differentiation between work done for one's own household and that done for others, so the question of doing this category of work for others does not arise. It is only in unfortunate circumstances that women of middle-classes, who have no other qualifications and skills, may be forced to do these jobs as a means of earning a livelihood; crafts like knitting, tailoring and embroidery are in some cases adopted by women to make small personal earnings, sometimes without the knowledge of husbands. Ideas of personal and family prestige are strong at this level; people take pride in the fact that their women do not go out of homes to work for others.

This traditional concept of women's role is gradually changing as girls have started taking up white collar jobs. In some families, the earnings of the girl are set aside for providing her dowry and marriage expenses, but gradually, the inhibition of the parents to be supported by the earnings of a daughter are also breaking down. There are extreme cases of parents not wanting the daughter to get married, as it would deprive them of her earnings.

Amongst the well-to-do also the spheres of men and women are well-defined and separate. Even though with domestic help, the burden of drudgery does not fall on the woman, but she is still expected to run the home and bring up the children. Her precise activities would depend upon a rural or urban setting, level of education norms of segregation and seclusion, notions of purity and pollution. Homemaking is raised to a fine art and trifling details assume exaggerated importance, but even here there is insistence on a role differentiation, according to conventions.

On the question intended to evoke responses on the pattern of division of labour by sex in the family, 84.1 per cent respondents said that cooking is entirely a woman's job; only 3.84 per cent said that it is shared equally. As for sweeping and cleaning the house only 3.94 per cent said that the work is equally shared and only 2.14 per cent said that the work of cleaning the utensils is equally shared. These two activities were undertaken only or mainly by men in less than 1 per cent cases. Washing of clothes is shared by men to some extent. In comparison to this, only 50.74 per cent respondents said that care of children was in the hands of women, either entirely or mainly; 28.90 per cent said it was shared equally, and 10.05 per cent said that men did it entirely. Sharing in decision making about the household expenditure reveals a different pattern. Only in 28.18 per cent cases, expenditure on food was decided entirely by women. Decision making seems to have been largely shared (48.48 per cent) by men and women. In 33.96 per cent cases decision about expenditure on education is entirely in the hands of men, as compared to 9.66 per cent cases in which it is mainly in the hands of women. Responses clearly indicate a pattern in which, besides equal sharing in decision making, more women take decisions about the kitchen, other domestic matters and matters concerning the future of the daughters. Men, rather than the women, more often exercise their judgement regarding choice of school, type of education and job the son should take. As is to be expected, various sociological and anthropological studies of village and of urban localities and communities clearly point towards male and female spheres of activity. For example, in Gore's sample of Aggarwal families in and around Delhi, women were expected to remain at home and look after the kitchen. 80 per cent of the women were busy exclusively with household work. They did not handle the money. Desai's findings based on the replies given by 369 married women students tell us that a majority of men did not share the household work. A study of 500 college students of Jhansi in UP brings out a sharp contrast between the daily routine of boys and girls, between the restrictions on girls and relative freedom of movement for boys and between the range of exposure to the outside world and to their travel.

Notions of distinctiveness between the spheres of men and women, patterns of division of labour, and expectations of differential behaviour between the sexes have a direct bearing on the process of socialization, on opportunities provided for the education and training of girls, on the kinds of ideals projected before them, on the kinds of expectations they come to have, from life, and on the way they conduct their lives.

In the process of preparation for adult roles the spheres are distinct. However, amongst the enlightened sections this distinction may not be emphasized, but even here feminine tasks and over all abilities are assumed to be different. A girl has to be prepared for feminine roles as conceived by the stratum to which she belongs. Parents also have to take note of the attitude of the world outside the home, and special protection is needed for girls.

In the middle-classes, distinction between femininity and masculinity gets crystallized for the children in the pattern of domestic responsibilities, distribution of financial resources, and planning for the future. Domestic work is the domain of women and in very few families are the boys asked to share it. They may be asked to lend a helping hand in making purchases and running errands, bringing medicine, and escorting sisters, but household chores are beneath their dignity. Boys interested in cooking, knitting, or embroidery hardly ever get any encouragement from the family members, instead they are often ridiculed and discouraged.

Girls are sent to school but they are not sufficiently motivated to achieve excellence; neglect of studies and lack of interest is easily condoned. Very few parents visualize a career for daughters. Their main interest lies in finding a good match for them. Still many parents view education as security for unforeseen eventualities. Even where school or college performance is praised, lack of interest in household work is not condoned. Girls have to live a constricted life. In allocation of scarce resources, a daughter's education is often the first casualty. Parents are not inclined to undergo the inconvenience and strains involved in giving proper facilities to the daughter for better performance. At this level also girls may have to drop out because of family circumstances such as mother's illness or death. Attending functions like weddings and other ceremonies are considered more important than a daughter's education.

In the middle-class families there is a premium on boys' education for it is essential to enable him to get a job. Parents are ready to make all kind of sacrifices for the education of boys. Despite all the misgivings of modern times, they still hope that their efforts will bring them comfort in old age. Various sociological studies clearly bring out the fact that if the family does not have enough resources, even if the girl is brighter her brother will be sent for higher education and she will be told that ultimately she has to mind the kitchen. In fact, what is not always stated in so many words is the culturally determined attitude, that conservative parents cannot and should not depend upon a daughter for support.

It is necessary to note the effects of this emphasis of feminine roles on the development of personality and identity formation for girls. Girls receive informal education for roles which they are expected to perform in adult life. Many give up their ambition to take up career as these are regarded as incompatible with smooth and peaceful family life. They learn early in life that society expects greater flexibility of mind, capacity to adjust, and submissiveness from a woman. In respect of ideologies and values, girls feel that it is no use their committing themselves to any particular ideology because they may not be allowed to adhere to it after getting married.

Thus the constraints, visible as well as invisible, that are placed on girls have an effect on their personalities. Some of these girls join the workforce of the country as white collar workers, in professions and even take up challenging careers like politics. This is either before marriage or after marriage. When married women work outside the home they encounter problems of harmonizing their two roles. They have to evolve a pattern in which they can perform the two roles satisfactorily.

At the relatively lower economic level, both in the rural and urban sections, girls start their contribution to the running of household much earlier than boys. They take care of the younger siblings, help the mother in various domestic chores, and also participate in work of production which falls in the feminine sphere, or activities which fetch some extra income.

Both as preparation for adult roles and as a contribution to the work of the household, the girls' share is important. It is depressing to find that a fairly large proportion of girls are still out of school. In the rural areas there is a lurking fear that education makes girls less useful for adult feminine roles. If they get a little education they develop a distaste for the kind of work expected of them in the village and aspire to get married in towns. In fact, this problem is very real for the cultivators and artisans. It was voiced before the committee in very strong words in Himachal Pradesh and Andhra Pradesh. Education does alienate its recipients from their environment and creates a distaste for manual work.

Women Workers

In a discussion of the dual role of women we may first take note of the quantum of labour, both domestic and extra domestic. In the rural areas, even those who are confined in the home, because of purdah or other norms of respectability, contribute hard labour in activities such as running a dairy processing and storage of grains and other foodstuffs, spinning, coir-making, preparation of cow dung manure, and so forth. It has been seen that a woman's direct contribution to the family economy and her actual control over many of the products gives her considerable power and initiative. Their economic value to the family and their own capacity to earn a living frees them particularly from rigid family controls, and bestows on them a certain measure of autonomy. In contrast the lower middle-class women of urban areas, who have little education and no independent source of income, are in a less advantageous position because of stricter norms of behaviour and almost total dependence on men.

In the social context, due to the low status attached to manual labour in our society and the cultural value associated with women's confinement to home, the work of rural and urban women as wage labourers, unskilled factory workers and menials is not conducive to a better status.

The average woman in rural areas can give little attention to the bringing up of her children. With dual roles and without any mechanical aids for housework, she is definitely overworked. So also are the women engaged in unskilled or semiskilled work in organised and unorganised sectors in urban areas. Overwork and more than a culturally acquired attitude of unconcern about public affairs, is responsible for the limited participation of women in activities like those of the trade unions or political parties. They may become vocal and assertive only when non-availability of essential commodities, or escalating prices threaten to upset their household budget and routine.

It is necessary to assess the status of housewives of the middle and upper economic strata belonging to the urban areas, and also the urbanized rural families. Closely allied to this is the appraisal of the gains achieved in terms of status, by the women who have joined the workforce in white collar professions. The reform movements for the education of women in the late nineteenth and early twentieth century, along with the realization of the need for a measure of economic independence towards the late twenties and thirties of this century, helped to improve the position of women of this class to a large extent. The passing of Hindu Women's Right to Property Acts of 1929 and 1937 was an important measure to give widows some economic independence. Later, organised efforts were made to provide remunerative work to such women. As the number of helpless women with education upto higher secondary or graduation is increasing, need for work which suit their earlier status and which they can take up only after a brief training is also increasing. Desertion and widowhood in this class often result in a sharp fall in the composite social status of the woman.

Initially society accepted a widow's gainful employment and gradually a young unmarried girl's employment till she got married received approval. Post 1940, the Second World War gave an impetus to women's employment and even married women came forward to take up gainful employment. In the post-Independence period, the structure of opportunities expanded, education qualified more and more women for a variety of jobs, and economic compulsions increased.

The socio-cultural environment of India has changed rapidly in the last five decades, especially in the quarter century after the attainment of India's independence. Forces of modernization continue to make a powerful impact and the society has to respond to the new needs and urges of the people. Mahatma Gandhi and other leaders who combined in them the roles of social reformers and political leaders projected the vision of a new society; the humble and the oppressed were to get a new deal and the women were to secure a measure of emancipation in the society visualized by them. It is true that their philosophy and action did not bring about an instant transformation in social attitudes towards the women but it did nevertheless have a powerful effect, and over the decades legitimized many of the new roles contemplated for women. A series of powerful forces are in operation today to bring about perceptible changes in the social milieu. Education, with all its inadequacies, has made a definite impact. It opens up an arena in which women can compete freely with men and prove themselves equally worthy. It also creates for them new avenues in the competitive employment market. The mass media, especially the film and radio, despite their faulty conceptualization and constricted reach have contributed towards refashioning social images and goals. The most significant impetus to change has been provided, however, by demographic pressures and economic compulsions. These have been responsible for women seeking to take advantage of the new structure of economic opportunities. Politicization and articulation of new ideologies has acquired a new meaning and a heightened significance in the changing economic context. In consequence, the legitimacy of the new roles for women is increasingly becoming a social reality. At least on the overt level, the attitude to women has undergone significant modifications, although on the covert level the alteration in the basic attitude structure does not keep pace with the more explicit changes. Thus we find that there is considerable role enhancement, or at any rate a role expansion for women. Beyond their traditional roles they are called upon to assume several new roles also. This is particularly true for the upper stratum of the lower class and for the middle strata of the entire society in which education has been taken up as a mark of social respectability and also as an instrument of economic gain.

The persistence of traditional norms in regard to women's essentially domestic roles and the addition of new work roles in the wider society has created problems of adjustment for them. It has added to their burdens. Everyday domestic chores plus full time employment imply a workload that cannot be managed easily by them. On the domestic front there is little help; they cannot neglect their responsibilities in this sphere. The in-laws and even the husband and the children do not extend to them the measure of sympathy and support they need. Added to this are the latest prejudices and built-in rivalries that are constantly at work in the home atmosphere. These contribute considerably to the psychological stress that a working woman has to undergo. The lot of the working woman, unless she has a really well-paid job and a set of educated family members who are attuned to her psychological needs and physical capabilities is still deplorable. She has in fact to carry on two full time jobs leaving her little time for rest and leisure or for self improvement. The pattern for social interaction demanded by her out-of-home job cannot be smoothly worked out: the demands of the home and the built-in prejudices create impediments that cannot be managed easily.

New lifestyles of women are now visible. In pre-independence days some women had voluntarily decided against marriage in order to devote their life to the national cause or social service. Today in the professions; services, and in the field of social work, we have a number of successful unmarried women who enjoy high status. Along with married women, who are primarily housewives, there are women who combine housework and job, and there are also those who may return to their work or take up a job after their children have grown up.

The pace of change in attitude to women working outside the home or participating in public life has been slow and uneven. These attitudes are related to conceptions about women's inherent attitudes and capacities, her proper sphere of work, and man-woman relationships. Thus, education as a field of employment is more popular because the hours of work are more or less fixed, work at home and outside can be satisfactorily combined, and the work involves less contact with men. Even in mixed schools and institutions of higher education, contact with male colleagues does not have to be close. Work in the field of education does not conflict with traditional norms of femininity.

Although nursing does not conflict with the feminine ideal of service, the job involves contact with impure objects, contact with male patients, doctors and paramedical personnel, and odd hours of work, during night and day. It is only in recent years that nursing is becoming a more respectable and therefore acceptable calling in some regions.

Entry of women in films or the professional theatre had been frowned upon by almost all sections of the community. In many regions participation in domestic performances was associated with particular castes and communities whose women were professional dancers and singers. Now the situation has improved, though the prejudice still persists. In the past, dancing and singing were associated with courtesans only, but gradually with the cultural renaissance, they are becoming more acceptable to society. Giving a remunerative performance before an audience may be accepted in large cities, but it would still be considered unbecoming for the wife or daughter-in-law in small towns. The All India Radio had greatly helped in weakening this prejudice. Teaching music or dancing or organising music programmes is now acceptable. However, living by music or dance performances alone is laden with problems which a woman finds difficult to manage as a career.

In small towns and villages, young women, more so unmarried girls, find it very difficult to work because of the attitude of the people. A touring job is even more difficult. If a girl has been brought up on a traditional home she is likely to be handicapped by her own personality, and if she has been brought up in a modern atmosphere she is likely to create more misunderstanding.

In recent years women have done well in administrative jobs. But in this field the difficulties are of a somewhat different nature. At the utmost, men are prepared to accept a woman as an equal, but men still do not relish working under a woman superior. The traditional conception of women's limitations and her proper place were responsible for the well-known episode in Uttar Pradesh when the former chief minister Charan Singh stated that women officers should not be entrusted with administrative responsibility. He thought that women were unfit for administrative jobs. The Press said that the chief minister was of the opinion that women were too 'delicate' to be entrusted with executive jobs. He also refused to meet a delegation of women officers wanting to convey their protest. Earlier, he had abolished the Mahila Yojana. According to press reports he exhorted the women to go back to their kitchens and look after their children.

This may be an extreme case but it does indicate a certain mind-set of thinking. There are many who share this view and relate the stories about the stupidity and failures of women in high positions, but who adopt a progressive posture in public. The view that women do not possess the essential attributes of an officer to function in high executive ranks cannot be attributed to male chauvinism or a conservative attitude alone. Even some women appear to assume it tacitly. For example, Shivani, a popular woman writer in Hindi, has portrayed a fictitious woman officer of the Indian Administrative Service in a manner that highlights the frailty of woman. Her novelette on this theme was serialized in a popular weekly and later issued in book form. The book leaves an unmistakable impression in the minds of the common reader that women do not quite measure up to positions of higher authority.

The problems connected with dual roles of women may be viewed as those of burden of work, interpersonal relations within the family, and of role conflict. Gainful employment of wives is often viewed with a degree of ambivalence by men. It is approved because it lessens the financial burden and raises the standard of living. However, it can be a source of disruption in the smooth running of the household. The other aspect is the economic independence of women, which is resented by many husbands. It is difficult to say how many women are in a position to take decisions regarding their own earnings. According to a study the freedom of association and movement which outdoor work involves, is not approved of in many homes and puts a stigma on working women. Even in those regions and communities which have had a long tradition of women working outside the home, husbands still do not tolerate women coming home late from office.

Most men do not want to give up their traditionally superior position in the family and do not offer any assistance to their wives in domestic chores. In middle-class families where they cannot afford domestic help and the husband does not share any work, the burden on the wife can become unbearable. A change in older attitudes and values is essential for achieving rationalization of the load of the work. During our tours, we were repeatedly told that men while living in the West helped their wives with domestic chores but when they returned to India, they stopped giving this practice.

Often women themselves do not like the idea of their husbands doing domestic chores as they consider that to be a feminine role. The attitude of relatives and neighbours is also unfavourable. They criticize working women as bad mothers and inefficient housewives. A study focussed largely on middle-class working women of Patna reveals that husbands of 131 respondents thought that it was the wife's duty to carry out household jobs and to look after children. Sixty six were of the opinion that since both were working, it was the duty of the husband to share some responsibility. Many women have to leave their jobs in order to be able to do their household duties satisfactorily. This, however, depends on the financial condition of the family.

Although the in-laws still tend to expect the same amount of attention from a working woman as they would from a non-working woman, there are positive indications that the situation is changing. When the woman's earning is an absolute necessity for the family or if the woman has a well-paid and high status job, she does get consideration.

It is often remarked that if the woman has to spend most of her income on servants and conveyance her employment is of no consequence. But it is seldom understood that a career in itself has its rewards and satisfaction.

The situation of women alternating between work and home leads to a role conflict. Some of them develop a feeling of guilt that they are unable to look after the children and home properly. Working women tend to pamper their children because they want to make up for what they consider to be lack of proper attention on their part. This is because of their role perception rooted in their socialization and the expectations of other members of the family. It is not realized that a child does not need the continued presence of its mother for its proper growth, nor is it realized that the other parent is as important for the healthy growth of the child. Role conflict makes working women tire themselves out giving personal service to the husband and attending to various tasks which are often beyond their physical capacity and endurance.

Besides the strains of shouldering the burden of dual roles and of facing a role conflict, there is often another kind of strain arising from a lack of adjustment between a woman's position at home and in the place of work. She may be better educated and lesser paid than the husband but he claims absolute superiority over her at home. According to Promilla Kapur (1970): "The husband's denial of the right of the wife over her own earned money or her privileges to relax or to move about freely.. was found to be related to his patriarchal attitude towards wife's privileges and obligations."

But the problem of status inconsistency is deeper than this. Unfortunately our society is extremely status conscious and status bound. If the wife enjoys a higher status in her work place, her circle of associates are also of higher status, and however the wife may try not to bring in her office status at home, the husband's adjustment with her becomes difficult. He tends to consider it a reversal of roles. Such a husband tends to become more domineering. Sometimes the wife is also to be blamed, for she too is a part of the status conscious society.

The situation in which the husband is employed in an inferior position in the same office or directly under the wife is perhaps the worst. Many wives are known to have deliberately refused promotions, in order to maintain peace in the family. Thus, when the position of the husband as not the principal breadwinner, as not superior to the wife, or his authority in the family being challenged is when serious problems can arise.

Another aspect of status inconsistency emerges in situations in which a wife has a relatively low status job with limited earnings. For example, nurses marrying doctors are found to leave their occupation mainly of reasons of status. Women working in low paid/status jobs generally leave their jobs after marrying businessmen or executives and thus waste their training, aptitude, and experience. It has been found that sometimes these earnings of the wife may be necessary for the household, and because of the presence of relatives or servants in the house, the wife may not be occupied fully at home, but still her working in low status jobs is not allowed, for it brings down the status of the husband. An idle wife attuned to the life pattern of the husband is more appreciated. It is seen that a woman is not allowed to work in low status positions even in an honorary capacity. By leaving their jobs women are forced to withdraw the support that they were giving to their needy parents or siblings prior to marriage.

It should be a woman's right to play a dual role. A woman should not be penalized for her important contribution as mother in the perpetuation of society. Childbearing is treated as purely a matter concerning women and hence the attitude that a woman must either give up her job or her right to bear children. A distinction between man's work and woman's work in respect of household jobs will have to be removed. If what are called woman's jobs come to be respected by society, men will cease to hesitate doing these jobs. This attitude needs to be built into the socialization process of children, both in the home and in the school.

It is necessary to make adequate provisions to give women opportunity to do both their jobs efficiently and satisfactorily. To this end, it is necessary to provide for creches, nurseries, and labour saving devices. Since all families cannot afford to buy gadgets it will be necessary to provide gadgets to do washing, vegetable chopping, preparing chapati and such other things which make household work a drudgery.

In the absence of many social and physical amenities like labour saving devices, easy transport, creches, inexpensive processed foods, as also conditions of service, such as transfers many women will have to remain principally mothers and housewives. Some may have to confine themselves to the role of a housewife while the children are young. If family is important, home-making is so too. The inputs of household work and the mothers' role in rearing of children need to be recognized by the family and the society at large.

The housewife certainly contributes, even though it may be indirectly, towards a stable national economy by consolidating the economic structure of her own home. Her efficient management of her home alone ensures the saving potentiality of her earning husband. Recognition of her work for the purposes of 'national accounting' would certainly enhance the status of woman and acknowledge the debt of society to her.

Different Issues

In a rapidly changing and culturally differentiated society, a slow process of adjustment in its social value system and rigidity of its institutions, results in various forms of incongruous behaviour. The changing social patterns without restructuring or redefining social values and norms always cause deviant behaviour. Structural changes in the socio-economic system are needed for a smooth process of adjustment.

The problems of women discussed in this section cannot be tackled by legal methods of penalization and prevention alone but by providing 'institutional infrastructure' for their reform and rehabilitation. The gap in the perception of their needs and available opportunities, are conducive to exploitation of the weaker section of society and cannot be offset by development programmes alone but by adequate understanding of the magnitude and intricacies of the problem and providing supportive institutional framework.

A Social Evil

Prostitution is the worst form of exploitation of women and as an institution it speaks of man's tolerance of this exploitation on an organised level in society. Women are viewed solely as a sex object and as an outlet for man's baser instincts. The condemnation of the woman and not the man is the continuance of the standards of dual morality which prevail in most countries with regard to men and women. Some societies have continued to regard prostitution as a necessary evil and have tolerated it as such.

The social anthropologists' explanation of prostitution is that it has been in existence in some form or the other as long, as society has attempted to regulate and control sex relationships through the institutions of marriage and family. Promiscuity or sexual communism preceded marriage and family, and sex was shared by all without any taboo or control. With the institutionalization of sex behaviour through marriage and particularly in society which lays great emphasis on the chastity of its women, prostitutes became an evil of necessity. In a way, they helped to retain the chastity and purity of women in society and hence performed a social function. Even now among certain tribal communities entrance of women into commercialized prostitution is a recent phenomenon and has only started with the advent of outsiders into the tribal community. In tribal communities which always, enjoyed a certain degree of sexual freedom, the institution of prostitution did not exist. According to Rao and Rao in Prostitutes of Hyderabad: "In India, the emphasis on chastity value prior to marriage compelled women of deflowered innocence to court prostitution. Dowry among the upper castes has been a constraint in marriage and some frustrated women were forced to become prostitutes." Rao and Rao further say: In parts of Andhra Pradesh, college girls, and young women practise prostitution and save their earnings. Some even have passbooks in which they indicate their savings which they say will form their dowry to enable them to make a decent marriage. "Child marriages and social discouragement of re-marriage of young widows have greatly helped in the recruitment of prostitutes from village in India. Caste inequality and sex exploitation by the economically well off castes are other factors."

In the 19th century, certain social customs were responsible for many women resorting to this profession, who were otherwise outside the hereditary and customary groups of prostitutes. The spread of child marriages, early widowhood, social taboos on widow remarriages, caste rigidity, dowry system and the practice of polygamy and polyandry among certain communities, the decay in the joint family system, and the generally low status accorded to women in society contributed to women being driven to prostitution as the only occupation for livelihood. At the same time, the beginning of industrialization and consequent urbanization in the latter part of the 19th and early 20th century, drew in large number of women other than hereditary prostitutes into this profession. One reason was the wide sex disparity in the big cities when the migrant worker who had to leave his family behind in the village for mainly economic reasons, became a customer for the prostitute.

Briefly, the following social and religious customs which may have contributed directly or indirectly to prostitution are enumerated as follows according to H.R. Trivedi from a survey on "Exploitation of SC Women" undertaken by the Harijan Sevak Sangh.

The Devdasi system which was so widespread in pre-Independence India that it necessitated legal measures such as the Madras Devdasi Prevention and Dedication Act of 1947 and the Bombay Devdasi Protection Act of 1954 is a system that continues today in parts of Tamil Nadu, Mysore, Andhra Pradesh and Orissa, practised particularly by the lower castes. A study conducted in Bombay in the mid sixties reported that as many as 30 per cent of the Bombay prostitutes were of Devdasi origin. In a study of the Bijapur district, girls are still dedicated to the temples amongst certain sections of the lower castes and enter the occupation with the consent of the parents. No social stigma is attached to this. The reason is mainly economic. These girls are also taken out of the town or village by an agent and a large part of the earnings of the Devdasis goes to the family members and agents.

Prostitution has been the traditional occupation among certain castes, for instance, the Naiks from the hilly regions of Uttar Pradesh where the woman is traditionally the breadwinner and the men have to marry from another caste, as their own womenfolk take to prostitution. The Uttar Pradesh Naik Girls' Protection Act was passed as early as 1929, but the practice continues even today and Punekar and Rao's study indicated that 43 per cent of the prostitutes were drawn from the Naiks of Uttar Pradesh.

Certain castes practise historical and traditional prostitution. A survey conducted in the Raipur and Raigarh districts for the Committee on the Status of Women found that very loose marriage ties in which adultery is scarcely regarded as an offence, encourage prostitution. "A woman may go and live openly with other men and her husband will take her back or two men each will place their spouse at each other's disposal". Women of the lower castes earn money and support themselves through prostitution which is carried on at the weekly bazaars or fairs. The women have historically been exploited by the higher castes, and are often handed over or mortgaged temporarily to creditors on return of loan. The men of such communities indulged in drinking and gambling and encourage their woman to earn money for them and also the emergence of the new industrial towns has encouraged commercialization of prostitution. The survey also found that agents and intermediaries come from outside the community and parents, in-laws and husbands take the initiative in getting women into prostitution for commercial gain. A large part of the income is sent back to the families. Prostitution is the only way open to women to earn a livelihood for the family. No stigma is attached to the woman if she brings wealth or income from prostitution to her natal or conjugal home.

A recent study of the immoral trafficking in women from the Purola Block of Uttarkashi district (UP) reveals that a large number of girls from the lower socio-economic communities go in for prostitution. In 1969, 45 women had entered and remained in this profession for three years. It was estimated that about approximately 500 families were dependent on this profession on account of extreme poverty. 60 per cent of girls from Rawain area were operating in Delhi and 77 agents were engaged in procuring women for prostitution. The causes for prostitution were the high bride-price and consequent indebtedness of the couple who were forced to work as bonded labour. The girl was then compelled to earn money to free the family from this debt through prostitution. In other cases, a man from a higher caste may pay bride-price and contract a marriage with one or more girls of a poor family and take her to Delhi and sell her into the trade. In other cases, Delhi brothel-keepers used girls from Purola to entice other girls or their cousins, etc., by showing them the easy life they could enjoy in the brothels. According to one report the history of this traffic in the Rawain area is about 60 years old, but it has increased recently, with the entrance of officials and traders.

Among the Bajgi caste in Purola region its occupation in service of the temple may be closely connected with the large number of women who go into the trade. Though the Devdasi system as such does not exist much now, certain castes closely connected with work of the temple are more prone to prostitution. Families of majority of these prostitutes are landless and up to 75 per cent bonded for life to upper caste money lenders. Many of these communities belonging to lower socio-economic groups practise polyandry due to high bride-price. This may be sociological cause for the ease with which the women descend into prostitution. Women generally occupy a very low social position and labour incessantly in homes and in the field once they are bought or sold. Trafficking is on the increase in these regions and sometimes higher castes or powerful men in the village act as agents and are in liaison with procurers and brothel-keepers for taking young girls into prostitution.

According to a sociological analysis of prostitution in India, there are about 10,000 dancing and singing girls in India usually known as "Nautch girls". This community practises the occupation on an hereditary basis in different regions. The majority of 'Nautch girls' in Delhi are Muslims. The study also mentions a recent addition to the poor and customary army of prostitutes from the middle-class. These women practise prostitution often with the connivance of their parents or husbands in order to secure huge sums of money to keep up an appearance of affluence. Educated and outwardly respectable, these women are prompted to take to prostitution because of the undue emphasis on values of affluence. Middle-class prostitution can ultimately be traded to the economic factor, though it is the cult of consumption which encourages this pattern of prostitution. Large number of prostitutes also come from a group of women who have been deserted or abandoned by husbands and have no other source of income or employment open for them. According to a former commissioner of police, Calcutta, a large number of middle-class families are surviving on income from prostitution in the absence of alternative avenues of income. A number of these women are educated and quite a few are even graduates.

The causes of prostitution may broadly be classified into the following six groups:

(a) natural events such as death of father/mother/guardian/husband or relatives;

(b) economic causes such as ill-treatment or neglect by parents, husband, or relatives;

(c) domestic causes such as ill-treatment or neglect by parents, husband, or relatives;

(d) social causes such as kidnapping, seduction, deception, bad influence;

(e) causes of physiological significance such as sexual urge, illegitimate pregnancy, etc.;

(f) causes related to mental disposition of attitudes such as ignorance, desire for easy life and normal moral values.

The present practitioners of this trade can broadly be divided into two groups – hereditary class, where prostitution is the ancestral profession and the non-hereditary class who are driven to prostitution or introduced to prostitution due to number of reasons such as economic distress, desertion, destitution, lack of protection, family problems or pathological reasons, desire for easy life, etc. The report of the Committee on Moral and Social Hygiene of the Central Social Welfare Board in 1958 divided the prostitutes into four groups, namely: (1) hereditary (community, customs and social patterns), (2) religious or traditional, (3) victims of social and sociological conditions and (4) highly sexed, pathological cases.

Prostitution must be viewed not from the traditional or historical aspect, but as a form of exploitation of women and girls. According to Mahatma Gandhi, "Man is primarily responsible for the existence of these unfortunate members of society". Prostitution has now been commercialized and a number of intermediaries, the brothel-keeper, the pimps and touts for whom the profit motive has become the guiding principle, has increased the exploitation of women and girls.

Taking into consideration the three elements of prostitution, payment, promiscuity and emotional disturbances there can be two broad categories – professional and non-professional (clandestine). Professional or the public prostitute derives her sole and only livelihood from this profession in a brothel or in red light districts in big towns. The higher type in this profession are street walkers and 'call girls' who find their clients in hotel lobbies, bars and luxurious establishments. Non-professionals are those who conduct their business in a clandestine manner.

Prostitution represents the exploitation of the poor by the rich and of women by men. If women have really to reach the level of equality with men, society should be in a position to ensure economic, social and psychological security for the traditionally exploited womenfolk. Prostitution is the worst form of women's exploitation and inequality.

What must be emphasized is the growing commercialization in the exploitation of women and girls. While the urbanization process and industrialization with its accompanying evils, particularly socio-economic insecurity, poor living conditions, etc., are important forces for the increase of Prostitution in recent years, this profession like any other, operates on a commercial basis according to the law of demand and supply. The growing incidence of prostitution in metropolitan cities and urban areas is an indication of the growing demand on the one hand and poverty on the other. Some sociologists have emphasized the role of economic factors over and above the traditional and customary factors, such as poverty, low wages, lack of gainful employment, partial or complete unemployment which are contributory factors that constrain helpless women to embrace prostitution.

The increasing commercial aspect is represented in the host of intermediaries and allied trades which gather around prostitution. The most important ones are the procurers, pimps, landlords, musical instrument players, intoxicant sellers, panwallahs, hotel-keepers, flower-sellers and the rough elements whose help is sought for protection. Some intermediaries work on a commission basis, like pimps. Procurers are engaged in the purchase and sale of women. The survey of exploitation of Scheduled Caste women has also emphasized that commercial prostitution has gained preponderance over the sacred or traditional prostitution, which used to be practised in the Bijapur region. An agent usually contacts a family and buys a girl or a fake marriage is declared and she is taken out of; the town or village to practise this trade.

Once these girls have been lured or enticed, and in some cases forced into this profession, they are taken to a brothel. If the girls are unwilling, they are mercilessly beaten and punished and even locked up if they do not conform to the brothel-keeper or *gharwali*. Their status is that of an employee and their income is divided between the brothel keeper and as commission for the pimps and procurers. The rest is taken up for rent, lodging and food, while the remaining income is so small that the prostitute has hardly any savings or security for old age. They are fully exploited by the brothel keeper who enters into a bargain with customers and the prostitute has no choice, but to follow his or her orders. They are kept strictly under control and surveillance of the brothel keeper and his hired men. The prostitute is not permitted or encouraged to save or keep any valuables which are usually stolen. As she grows older, a prostitute desires to set herself up as a brothel keeper, if possible, or amongst some of the traditional communities like the Barias, the Bednies and Takyaies, they admit their daughters into the profession when they are grown up. She herself initiates her into the profession so that she may continue to support herself through the daughter's earnings. Amongst Deredar girls' they are given training in music and dance by their mothers from girlhood so that their mehfils and *muftas*, get large number of customers. In some cases, after a woman has been in the profession for 10 to 15 years, and is not able to attract customers, she is thrown out on the streets by brothel-keepers, and is reduced to beggary.

In certain tribal regions, particularly where new projects for construction, industry or mines, etc., have been established, contractors, traders and petty officials have seduced and then abandoned tribal girls. These girls have been forced into prostitution because they have been alienated and thrown out of their own tribal society. In Baladila (MP), for example, a serious situation was created, but the management forced the men to marry these tribal girls and thus saved them from drifting into prostitution. Generally such strong measures are not resorted to and the fact remains that a very large number of tribal girls are being lured into prostitution by unscrupulous men who have made this a very lucrative business for themselves.

The Suppression of Immoral Traffic in Women and Girls Act, 1956 repealed all previous enactments passed by the State and brought uniformity in the law. According to Beotra (1970): "The Act aimed at the suppression of commercialized vice and not at the penalisation of the individual prostitute, or of prostitution itself." In one case, the individual prostitute can be penalised if she carries on prostitution "within a distance of 200 yards of any place of public, religious worship, educational institution, hostel, hospital, nursing home".

According to M.L. Sahney (1974), a senior police official, this section has severely restricted their powers for suppression of this traffic. He opines that:

> "This restriction needs immediate amendment as the vice of prostitution has gone to posh colonies where the pimps have hired modern houses to run this profession. In the absence of these premises situated within 200 yards from the places as envisaged above, it is not possible to prosecute such women or girls soliciting their bodies for immoral purposes".

Police officers have pointed out that this proves to be extremely difficult particularly in the case of a woman witness. Considering the social conditions existing today in our country, no respectable man/woman would like to help the police in the prosecution of sex offences. If anybody turns up for such help, he has to face harassment and even repent for his action, as the persons prosecuted are themselves criminals or are supported by them. At first these witnesses are lured with money, wine and women. If these tactics fail they are threatened with dire consequences with immediate danger to their lives and properties. Efforts were made to procure witnesses through welfare associations and agencies but all in vain. A letter was written to the Association for Moral and Social Hygiene in India for furnishing some names of social workers including lady social workers so that they could be contacted at the time of raids on brothels and places of disrepute. They have replied that although the members of the association were very sincere workers they were not certain whether any of them would be prepared to come forward during raids and face cross-examination in courts.

Social workers and police officers have repeatedly brought to our notice that the punishment imposed under the Act is inadequate to deter people from this crime particularly in view of the enormous income that can be earned from this traffic.

It has been realized that the Act was itself not sufficient to control this commercial exploitation and traffic in women. In fact the number of prosecutions under this Act have been very small in comparison to the volume of the traffic. A report of the Central Bureau of Correctional Services indicates that while the number of prosecutions under the Act has increased from 6428 in 1965 to 7573 in 1969, i.e. by 17.8 per cent, the rate of prosecution for the same period has gone down by about 10 per cent. About 58 per cent of these persons were only fined, 14 per cent acquitted and 8 per cent were released on admonition. Only 11 per cent were sentenced to imprisonment with a fine which is nominal (Rs. 200) and 4 per cent without fine. 78 per cent were charged under the Act for seducing for purposes of prostitution (Section 8 of the Suppression of Immoral Traffic Act). During the same period the number of such women rescued declined sharply. Only 7.2 per cent were charged under Section 4, which prosecutes persons over the age of 18 years for living on the earnings of prostitutes but exceptions are made in favour of mother, son, daughter and sister or other persons unable to support themselves on account of age or mental and physical incapacity.

The Department of Social Welfare set up an expert committee in 1968 to consider various proposals and suggestions for enlarging the scope of the Act with a view to make it more comprehensive; various amendments are under consideration.

It is important that certain changes be made in the Act to help eradicate this social evil. It is essential to prevent the women caught under this Act from returning to the profession by adequate rehabilitation arrangements. The persons who pay for their bail are invariably the procurers or brothel-keepers. Instead of sending the women and girls to jails, it is necessary to send them to protective homes. The age limit should also be lowered from 21 year to 18 years. Adequate arrangements should be made to give protection to girls and women in moral and social danger particularly destitute women, unmarried mothers and helpless young widows. At an orientation camp of the Association for Social Health in India held in March, 1974, one of the participants suggested improving the existing institutionalized services providing proper protection for abandoned and illegitimate children, especially girls, as a method that may help control prostitution. As far as the rehabilitative aspect is concerned, the Rama Rao Committee, 1954, had said that the after care homes are not adequate and they should be associated with some programme to help prostitutes earn a decent living. Those who are detained under the Act require long-term treatment for rehabilitation. Special counselling service towards better understanding of the problems of prostitutes is important. The children of prostitutes should be prevented from entering the profession, especially the girls. They should be segregated from their mothers and institutionalized, but not in special homes which would put a social stigma on them. Women and girls, who do not wish to continue in this profession, but are compelled to do so for economic reasons should be rescued and engaged in remunerative work. There is, therefore, greater need for understanding the cause underlying prostitution and to make efforts to prevent more women from entering this profession as well as to rehabilitate those who are already victims of the trade.

These women need to be rehabilitated and their emotional and psychological problems are to be tackled with understanding.

The most significant aspect is preventive. This applies particularly to women and girls in moral danger. An important segment of this group are women who are victims of family discord. Counselling services could help them and prevent their taking recourse to this profession. Counselling centres should also have homes for such women.

According to an estimate, women members constitute about 4.3 per cent of the convicts and 3.2 per cent of the under trial prisoners, 73 per cent of female convicts and 54 per cent of undertrials are from Andhra, Maharashtra and Tamil Nadu. Since they constitute numerically a small segment of the total convict population, the condition of women prisoners has not received adequate attention. 72 per cent of the female convicts are between 21-40 years of age, and around 10 per cent are between 16-20. 12 per cent of women convicts are illiterates, 73 per cent of them are married, 15 per cent unmarried and 12 per cent are widowed. This means that a large section have children, who are either deprived of maternal care or in the case of very young children, are living with their mothers in prisons.

It has been found that more women serve short sentences as compared to men. Habitual proneness to crime is found to be less among them. This also means that a large majority of women prisoners are 'freshers' and are exposed to the influence of prison life for the first time. We would like to draw attention to the fact that the Law Commission has recommended that convicts on short-term sentences should not be sent to prison, where they are exposed to the unhealthy influence of hardened criminals.

Separate living quarters or wards with female wardens or matrons are provided for women as a rule. In rare cases child care services or creches for mothers in prisons are available in a few States. Training in skills such as niwar and dari making, tailoring, spinning, weaving, bidi-making, embroidery, etc., are not necessarily in tune with market labour requirements or conducive to self-employment.

The background of women prisoners studied by one or two experts reveals that their crime comes mainly from poverty or social helplessness. Most common are pickpocketing, attempted suicide, family feuds and domestic quarrels, questions pertaining to the custody of children, infanticide, destitution or vagrancy and murder of a lover.

The generally low level of literacy among women convicts, except for Kerala, where 45 per cent of women convicts were illiterate, reflects the lack of effort by prison authorities to educate them. In general, the women sections of the jails have practically no positive education or work programmes, presumably due to few prisoners; they cannot participate in the general routine of work due to strict segregation. Sometimes the women prisoners have dependent children with them for want of any family arrangement outside. Life for these young ones can be equally futile. Efforts to set up creches for children of women prisoners did not succeed due to very small number of children. Discrimination against women is prevalent, since they hardly share any of the privileges available to men convicts such as wage system, canteen, outdoor work, PT drill, library or prayer meetings or general recreation, or holidays. This is explained by the problems of segregation and inadequate staff to organise such activities for women.

It has been reported to us by senior officials of the police force that in some prisons, lunatics, both criminals and noncriminals, are housed along with other women prisoners. This appears to us to be not only unhealthy, but a dangerous practice. We fail to understand how any reform or rehabilitation of these convicts or the treatment of these lunatics is at all possible under these circumstances. Another problem that has been brought to our notice is that women prisoners are often sent to places away from their normal residence. This makes it impossible for their family, particularly children, to visit them. This isolation increases the difficulties of rehabilitation and readjustment to family life on their release.

The committee feels that the problems of women prisoners deserve special attention, particularly with regard to the care of the children if any, their rehabilitation and education. Since most of the women prisoners cannot return to their families or do not have families to return to after they are released, suitable arrangements for their rehabilitation needs to be considered along with after care programmes. While in prison, these women must be taught some activity or imparted training in a skill which would enable them to earn their livelihood on release. A suggestion made to us is to involve women's voluntary organisations for arranging useful educational, recreational and work programmes for women in prisons. Successful results have been seen in Maharashtra and Gujarat State where long-term women prisoners are released to the care of recognized women's institutions run by social welfare agencies.

Suicide is a social problem affecting both men and women. However, a study of the causes and factors for committing suicide provide an indication of the status of women. Suicide is a reaction to problems that apparently cannot be solved in any other way a final response which a human-being makes to inner emotional distress. Cultural patterns, socio-economic conditions, and group activities influence the extent of suicides and act as inhibiting or encouraging factors. In India, the medieval Hindu institution of 'Sati', which was finally stopped due to vigorous efforts of social reformers like Raja Ram Mohun Roy in the 19th century, was the earliest institutionalized form of suicide for women. Though it was thought to have had religious sanction, it arose out of a social system which had degraded and dehumanized the widows. Regardless of age, a number of those widows had to mount on the funeral pyre of their husbands forced by relatives and others. The prohibition of widow remarriage, the austerity imposed upon a widow and the cruel treatment meted out to her must have persuaded some of them to end their lives on the pyre in preference to leading a miserable existence. According to the vital statistics deaths by causes and sub-causes prepared by the Registrar General's Census (Sample Registration System), suicides were reported to be the highest for women in the age-group 15-34, both in 1966 and 1969. The overall incidence of suicide for women was reported to be higher than males in 1966 and 1969, but it declined in 1967 and 1968.

In 1970 on an 'average 41.4 per cent of the persons who committed suicide were women. Among causes for suicide, the following were listed: (1) despair over dreadful disease 14.1 per cent (2) quarrels with parents-in-law 8.6 per cent and (3) quarrels with married partners 6.3 per cent as the major factors. An analysis of the percentage distribution of total deaths by the cause and subcause for women indicates that the maximum percentage of suicides occurred in the age group 15-34, the second largest being in the 35-54 age group.

In Status of Women and Suicide by Dr. Jyotsna Shah, it may be assumed that in this age group, "suicides committed by females were mainly due to quarrel with parents-in-laws and quarrels with married partners. The joint family system still prevails in India, therefore, the suicides by females may be taken to reflect the extent of oppression of the daughter-in-law in the joint family at the hands of the in-laws".

Though no national survey or in-depth study on a national scale on the causes of suicides have been done so far, the report of the Suicide Enquiry Committee in Gujarat studied the problem of suicides between 1960-64 in the State. The study found that the number of women committing suicide for physical factors, mental factors and social and domestic factors, were larger than men, being respectively 514 males, per 516 females, 431 males per 513 females, and 562 males per 1,192 females. As far as the economic factors were concerned, 256 men committed suicide as compared to 196 females.

A further analysis of the social factors indicates that out of 1,784 persons, 1,192 women committed suicide, and out of these the largest number were due to failure to adjust in matrimony, domestic unhappiness or ill-treatment at the hands of relatives. These were further cross-analysed with levels of education and a definite negative correlation between the educational level of women and the number of suicides was observed. The percentage of illiterate females constituted 61.9 per cent of the total cases of female suicides. As the educational level increased, the number of suicides decreased. Among the number of persons who committed suicide due to unhappy human life and other factors, the largest were from the illiterate group, next being literates below primary level followed by primary, middle and higher categories. Significantly 1,058 married people against 95 single people commit suicide due to domestic unhappiness and out of these 836 were females which corroborates the statement about suppression of women in married life particularly by in-laws. The study established that more women in the 15-34 age group commit suicides due to domestic unhappiness.

This report pointed out the 'cultural lag' in our social institutions which have not kept pace with educational and technological advance as the basic cause behind the suicides. It listed as reasons, the lack of freedom in the choice of the marriage partner, changes in the family units and especially joint family relationships, child marriage, dowry and lack of education about sex and married life among others.

The report recommended homes for women to which they can resort in times of extreme hardship or family estrangement. Some voluntary homes have been established in Gujarat.

An earlier survey of suicides in Bombay State in 1954-57, indicated that the existence of suicide per population is 3.4 males and 3.9 females in Ahmedabad range, 4.1 males and 8.9 females in Rajkot range per one lakh of the population. The highest number of suicides was in the rural areas. 2,006 females who commit suicide out of 5,173 were in the 15-24 age group. The highest number of suicides was by women due to domestic quarrel. 75.8

per cent of females were from the literate group. The Suicide Enquiry Committee of Saurashtra in 1952-55 also bore out the fact that twice as many women commit suicide as men.

Though apart from Maharashtra and Gujarat, data on suicide and causes are lacking from other states, suicide remains a widespread social problem. There are various items appearing in the daily Press from time to time giving news of women who die to injuries received from bums, etc. Some of the reported accidental deaths due to bums, etc., may very well be self-inflicted. The majority of these women are housewives in the susceptible age group mentioned above. The causes have to be searched for in our social structure, enjoining upon women an inferior status and position, socially, economically and culturally.

Another cause that in our opinion also pushes many women to end their lives is breakdown of family economy. In recent years there have been reports of women committing suicide along with their children. The burden of economic insecurity and grim poverty presses more heavily on women's minds particularly when she has children to feed. This increasing strain causes complete breakdown in many cases. The absence of social security or adequate employment opportunities leave a woman utterly helpless, in the absence of a breadwinner in the family. Rather than see her children starve, it is not unnatural for, her to prefer ending her life. Suicides thus represent a serious malaise in social organisations, which will increase as life becomes harsher with increasing poverty and destitution.

Sans Marital Bonds

Data on unmarried mothers is not available as there has been no attempt to examine the prevalence of this problem by any agency. Nevertheless it remains a social problem. Some indication is available in the Report of the Suicide Enquiry

Committee which studied suicides in Gujarat between 1960-64. One of the causes of high rate of suicide among women was due to illegitimate pregnancies. Some time back, a leading gynaecologist had observed that there was an increase in the number of abortions asked for by unmarried girls after passing of the Medical Termination of Pregnancy Act. Social workers have long been aware of the problem of illegitimate pregnancies and unmarried mothers. Before the liberalizing of the Abortion Act these women and girls had either to resort to quacks for abortions and in the process a number of women may have lost their lives. The other alternative was to abandon such children in the destitute homes. Very often these unmarried mothers joined the ranks of the destitute women and were exposed to moral and social danger. Some of the women in the brothels may have initially joined the profession because of this stigma. While for some these illegitimate pregnancies may be due to rape, others were due to unhappy or maladjusted family life, broken homes, sexual maladjustment or even ignorance. A large number of women who were pushed into prostitution or into committing suicide did so because society does not accept an unmarried mother.

At an orientation camp held by the Association of Social Health in March 1974, some experts have advocated sex education since a great deal of confused thinking prevails with regard to sex. A medical expert citing case histories and research findings said, "there is either complete ignorance or complete misunderstanding about the role of sex and this results in social and sexual maladjustments. This calls for evolving an intelligent and comprehensive programme for sex education."

A medical expert at the same seminar cautioned against the alarming rise in venereal infliction among teenagers, due to profound socio-economic changes in society over the past few decades. They advocated sex education, health education to control this. Apparently prostitution accounted for only 20 per cent in the spread of venereal diseases.

The committee in the course of its tours met a few such cases in women's homes. Some of them had conceived as a result of rape, but the refusal of the family to accept them or assist them in any manner had wrecked their lives completely. In one instance, in Andhra, the father wanted to kill his daughter, but the mother; with the assistance of a school teacher, got her admitted into a women's home for safe keeping. The number of such homes are most inadequate and very little is known about them, particularly in the villages.

The problem of unmarried mothers is a result of rapid socioeconomic change. The value system is changing and the struggle for existence brings out tensions leading to deviant behaviour. In Western countries it was found that the existence of this problem rapidly increased with increasing urbanization, growing affluence and the cult of materialism. The resultant breakdown of the moral order systems leads to the disintegration of traditional social values. Indian society even now practises segregation of the sexes and tremendous emphasis is placed on the chastity of women. Under such circumstances the tensions are often aggravated and problems become manifest.

We feel that this problem requires much greater attention than it has received so far from both official agencies and voluntary welfare organisations, particularly as the indications of its increasing incidence are already manifest. It is important to provide adequate assistance to these women for their rehabilitation and care for their children. Counselling services are essential to persuade families to take a more humane view of this problem.

The Oldage

Traditional Indian society had through the joint family system provided for the care of aged persons. Even in the absence of the joint family, traditional norms of behaviour required the children to take adequate care of their aged parents and grandparents. The pressure of socioeconomic changes, the breakdown of the joint family and of traditional values have increased the significance of the problem of care of aged persons. It is easier for old men to live on their own but it is much more difficult for women. Most of them are economically helpless; even the minority, who may have some source of income are not in a position to look after themselves or protect themselves. This problem was brought to our notice by the Ramakrishna Mission in Varanasi which is running a home for old women.

The committee also visited an old-age home in Pune where all the inmates were from well-to-do families. Their relatives were paying Rs. 125 per month for food and lodging and some of them were paying for extra services like milk, etc. These women had been sent to the homes because they could not get along with their daughters-in-law. We also heard of cases where old women were living in destitute homes, not because they were destitutes but because there were no other homes available for them and the only way they could enter these homes was by declaring themselves destitutes. It was also brought to our notice that these women, even if they had any family, are seldom visited by the latter.

A number of State Governments are operating schemes for old age pensions and the annual expenditure on such schemes is now about Rs. 10 crores. The reports received by us in most of the States indicate, however, that the amounts are very meagre, and the number of pensioners falls far short of applications or even recommended cases. We were also informed that because of their helplessness these pensioners have to give a share to the intermediaries, who assist them in obtaining the pension. This becomes a continuous process, because the women are threatened that without the commission the government will be informed of their death so that the pension will cease. We were also told that payments are not always regular causing great hardship.

In the changing social milieu the problem of aged women who are regarded as encumbrances by their families is going to increase. Greater attention to their assistance and care is necessary from the State and voluntary agencies.

The number of destitute women has been increasing in recent years. According to one report, a large number of such women were found scrounging for small fish in the nullahs along highways leading out of Calcutta. A majority of them are elderly women. In a village in Birbhum, we met a group of Santhal women who had been reduced to complete destitution because their ill health and age prevented them from obtaining any employment. They were agricultural labourers whom the landowners would no longer employ.

A large group of destitute women were widows and deserted women who have no means of support for themselves or their children. They swell the ranks of beggars and are exploited for immoral traffic. The Department of Social Welfare has estimated that about 1 lakh women, in the age group of 20 to 44, join the ranks of destitutes every year. We believe this to be very short of reality. Institutionalized services now available for them are highly inadequate, both in numbers and in the type of services provided for rehabilitation. Services for this group have only touched the fringe of the problem. It is imperative to obtain more reliable data to assess the magnitude of the problem and organise adequate services for their rehabilitation.

The reviews of the disabilities and constraints on women, which stem from socio-cultural institutions, indicates that the majority of women are still very far from enjoying the rights and opportunities guaranteed to them by the Constitution. Society has not yet succeeded in framing the required norms or institutions to enable women to fulfil the multiple roles that they are expected to play in India today. On the other hand, the increasing incidence of practices like dowry, indicate a further lowering of the status of women. They also indicate a process of regression from some of the norms developed during the freedom movement.

We have been perturbed by the findings of the content analysis of periodicals in the regional languages, that concern for women and their problems, which received an impetus during the freedom movement, has suffered a decline in the last two decades. The social laws that sought to mitigate the problems of women in their family life have remained unknown to a large mass of women in this country, who are as ignorant of their rights today as they were before independence.

The changes in social attitudes and institutions cannot be brought about very rapidly. It is, however, necessary to accelerate this process of change by deliberate and planned efforts. Responsibility for this acceleration has to be shared by the State and the community, particularly that section of the community which believes in the equality of women. We, therefore, urge that community organisations, particularly women's organisations, should mobilise public opinion and strengthen social efforts against oppressive institutions like polygamy, dowry, ostentatious expenditure on weddings and child marriage, and mount a campaign for the dissemination of information about the legal rights of women to increase their awareness. This is a joint responsibility, which has to be shared by community organisations, legislators, who have helped to frame these laws and the government which is responsible for implementing them.

8

Working Conditions

While part-time employment presents a partial solution of the employment needs of many women, there is no generally accepted definition of such types of employment in terms of hours, remuneration and other facilities. The ILO described two occupational categories which employ the largest number of part time workers in both developing and developed countries, cleaning and related work both in private households and institutions, and professional and technical services. Other areas where part time work is common are agriculture and commerce and manufacturing. Particularly in consumer goods industries. The available statistical data does not make it possible to obtain an accurate picture. Since the arrangements for part-time employment are largely determined by the nature and pressure of work, it can only be conceived within the framework of the broader policies guiding and governing the integration of women in economic life.

Part-time Employment

In response to the ILO's enquiry regarding the possibility of providing part-time employment to women with family responsibilities, many governments expressed their reservation. They felt that providing such employment to women only may adversely affect full-time employment opportunities, or may result in discrimination and exploitation in respect of employment and promotion. It was stated that part-time employment should not be imposed on women with family responsibilities who, if given suitable child-care services, would prefer full-time employment.

Such views ignore the repeated advice of expert bodies like the ILO or the National Committee on Women's Education in India and reflect the attitude of employers and workers who fear the invasion of the labour market by part-time workers. Part of this apprehension is also due to the difficulties in making administrative arrangements for such workers. It should be noted that this kind of resistance is found mainly in the organized sector whose wide structure, labour policy and legal provisions are geared to the needs of full-time workers only. In the unorganized sector, part-time employment is very much of a reality. As we have pointed out earlier, very little is known about dimensions of this group either in numbers or in the nature of their problems. The studies conducted by the ILO in 1952 and 1962, referred to the serious gaps in national information regarding employment opportunities, number and characteristics of persons engaged in or seeking part-time employment. The International Labour Conference recommended that surveys need to be conducted in cooperation with employers and workers, regarding the scope of part-time employment.

The International Labour Conference resolution concerning part-time employment and the employment of older women, adopted at the 38th session in 1955, drew attention to the basic principles that it should not adversely affect full time employment and general level of wages, contrary to the provision of the Convention on Equal Remuneration. It further mentioned that adequate attention should be paid to the conditions of employment. With particular reference to the need of equality of opportunity and treatment with full-time workers, equality of remuneration and rights in respect of holidays with pay, sick leave and maternity leave, and adequate social security protection. Obviously these points raise many problems in practice, because of adequate information relating to the demand and the opportunities for part-time work, needs and preferences for such work and the size and characteristics of part-time workers.

While empirical investigations are necessary to assess the need, scope as well as problems of part-time employment, conducting such enquiries among women already in full-time employment can yield misleading results. A pilot study conducted by the Tata Institute of Social Sciences and the Delhi School of Social Works found 74 per cent of the women reluctant to accept part-time employment because of its low remuneration. Such responses are obvious when it is noted that one-third of the 'respondents earned 50 per cent of their family income. Some were either the major or the only source of income of their respective families.

For women who need employment to augment the family's income, and whose inability to arrange child care or home responsibilities, make full-time employment a burden on their physical and mental resources, part-time employment could be a boon provided it carried adequate remuneration and greater security and protection than it does at present. The first step to provide support to such women is to investigate the existing models of part-time employment prevalent in the unorganized sector and to provide legal and social support against their exploitation. We have been informed that the National Labour Institute proposes to initiate some experiments in offering part time employment to women workers.

We suggest that an all-India survey should be undertaken to investigate in which areas and in what manner part-time employment of women, is possible, keeping in view their special problems. Availability of this data will help in adopting legal measures which will provide security of some employment benefits.

The ILO has drawn attention to the problem of re-entry into employment after a lengthy absence mainly caused by family reasons. Some countries have already provided safeguards for working mothers protecting their right to employment in jobs previously held or comparable ones, for a stipulated period of absence on prolonged maternity leave.

The ILO's questionnaire regarding adoption of an international instrument on this issue "evoked high proportion of negative replies, and of replies giving strictly qualified agreement". Most countries felt that in the early stages of social and economic development, an absolute commitment of this kind would not be justified as it may affect women's employment opportunities in an adverse manner, more so in the case of labour surplus economies, where law of supply and demand plays a decisive role. The general reaction from most Governments suggests that there would be considerable resistance to any uniform measure on this issue. Labour shortage economies may find it necessary to attract women into industries. But most countries believe that any such pressure may create resentment in the male labour force as discrimination.

The Government of India while supporting such policies as an ultimate objective felt that "in developing countries the more pressing problem is the expansion of employment opportunities for the vast numbers of the unemployed and the underemployed. This must inevitably be a prior pre-occupation of all policies in these countries."

Re-entry after a prolonged absence caused by definite withdrawal from employment for family reasons may pose a greater problem, particularly in white-collared jobs and professions. Technological, scientific and organizational development during the period of their absence tends to make the previous experience of such women obsolete.

It should be noted that this type of withdrawal and return to employment is found mainly among middle and upper class women. Working class women, whose survival depends on their earnings cannot afford such behaviour. With greater acceptance of small family norms and higher cost of living, the need for such return to active economic participation will increase for both economic and social reasons. In our opinion, provision for part time employment will reduce the problem of lack of continuity in such cases.

Such measures, however, cannot solve the problems of women who seek employment at a later age without previous experience, primarily for economic reasons. Loss of financial support, due to widowhood or separation from husbands make their need for employment more acute. In many cases such women also lack educational qualifications. The condensed courses have tried to meet their educational problems to a certain extent, but unless the age limit for recruitment for this group is realized, it would be difficult to solve their employment problems.

Placement and Training

A great necessity for all these groups is assistance and counselling for placement and training. The present employment service is ill-equipped for such assistance. Special efforts will have to be made to provide adequate information and assistance to such women seeking work. It will also necessarily combat existing prejudices among employers and workers against them.

The need for child care services for employed women has already been accepted though legal provision for it has been made only for women in organized industry. No such arrangements are available for women working in offices or the vast mass of women employed in the unorganized sector.

During our tours, groups of working women, particularly in the urban areas, referred to the great difficulty which they experienced in the absence of creches or day nurseries for their children. Women office workers in the urban areas, do not enjoy any facilities of this kind for the care of their children during their working hours. The few private creches or nurseries, being operated by voluntary organizations or individuals, are highly inadequate and generally, too expensive for women who need them most. A suggestion that was made to us by many office workers was to provide a room in offices where children could be looked after. Many of them were even prepared to make necessary arrangements to provide an attendant out of their own resources.

In big cities, where the problem of distance and overcrowding on public transports makes it difficult for women to carry their children to their place of work, the best solution lies in community or neighbourhood creches in the residential areas. The urgency of providing these institutions have been repeatedly emphasized by all expert bodies studying problems of women's employment. The ILO has suggested that governments should take steps to coordinate the provision of these facilities by employers, voluntary agencies and community effort to ensure their even distribution and at least minimum standards of services.

Adjustment and Safeguards

The problem of accommodation has become acute for working women both in urban as well as rural areas. This was emphasized in a National Seminar on Social Problems of Working Women in 1973. Educated women are reluctant to go and work in rural areas because of accommodation difficulties., though efforts are being made by Government to provide accommodation to Government functionaries in education, health and other developmental services. These efforts have not, however, always taken into consideration the questions of security and distance from place. The problem is acute for both single women who are not fully accepted by rural society; and for married women with families.

In urban areas, working women living in slums face high incidence of disease and socially deviant behaviour, the primary cause of which lies in bad housing. The employers' responsibility for providing adequate housing is generally not fulfilled. For unmarried working women some efforts have been made during the last two decades to provide hostels with the aid of voluntary agencies. The Central Social Welfare Board's programme in this connection is being supported by the Department of Social Welfare, with building grants for such hostels. Their numbers are, however, still very limited, and they can cater to the needs only of middle class working women. The problem needs to be solved by co-ordinating efforts of Government, employers and voluntary agencies.

The problem of security to which women workers, particularly young ones, are exposed, has been pointed out in the reports of certain Committees of the Government and Social Welfare Organizations. A Committee of the Maharashtra Government examined the difficulties that women government functionaries have to face, particularly in rural areas, and recommended that women functionaries posted in rural areas should be of a more advanced age. A similar Committee, appointed by the Government of Karnataka, recommended posting older women as supervisory staff and involvement of senior local women, including wives of senior official. The Committee of the Maharashtra Government also advised setting up of enquiry committees at divisional headquarters for such grievances of women officials on a priority basis.

While we realize that these problems are essentially related to the transitional state of our society, some supportive measures to look into these difficulties and to provide assistance, is a necessity at present.

Both the Committees of Maharashtra and Karnataka, referred to above, recommended changes in the cadre and recruitment rules for various categories of women workers needed for developmental activities. The existing rules, in their opinion, kept out "really qualified and experienced women from the purview of these posts." The Maharashtra Government has relaxed the maximum age limit for recruitment with a view to recruiting women of greater experience for work in rural areas. Possibilities for similar relaxation in other states need to be examined. In Uttar Pradesh, local women are trained and posted to their own villages to ensure greater acceptance by the society.

During our tours, we received complaints from various categories of women employees regarding service conditions. Many of these cadres are working on an ad hoc basis from plan to plan or sometimes even on annual extension of their services. They are denied promotion opportunities and adequate pay scales. This is particularly the case with women recruited for the rural development programmes of the Central Welfare Board and Department of Community Development. Similar complaints of lack of promotion opportunities were made by telephone operators, clerks, typists and stenographers. The representatives of the Trained Nurses Association pointed out the absence of gazetted posts in their profession. Nurses we met during our tours also complained of overcrowding in hospitals, long hours of duty, and lack of accommodation for married nurses. The Auxiliary Nurse Midwives posted in rural areas face an additional problem of transport and security in case of night calls.

There is a general feeling among many of these women workers that even where promotional possibilities exist, the claims of the women are discriminated against not only by private employers but even by the Government.

A major problem repeatedly brought to our notice was on the question of transfers. Though most of the State Governments have adopted conventions, to post husband and wife to the same place, if they are both in Government service, this has not always been possible. This convention has sometimes resulted in single women being subjected to frequent transfers causing great hardship. While we appreciate the administrative difficulties of fulfilling such a convention, frequent transfers of low paid women employees should be avoided as they cause innumerable difficulties.

Some consideration is also needed for provision of adequate transport or transport allowance to women who have to carry out touring duties. The inadequacy of this provision often results in inefficiency. The assistance of local authorities, including local self-governing bodies, could be obtained to provide suitable accommodation during night halts for these touring officials.

While we realize that many of these difficulties may be inevitable in a transitional situation, it is our belief that a commitment to the national objective of integrating women into the process of development at all levels can help to solve them in due course. The constitutional guarantees and the objectives of the nation, require acceptance by the society of the multiple roles of women as home makers and mothers as socially and economically productive in the same manner as direct participation in the economic process. It is, therefore, imperative that society in general, and the State in particular, provide the necessary conditions and support to enable women to perform their various roles successfully. As citizens they deserve the protection of society. Marriage and motherhood, which contributes to the continuation of the nation should not become disabilities in the gainful participation of women in the economic process. Without the type of supportive services and institutionalized aids suggested above these, dual roles will continue to impose a tremendous strain on the physical and mental resources of women. It will also affect the welfare and development of the future generation through inadequate care in childhood.

The Indian Constitution guarantees equality of opportunity in matters relating to employment and directs the State to secure equal rights to an adequate means of livelihood, equal pay from equal work, and just and humane conditions of work. Our Labour Laws concerning women reflect the attitude of protection and welfare through provision of maternity benefits, creches and restriction on types of work that are considered unsuitable to their health. Though the Government of India ratified the ILO Conventions regarding equal remunerations and against discrimination, this shifting emphasis towards equality and greater employment opportunities has not as yet found reflection in Indian laws. Executive actions initiated in this direction, have made some impact in the organized sector, but in the vast unorganized sector no impact of these measures have been felt either in conditions of work, wages, or opportunities.

The impact of transition to a modern economy has meant exclusion of an increasing number and proportion of women from active participation in the productive process. A considerable number continue to participate for no returns and no recognition. The majority of those who do participate fully are on sufferance, without equal treatment, security of employment and humane conditions of work. A very large number of them are subject to exploitation of various kinds with no protection from society or the State.

Adequate means for livelihood or employment is the chief objective of development. There has been little progress in the achievement of this right for both men and women, but estimates of employment and underemployment clearly indicate that the position is worse for women. While the Constitution has guaranteed equal rights, the measures initiated since independence to remove women's disabilities and handicaps, particularly in the field of economic participation, have proved to be extremely inadequate.

While the draft Fifth Five-Year Plan emphasizes the need to utilize all idle manpower to speed up the process of development, its priorities for women's development omits employment generation as a specific objective. It is assumed that the ratio of females to males in the labour force will remain constant at 16 per cent for the next years, visualizing no structural changes by which a greater participation of women in the productive process can be ensured.

The experience of some countries has shown, that it is possible by public policy to accelerate women's employment in new areas of work, by finding solutions to their problems of family life and child care. These countries see no necessary contradiction between encouraging women's work at all levels and maintaining laws protecting women's health and welfare, in view of their role as mothers. What is more distinctive about socialist countries is the effective institutionalization of the rights of a working mother by protecting her right to return to her job.

While several factors have handicapped Indian women from being effectively integrated into the process of development, the lack of a well-defined policy indicating areas where they require special assistance and protection leave them without access to knowledge, skills and employment. The replies received to our question regarding the policy followed in employing women in various concerns, indicate the continuation of old prejudices regarding women's efficiency, productivity, capacity for skills, and suitability that debar them from employment in many areas. Wage discrimination is the result of this restrictive confinement of women to limited types of work. The replies clearly indicate that while there is a definite policy for excluding women from various types of jobs, the criteria for determining their unsuitability are not clear or uniform. Certain industries declare them to be unsuitable for technical as well as manual jobs, others declare them to be unsuitable for managerial and administrative jobs as well as unskilled work, yet another group finds them unsuitable for field duties. The general tendency appears to be, to find them unsuitable for all jobs other than clerical. The West Bengal Public Service Commission even finds them unsuitable for certain teaching posts, though teaching is generally accepted as the most suitable profession for women. The Defence Forces find them unsuitable even for posts of legal officers in the office of the Judge, Advocate General which involves no combatant duties. We have pointed out many industries and administrative agencies where women have been found to be suitable for all these types of work.

The objective of a labour market policy is full, productive and freely chosen employment. Recasting the employment policies for women requires re-examination of existing theories regarding their suitability for different types of work on scientific lines, and a deliberate effort to promote equality of opportunity by special attention to women's disabilities and handicaps. The recommendations that we make are directed towards making the Constitutional guarantees meaningful and for arresting the trend towards gradual exclusion of women from their right to a fuller participation in the economic process.

We therefore recommend:

(i) The adoption of a well-defined policy to fulfil the Constitutional directives and Government's long term objective of total involvement of women in national development. Such a policy should be framed by a government resolution. This policy will need to be implemented carefully to avoid evasion by direct or indirect methods. Apart from specific occupations from which women are debarred by law, employers should not be permitted to exclude them from any occupation unless the basis for unsuitability is clearly specified.

(ii) The creation of a cell within the Ministry of Labour and Employment at both Central and State levels under the direction of a Senior Officer to deal with problems of women.

(iii) We further recommend the following changes in the existing laws.

9

Justice for All

The statutory law in all matrimonial matters follows the adversary principle for giving relief i.e. the petitioner seeking relief alleges certain facts and, the respondent in his own interest refutes them. In addition to this, as we have already noticed, most of the grounds in these statutes are based on the fault principle instead of the breakdown theory. The combined result of these two factors is that strong advocacy is often the determining factor In these cases. This is particularly unfortunate in the field of custody and guardianship, where the welfare of the child is often relegated to the background and the decision arrived at, is based on the well argued points of the lawyer. In the present system, the judge has no option but to give his decision on the point raised and argued. If he were to base his decision on social needs or in the interest of one of the parties, it may be considered as biased and hence reversed in the appellate court.

There is also no distinction drawn between matrimonial causes and other suits. This frequently leads to unusual delay, which stands in the way of conciliation and further embitters the relationship of the parties. In a case filed for restitution of conjugal rights by the husband, the appellate judge referred to the "unfortunate fact that it has taken more than eight years for the appeal to come to me, such long delay.. is extremely regrettable, because in such cases the time factor is of vital importance."

Conciliation which needs to be the main consideration in all family matters, is not a guiding principle in the statutes dealing with them. The legislators of the Hindu Marriage Act recognized the need but made only a half-hearted attempt to break away from the traditional approach. While they mentioned the need for conciliation, by emphasizing that the duty of the judge is to make every endeavour to bring about a reconciliation between the parties, they failed to provide the infrastructure necessary, like pre-trial investigation, specialized opinion of psychiatrists or social workers, which would help the judge to perform this role. The results, therefore, have not been satisfactory. The Parsee Marriage and Divorce Act, 1936, by its provision of special courts, also attempted to adopt a different procedure but that experiment too has not been a success.

The solution lies in establishing Family Courts for settlement of all problems dealing with personal law, where the role of the lawyer in adversary procedure is substituted by conciliation. The case of Japan which has successfully adopted this system is specially relevant as it is an Asian country and the emancipation of Japanese women, after the Second World War, almost coincided with the Constitutional recognition of equality in our country.

In Japan, the proceedings in a family Court are informal. There are usually two conciliation commissioners of whom one is usually a woman, and the proceedings are not open to the public. A person having an interest in the case should appear before the Family Court and only under very special circumstances will the appearance of a representative be permitted.

The need for a Family Court in India has been expressed by many scholars. The Law Commission has also referred to it. The recent report of the Legal Aid Committee has strongly urged the need for such courts. In this connection, two institutions should be mentioned where the informal conciliation or compromise procedure has almost totally replaced the formal court procedure. In Rangpui (Gujarat) the 'Lok Adalat' deals inter alia with all family problems. Similarly, in Ahmedabad one section of the Jyoti Sangh work, dealing with all complaints pertaining to family problems, has acquired the status of a woman's court. They listen to both the parties and try to solve the problem by a compromise, failing which, other alternative solutions are suggested.

Indigenous system in India for settlement of disputes indicate that acceptance of this will be easier in our country. We, therefore, strongly recommend that the established adversary system for settlement of family problems be abandoned and established which will adopt conciliatory methods and informal procedure with the aim of achieving socially desirable results.

Article 44 of the Constitutions states that "The State shall endeavour to secure for the citizens a uniform civil code throughout the territory of India".

During the debate in the Constituent Assembly, several members had expressed the fear that implementation of this article might lead to the abrogation of their personal laws. Shri K.M. Murishi had explained, that there was nothing sacrosanct about the personal laws, as they covered secular activities like inheritance and succession. Dr Ambedkar had also emphasized that India had already achieved uniformity of law over a vast area, and the only area of Civil law which continued to have diverse laws were the areas governing matters like marriage and succession. The other point which had been argued, was that such diversity violated the principle of Fundamental Rights that there should be no discrimination between citizens.

These arguments remain as valid today when they were placed before the Constituent Assembly. The absence of a uniform Civil Code more than fifty years after Independence, is an incongruity that cannot be justified with all the emphasis that is placed on secularism, science and modernization. The continuance of various personal laws which accept discrimination between men and women violates the fundamental rights, and the Preamble to the Constitution which promises to secure to all citizens' equality of status, and is against the spirit of national integration and secularism.

Our recommendations regarding amendments of existing laws are only indicators of the direction in which uniformity has to be achieved. We, therefore recommend expeditious implementation of this Constitutional directive by the adoption of a Uniform Civil Code.

The Penal laws of a country reflect more clearly the conditions of its society and its values than most other branches of law. It is, therefore, inevitable that the Indian Penal Code, enacted over a century ago would reflect values and protect interests which are out of tune with the norms prevailing today.

Certain penal provisions in the law are definitely influenced by the established patriarchal system, the dominant position of the husband and the social and economic backwardness of women. By amendments to the original Code, attempts have been made to reflect the socioeconomic changes in the country, but a major revision was needed. The Law Commission undertook this task and submitted the draft of a new Penal Code.

Criminal law has always given the same protection to men and women in respect of their personal safety, individual liberty, property and reputation. But along with this principle of 'equality before law', it has made special provisions to protect women inter alia against attacks on their modesty. Some of these measures require more stringent punishment to meet the present needs of our society, than the law provides today.

Rude or insulting behaviour by itself does not come within the purview of criminal law, unless such behaviour is likely to lead to a breach of peace. But an example of special provision is that it is an offence whenever anyone by words, sounds or gestures "intends to insult the modesty of any woman". When enacted, it was not necessary to classify this offence as a serious one, and therefore, the punishment provided was fine and/or imprisonment for a period which could extend to one year. Today eve-teasing in most cities has become a social evil. But the offence in the last century was categorized as a noncognizable one and the police could not arrest without a warrant nor carry out any investigation without the specific order of a competent magistrate. This was one of the reasons why no effective steps could be taken to combat this menace effectively. The Law Commission took into account this drawback and recommended that it should be made a cognizable offence "so that in the changed social circumstances of the day, when women are coming out in larger numbers and taking greater part in various professional and business activities, they may have a sense of security." We welcome this change in the Criminal Procedure Code, particularly because, as we have discussed later, the lack of security of women acts as an obstacle to their taking up jobs away from home.

In all legal systems, sexual intercourse with a woman without her consent or against her will is regarded as a serious offence. Our law also does so by providing a punishment of imprisonment for life or imprisonment upto ten years, and fine for this offence of rape. Consent, which would negate the offence, is however very strictly interpreted and, therefore, consent, if given by the woman under duress or fraud, will be clearly disregarded by law. But under the present law, no provision is made for consent obtained by putting someone else in fear in the presence of the woman. The Law Commission has recommended adding this and the Indian Penal Code (Amendment), 1972 has included "anyone else present".

We welcome this change as a woman would, in order to save her child from a threat of injury, give her consent to sexual intercourse. This cannot be her consent as consent requires voluntary participation, not only after the exercise of intelligence, based on the knowledge or significance and moral quality of the act, but after having exercised a choice between resistance and consent.

Originally, the age of consent for sexual intercourse was 10 in the case of a girl, but successive amendments raised this to 16. The policy behind these changes was to protect girls of immature age from sexual intercourse.

The Medical Termination of Pregnancy Act 1971, however, holds that the termination of a pregnancy can be performed on a girl below 18 without her consent as long as the guardians's consent to the operation is obtained. In our view, consent to have sexual intercourse requires more maturity than to have an abortion, particularly when the girl is unmarried. The same age limit should be applied in both cases. In conformity with our recommendation made later, we recommend that the age of consent below which a girl's consent to sexual intercourse is not legal should be 18, permitting some degree of flexibility to the court in border-line cases to decide whether the girl is mature enough.

The offence of bigamy may be punished with imprisonment upto seven years and a fine. This indicates the seriousness of the offence. But as already discussed, limiting the right of initiating prosecution to only the aggrieved person, in our social context, defeats the purpose of the law. To remedy this we have recommended permitting any person to initiating prosecution for bigamy with the permission of the court. Apart from this, the present law restricts the jurisdiction of the court to the place where the bigamous marriage was performed or where the husband and wife last resided. This is likely to cause difficulties to the wife. On being abandoned, a wife will usually either go back to her natal home or if feasible, take up a job, which may be away from where she resided with her husband. The present position, therefore, restricts her right to prosecute in many cases. We recommend that in addition to these two jurisdictions, provision be made for enquiry and trial for bigamy in a court within whose jurisdiction the wife is residing.

Retention of adultery as an offence is perpetuating the principle enunciated over a hundred years ago that the "dearest interests of the human race are closely connected with the chastity of women and the sacredness of the nuptial contract ..." The law today permits the husband to prosecute the adulterer of his wife though it exempts the wife from punishment as an abettor. By doing this it brings out clearly the values of the last century which respected the dominant position of the husband and regarded the wife as his property. The Law Commission in its recommendation has only sought to remove the difference between the husband and wife by withdrawing the 'privilege' a woman enjoyed earlier of not being punished under this provision. Adultery in our opinion is a matrimonial and not a criminal offence. The aggrieved is free to seek a remedy in divorce. Treating adultery as a criminal act, apart from reflecting outmoded values, sometimes deters the person of the opposite sex from giving help to a woman appraised by her husband. This was brought to our notice by several lawyers particularly in Andhra Pradesh. They mentioned many cases where lawyers, or house-owners were reluctant to assist a woman seeking divorce or separation from her husband because the latter had threatened to bring a charge of adultery against any man who gave her help.

We recommend that continuing to regard adultery as a criminal offence is against the dignity of an individual and should be removal from the Penal Code.

With the growing importance of human rights in the international sphere, the concept of nationality has come to acquire great importance. In Article 15 of the Universal Declaration of Human Rights 1948, the General Assembly of the United Nations declared that 'every one has the right to nationality and that no one shall be arbitrarily deprived of that nationality.'

Often the term 'Nationality' and 'Citizenship' have been used synonymously. The term citizenship refers to the relationship of an individual with the State from the internal aspect, while the term 'nationality' refers to similar relationship from the international aspect. Nationality is the status or quality of belonging to some particular nation or State. Therefore, the nationals of a State comprise all people who are politically members of the State but all of them may not possess full civil rights and privileges, which are conferred on 'citizens.' Nationality gives the State a limited right to protect its nationals while they are outside the country. The State is also entitled to allegiance from its nationals even when they are abroad as also obedience to certain laws.

In India, the matters of citizenship are governed by the Citizenship Act 1955, and the Rules 1956 as also certain provisions of the Constitution.

The Citizenship Act 1955 deals with the acquisition and termination of citizenship. Under Sec 5(l)(c), a woman married to a citizen of India does not automatically become a citizen, but may make an application and be registered as a citizen. An application by a woman for registration as a citizen under the provisions requires documentary evidence that she has either renounced her previous nationality or has lost it by operation of law. If she has neither lost nor renounced it; her application must be accompanied by an undertaking that she will do so on getting her Indian citizenship. This requirement is essential, as our law does not recognize dual citizenship. But the question of whether an alien woman married to an Indian citizen will get Indian citizenship or not is left to the discretion of the Central Government and can not be challenged in a court of law. This provision of the Act is in accordance with the United Nations Convention of 1957 on the Nationality of Married Women. Under the Convention, all contracting parties agree that the alien wife of a national may acquire the nationality of her husband, through specially privileged naturalization procedures, but it must be at her request.

The grant of nationality, however, may be subject to limitations imposed in the interest of national security or public policy. According to the information supplied by the Home Ministry, there were no statistics of the number of applications made by alien women married to Indian citizens or the number rejected, but 2151 alien women married to Indian citizens had been granted Indian citizenship under the Act.

The lacuna in the Act is the absence of any provision dealing with the case of Indian women marrying foreigners. Her rights are governed by the general provisions, which deal with renouncing Indian citizenship. Till she renounces it, she continues to retain her Indian citizenship, even if her husband has renounced his. But it is in the interpretation of what constitutes renunciation that the hardship may occur. The provision, which applies to all persons is that voluntary acquisition of citizenship of another country will amount to renunciation of Indian citizenship, as we do not accept dual nationality. On the face of it, the provision is unexceptionable but in practice this results in great hardship. If the law of the husband's country requires her to acquire her husband's citizenship by registration or any other way, her registration will be treated a voluntary act as it is not by operation of law. This is unfortunate as often an Indian woman marrying a foreigner requires special protection. Some countries specifically provide that a woman "shall in no case lose her nationality as a result of her marriage to an alien". If for some reason according to the law of her husband's country, a wife is deprived of her nationality, she becomes stateless as she had already lost her Indian citizenship the moment she registered for her husband's nationality. There is consequently no protection given to a woman marrying an alien to prevent this situation of statelessness.

According to the Home Ministry, "No Indian woman has yet lost her Indian citizenship by the sole reason of her having married a foreign national", though they agree that if she "acquires her husband's nationality by some other act, for example, registration, her Indian citizenship will terminate." The Ministry is however silent on the point as to how many of them have lost their Indian nationality by this process.

The right to determine whether the Indian women's act acquiring her husband's citizenship is voluntary or not, vests with the Central Government, which will apply rules of evidence specified in the Rules of the Act. One such piece of evidence is the obtaining of a passport from the Government of another country. Merely getting a passport from a foreign country should not be termed a 'voluntary' acquisition. Even the Supreme Court has expressed this opinion. Many jurists have also challenged the 'Rule', which lays down that getting a passport is a voluntary acquisition. In cases of emergency where time is important, many women would opt for getting a passport which is quicker but this can scarcely be termed a 'voluntary' act. 'From the practical point of view, an Indian woman married to a foreigner and living outside the country, may have to return for purely personal reasons like illness of a family member, and in such a case 'one would not hesitate to travel on any passport — the end being important and not the means of getting there.

Hardship to an Indian woman by arbitrarily applying the rules is best illustrated by the citizenship laws of Afghanistan. According to Afghan law, a woman acquires her husband's nationality by marriage. As long as this is the law, our law will accept the position that an Indian woman has both Indian nationality and Afghan nationality as she has not voluntarily acquired Afghan nationality. But the moment she returns to India on an Afghan passport, she loses her Indian nationality, because she will be deemed to have voluntarily acquired the citizenship of Afghanistan. Under no circumstances should she become stateless. We therefore recommend that the Citizenship Act be amended to provide a special rule for Indian woman marrying an aliend, stating that she will in no case lose her Indian nationality as a result of her marriage to a foreigner. (a) Further, that her acquiring the passport of her husband's country should not be regarded as evidence that she has voluntarily acquired another nationality; (b) In the eventuality of her having been declared stateless, she should revert back to Indian citizenship automatically.

Another rule which operates against the interests of Indian women marrying foreigners, is that their children cannot be regarded as Indian citizens, because the Act clearly states that a child will be considered an Indian çitizen only if his father is one at the time of his birth. Explaining this rule the then Home Minister had said that this provision was to prevent dual or multiple nationality and not to discriminate against women, and in any case, the cases of Indian women marrying foreigners was very rare. This does not really explain the basis of the rule. Where the father and mother are separate and the mother is either de jure or de facto guardian, there is no justification to have the rule that child's nationality will be transmitted through the father. As a mother may be a legal guardian in preference to the father, if it is in the interest of the child, there can be no justification for this rule. We therefore recommend the amendment of Sec. 4(l) of the Citizenship Act to read as follows: "A person born outside India on or after the 26th January, 1950, shall be a citizen of India by descent if his father is married to a citizen of India at the time of his birth."

Under the modern day material pressures and industrialized world women are compelled to think of their legal right for their happy and peaceful life.

In good old days different social and religious traditions laid down certain norms of behaviour for women in India. But compulsions of changing human values and mass education programmes for women have brought about a changed outlook and a new angle of vision to the Indian women. They are now no longer content with their traditional roles and are not prepared to tolerate denial to them of the basic rights. Moreover, it is now agreed that only a harmonious development of a regime of rights can provide the necessary conditions for peace and such a harmony is to be achieved not merely by declaring rights for women on paper but inculcating a culture of rights and responsibilities among the people. Womens problem is a human problem and its future prospects are prospects of humanity at large and not of women alone.

Let us conclude this chapter with a recent article from Hindustan Times.

Article 14 of the Constitution of India guarantees equal rights to all citizens and equality before law. No discrimination can be made on grounds of sex, religion, race, caste, creed, etc. "The State shall not deny to any person equality before the law or equal protection of laws". The rule is that "like should be treated alike and not that unlike should be treated alike".

In the light of Article 14, the Government has been trying to help women find gainful employment. They work in government service and also occupy posts in the judiciary, the army, police and in other departments. And yet women are made to feel inferior to men especially around the time they marry. Demands for dowry are not unusual, keeping in view, the social status of the bridegroom and his parents.

Husbands and in-laws further tend to harass women in numerous other ways. They resort to cruelty in their conduct and in the treatment they mete out to women. Thus, husbands cause harassment by forcing wives to do things that the latter may not like. The Supreme Court has held that cruelty in the legal sense need not be a mere physical assault. The Court holds that the conduct adopted by a married lady's husband or by any other relative, or treatment meted out to her which tends to undermine her health or reasonably affects her happiness can be termed 'cruelty'.

Even imputing unchastity to a woman is a very serious charge and, if established, may result in serious consequences.

Such a woman would stand condemned in society, amounting to mental agony.

The Supreme Court has held that injury to reputation is an important consideration in determining the question of cruelty. Husbands and in-laws often level false accusations against a woman by questioning her integrity, resulting in extreme mental agony. They even institute false cases to terrorise women by greasing the palms of the law enforcement staff and many others.

Newly married girls often fall victim to the machinations of unscrupulous in-laws who create all kinds of trouble for them. Both husbands and in-laws cause such mental torture that they are left with no alternative other than committing suicide. When cruelty for dowry is prima facie proved by certain acts or documentary evidence, a case under Section 498A, 304B, IPC, and under the Dowry Prohibitions Act is registered. Though this Act has been amended from time to, time, the unscrupulous manage to escape the clutches of law. It is therefore imperative to amend the law.

Some women suffer mental agony owing to polygamy. It has been argued whether a Muslim husband has a vested right to marry more than one wife and give universal divorce. It was held by the Supreme Court, that so far as polygamy is concerned, the Mohammedan law is only permissive or optional in nature, and not obligatory. It levies a ceiling on wives and does not lay down that every Muslim should have four wives as a matter of right. It is in the form of an exception.

Divorce or judicial separation are sought in court on grounds of harassment, cruelty, misbehaviour, desertion, adultery and so on. Even court proceedings are unduly delayed, causing great harassment and financial losses to the aggrieved women. Poor women who do not have the means to spend on litigation are the worst hit. The police too does not usually move swiftly to secure justice for destitute women. Neither are the FIR's recorded speedily nor any prompt action initiated unless some pressure is brought on from higher levels.

The fact that women's problems are not attended to even when the complaints are lodged with the local police or with various women's cells needs no reiteration. (Hindustan Times, 27 Feb., 98)

Legislation represents national intent and policy and it is necessary that existing legislation and personal laws be reviewed, appropriately amended or new laws formulated, to ensure equality before law among sexes. Equally important is the need to provide free legal services to weaker sections including women in need. A great deal has been done in recent months particularly regarding equal pay for equal work and steps are being taken for providing legal aid, etc. Needless to add, as has been emphasized in earlier chapters, legislation in itself cannot achieve results, unless it is supported by socioeconomic changes, an awareness of right and responsibilities by the weaker sections, effective legal implementation and follow-up machinery.

Law for Matrimony

The legal system should ensure full equality of sexes even in terms of the personal laws. There should be no compromise about the objective of having monogamy as the rule for all communities in India. Any compromise in this regard will only perpetuate the existing inequality of the status of women. Towards this end, the following measures are suggested:

Law for Reforms

Among some sections of the population, polygamy has legal sanction. However, before necessary changes in the law relating to polygamy are brought about, vigorous effort should be basically directed to generating initiative from among the affected groups so that by the end of the millennium, it would be possible to have uniform legislation for all communities. For this purpose, the practices adopted in other countries with Muslim/ Christian majority should be studied and made known widely.

The right to initiate prosecution for bigamy should be extended to persons other than the girl's family with prior permission of the court to prevent the current violation of this very salutary provision of the law which presents the socially accepted policy of the country. The approach should be towards making it a cognizable offence.

Registration of marriages should be made compulsory for all marriages. For this to be operationally effective, suitable administrative machinery will have to be designed particularly in the rural areas. Enforcement of this could be made operational through amendment, to Registration of Births and Deaths Act, 1969, to include compulsory registration of marriages.

The Child Marriage Restraint Act should be amended to raise the age of marriage for girls to 18 and that of boys to 21. However, for effective implementation proper machinery for enforcing the minimum age at marriage should be designed.

Penalties for offence under the Dowry Prohibition Act, 1961, should be suitably enhanced to make the implementation of the Act more effective. To bring about greater awareness of the evils of dowry, socio-educational programmes should be launched by social welfare organisations.

Government servants giving or taking dowry should be treated as having violated the Government Servants' Conduct Rules similar to the Government Servants' Conduct Rules relating to bigamy.

Although there is right to divorce, but variations and unequal treatment of sexes, vis-a-vis divorce, characterize the various personal laws. As a general principle, efforts should be made to bring about parity of rights for both partners regarding grounds for seeking dissolution of marriage by 1985. Here too, vigorous efforts should be made so that there is a demand from the affected group for uniformity of legislation.

Action should be taken in conformity with the broad principles or equal rights of sons, daughters and widows to ancestral property.

The Indian Succession Act is not uniformly applicable to all sections of women. Efforts should be made for generating the initiative from among the affected groups of women, for bringing about necessary changes in the Succession Act so that by the end of 1985 it is possible to have uniform legislation for all communities by the end of the twentieth century.

On divorce and separation, the wife should be entitled to some part of the assets acquired at the time of and during the time of marriage.

The present rule prevents the children of such Indian women from being considered as Indian citizens. Where the father and mother are separated and the mother is the guardian, the justification for the applicability of the rule that the child's nationality will be transmitted through the father is required to be re-examined with reference to the relevant aspects which have a bearing in Private International Law. The Citizenship Act will therefore, be modified if need be.

The procedures for regaining Indian Citizenship in the case of women of Indian origin, declared as Stateless are tedious and cumbersome. Efforts should, therefore, be made to design simpler procedure in this regard and what is more, there must be a sympathetic and helpful orientation at its implementation stage.

The present law restricts jurisdiction of the court to the place where the bigamous marriage was performed or where the husband and wife last resided. This causes difficulties to the wife who may have to move on after being abandoned by her husband. Therefore; the provisions of the Criminal Procedure relating to jurisdiction should be widened to include trial for bigamy in a court within whose jurisdiction the wife ordinarily resides.

Other Issues

There is need to have a uniform secular and enabling law of adoption.

In dealing with the question of guardianship of a minor child, two principles should be kept in view the interest and protection of the child, and parental right. It was assumed, at one time, that both these principles coincided and there could never be a conflict. For example, the offence of kidnapping is committed when the minor child is taken out of the keeping of the lawful guardian without his consent. The motivation of the person who takes the child and whether such an act is in the child's interest, are factors which do not negate or even mitigate the culpability of the offence. Today, however, there is a shift and the interest of the child is in many cases of paramount consideration that law bears in mind. Therefore, legislation protects a person who reports and often takes to the police a child who is neglected. Such a child can be removed from parental custody and kept where his best interests would be served.

In earlier years, parental authority was synonymous with paternal authority and "social and legal thought rigidly adhered to the proposition that the father by his natural right is entrusted with the care and control of his children." Contemporary thought reflected in legislation of various countries has shifted to regarding the child's interest as of prime consideration and parental rights as being subordinate to it. But unfortunately our law does not clearly reflect this trend. In this branch of law, perhaps more than anywhere else, the judiciary has to set the pace in changing our prevailing norms.

A guardian may be natural, testamentary or appointed by court. While deciding the question of guardianship, two distinct things have to be taken into account—the person of the minor and his property. Often the same person is not entrusted with both. As in other spheres of family law there is no uniform law. Three distinct legal systems are prevalent — Hindu Law, Muslim Law and the Guardians and Wards Act, 1890.

The Hindu Minority and Guardianship Act, 1956 has codified the law but as in the uncodified law it has upheld the superior right of the father. It lays down that a child is a minor till the age of 18. The natural guardian for both boys and unmarried girls is first the father and after him the mother. The prior right of the mother is recognized only for custody in the case of children below five, but even this right is qualified by the word 'ordinarily' It has, however, taken away the right of the father, which he enjoyed before, of appointing a testamentary guardian and thereby depriving the mother of the right. Under the present law, the father cannot resort to this device. In the case of illegitimate children, the mother has a better claim than the father.

Hindu law, however, makes no distinction between the 'person' of the minor and his property and therefore guardianship implies control over both.

The Act, however, directs that in deciding this question, courts must take the 'welfare of the child', as of 'paramount consideration'. It is under this principle that the judiciary has an important role to play, when there is a conflict between the paternal right and the welfare of the child. Recently, the Supreme Court held that in special circumstances the mother could be held to be the natural guardian even when the father was alive. Though the Supreme Court has used words like 'may be considered' and 'special circumstances', we hope that this judgement of the highest court will guide the lower courts, and prevent them from invariably upholding the father's right, even when it is against the interest of the child.

Under Muslim law the father's dominant position is recognized and his rights are very wide, but there is a distinction between guardianship and custody. The term guardianship is usually used with reference to the guardianship to property. This belongs preferentially to the father and in his absence, to his executor. If the father had not appointed any executor the guardianship passes to the paternal grandfather. Among the Shias the difference is that the father is regarded as the sole guardian but after his death it is the right of the grandfather to take over the responsibility and not that of the executor. Both the schools, however, agree that the father while alive is the sole guardian. The mother is not recognized as a natural guardian even after the death of the father.

There is some difference of opinion as to whether the right of the natural guardian extends only over the property rights of the minor or also over person. In the case of the father, there is no doubt that his right extends to both property and person. Even when the mother has custody of the minor child, the father's general right of supervision and control remains. The father, if he so desires, may appoint the mother as a testamentary guardian. Therefore, though the mother may not be recognized as a natural guardian, there is no objection to her being one under the father's will. When she is a testamentary guardian, she will have the right to control both the person and the property of a minor. The Shias, however, do not recognize the right of mother to be a testamentary guardian if she is a non-Muslim. Under both the schools, a mother has no right to appoint a testamentary guardian, except when she herself has been appointed as a general executrix under her husband's will.

Though a mother cannot be a maternal guardian, Muslim law recognizes that she has the prime right to custody of minor children (hizanat). This right is recognized by all authorities under Muslim law. "The mother is of all persons best entitled to the custody of her infant children." (Fatwai Alamgiri).

In the case of a woman custodian, the following qualifications are required:

(a) of sound mind

(b) of good moral conduct

(c) living in such a place where there is no risk, morally or physically to the child

(d) of such an age which would qualify her to bestow on the child the care it may need.

The last does not apply when the custodian is the mother. There is no general agreement however, about the qualifications necessary, if any, when the custodian is a man.

The mother's right of custody or hizanat appears to be an absolute right and even the father cannot deprive her of it. Misconduct is the only condition which can deprive the mother of this right. There is, however, no unanimity as to whether this is a maternal right or a right in the interest of the child. The distinction though subtle, is relevant because if it is a maternal right then only her positive misconduct can lead to her deprivation of the custody; if it is a right in the interest of the child, then even when there is no misconduct on her part she may be deprived on the ground that some other person is more suitable as a custodian. This question still remains an open one. There has been no clear-cut judicial pronouncement on this matter in India. In Pakistan, it has been decided that hizanat is based on the presumption of welfare of the minor and therefore could be rebutted.

There is a difference between the Shia and Hanafi schools about the age at which the right of the mother to custody terminates. In the case of a minor son, the Shia school holds that the mother's right to hizanat is only during the period of weaning which is over when the child has completed the age of two. The

Hanafi school, on the other hand, extends the period till the minor son has reached the age of seven. Both schools agree that the same age cannot be applied when the minor is a girl. The Shia Law upholds the mother's right till the girl reaches to puberty and the Hanafi school till she attains puberty. Both schools agree that only the mother has the right to the custody of a minor married girl till she attains the age of puberty.

The Muslim concept of hizanat is definitely an advance on the other legal systems, because it recognizes that for a minor child the mother's care and control is more desirable. The father, therefore, is required to pay maintenance to the mother for the child for this period.

The supremacy of paternal right is the keynote of the Guardians and Wards Act which governs all communities other than Hindus and Muslims. It clearly lays down that the father's right is primary and no other person can be appointed unless the father is found unfit. However, as in the Hindu Law, the Act provides that the court must bear in mind the welfare of the child, though this is not mentioned as being of paramount consideration. In recent years, however, some of the decisions have broken away from the past attitude of looking upon the father not only as a natural guardian but as having "an inalienable right over his child". They now hold that "the welfare of the minor is of prime consideration and even the paramount right of the father should be subordinated....

1. that the control over the person and property of a minor cannot be separated and should vest in the same person;

2. the question of guardianship should be determined entirely from the point of view of the child's interest and not the prior right of either parent;

3. the parent who does not have guardianship should have access to the child;

4. whatever the decision taken earlier, the child's choice of guardians should be obtained when the child reaches the age of 12.

We support the recommendations of the UN Commission on the Status of Women which are as follows:

(a) Women shall have equal rights and duties with men in respect to guardianship of their minor children and the exercise of parental authority over them, including care, custody, education and maintenance;

(b) Both spouses shall have equal rights and duties with regard to the administration of the property of their minor children, with the legal limitations necessary to ensure as far as possible that it is administered in the interest of the children;

(c) The interest of the children shall be of paramount consideration in proceedings regarding custody of children, in the event of divorce, annulment of marriage or judicial separation.

(d) No discrimination shall be made between men and women with regard to decision regarding custody of children and guardianship or other parental rights in the event of divorce, annulment of marriage or judicial separation.

10

The Privileges

(i) This Act should be extended to all industries not covered by the Act at present and the provision of maternity relief ensured by the creation of a Central Fund by levying contributions from employers. The administration of the Fund should follow the pattern already established by the Employees State Insurance Corporation.

(ii) The Act should also cover agricultural labourers in the same manner as suggested for other industries. To facilitate its implementation the Central Fund should also include a levy on agricultural farms employing hired labour, the quantum depending upon the size of the holding as recommended for the Agricultural Holding Tax by the Committee on Taxation of Agricultural Wealth and Income.

(iii) The anti-retrenchment clause already included in the Employees State Insurance Act 1948 should be incorporated in the Maternity Benefits Act.

(iv) For women retrenched for short period and re-employed on the same jobs, the period of unemployment should not be treated as discontinuation of service for their eligibility for this benefit. For casual labour, a minimum of 3 months of service should considered as qualifying them for this benefit.

(v) As decided by the Supreme Court in the case of bidi workers, the provision of maternity benefits should be extended to home workers in all other industries.

(vi) In order to eliminate unjust denial of maternity benefits, scrutiny of applications should be done by Committee of the management and trade union representatives. The latter should preferably include a woman. This will provide greater incentive to women workers to participate in trade activities.

(vii) The penalties for evasion of this law should be made more stringent.

(viii) The system of paying cash benefits in a lump-sum sometimes give rise to inadequate attention to the nutritional needs of the mother and the child. Payment of maternity benefits should be made in two instalments, before and after confinement, as already prevalent in many industries.

Creches

(i) The present limit of 50 women workers for the application of this provision under the Factories Act should be reduced to 20.

(ii) Women employed as casual labour or as contract labour should be entitled tc [illegible]e this benefit.

(iii) Wherever there is a demand, a day centre should be provided for keeping small children for other groups of women workers, e.g., workers in offices, hospitals, shops and commercial establishment.

(iv) As far as possible, creches should be established near the residence of women workers rather than the place of work. The ideal arrangement, in our view, would be neighbourhood creches. This will benefit women in all occupations, both in the organized and unorganized sector.

Basis of Equality

Permission to work up to 10 p.m. should be granted provided arrangements for transport and security are made.

We further recommend effective implementation of the Maternity Benefits Act in all States, and the extension of the Employees State Insurance Scheme to those areas which are not covered by it at present.

(i) We recommend legislative enactment of Article 39 (d) of the Constitution – equal pay for equal work to add the weight of legal sanction to what is only a policy at present.

(ii) We further recommend incorporation of this principle in the Minimum Wages Act.

Training and Employment

(i) We recommend reservation of a definite quota for women for training within the industry in order to arrest their retrenchment as a consequence of modernization.

(ii) A similar quota should be reserved for women for training of apprentices under the National Apprentices Act.

(iii) We further recommend developing programmes of vocational training in close relationship with industries and resources located in the area. Links with possible employing agencies have to be developed from the beginning so that the training does not end in futility.

(iv) As recommended by the Committee of the All India Council for Technical Education, polytechnics for women should include a production centre with assistance from the Small Scale Industries Department of the State concerned.

(v) Development of training programmes in production and market organization to develop self-employment.

(vi) Special efforts have to be made to develop vocational training for both illiterate and semi-literate women workers.

(vii) We further recommend development of training-cum-production centres in small scale or cottage industries in both rural and urban areas to provide employment to women near their homes.

We recommend specific provisions for part-time employment of women by suitable revisions in recruitment rules and service conditions. We also recommend detailed investigation of areas where part-time employment could be generated by agencies like the Directorate General of Employment and Training, the Institute of Applied Manpower Research, the National Council of Applied Economic Research, etc. Such studies should include examination of existing avenues for part-time employment, viz., in the unorganized industries and occupations.

We recommend expansion of the national employment service, particularly in rural areas, and the development of a women's cadre in the service to provide employment information and assistance to women.

We recommend that provision for special leave without pay, subject to a maximum of 5 years during service, should be made in all occupations, in order to enable women to devote full-time for the care of their families. Their hen should be protected.

Protective Rules

We recommend increase in the number of women on the inspectorate of different labour Departments as well as provision for women welfare officers wherever women are employed.

We further recommend:

(i) That trade unionists and labour leaders should take steps to organize labour unions in the field of agriculture and other industries where such organizations do not exist at present.

(ii) Formation of women's wings in all trade unions, to look after the problems of women workers and to improve women's participation in trade union activities.

In India, rural women constitute nearly 80 per cent of the female population. They contribute largely to the country's economy which is mainly agriculture based. Although distributive justice has been categorically underlined in all the development plans, the needs of women have not been adequately addressed. While laying emphasis on enhanced agriculture production in which the involvement of women is high, the plans have fostered a target group and area oriented approach to reduce regional and ecological imbalances disregarding women's equality as embodied in the Constitution. Rural development programmes for women have only in recent decades recognized the crucial role of organization and mobilization as strategies for women's empowerment and development. Rural women's organizations are also mechanisms for restructuring and redistributing power and have been utilized pressure groups that influence and/or bargain on behalf of rural women.

The launching of the Community Development Programme in 1952 was a landmark in the history of India and ushered in an era of development with the participation of the people. The Community Development Programme adopted a systematic integrated approach to rural development with a hierarchy of village level workers and block level workers drawn from various fields to enrich rural life. Agriculture, animal husbandry, public health, women's development, rural industries, etc. found a special niche in the framework cast for this purpose. Five thousand National Extension Service Blocks were created under the Community Development Programmes by the end of the Second Five-Year Plan. During the Third Five-Year Plan the momentum was maintained through a series of developmental schemes though allocations under the NES programme tapered. This was succeeded by the Small Farmers Development Agencies, Cash Schemes for Rural Employment, Food for Work Programme, Drought Development Programme and Desert Development Programme in the early seventies. The contents of all these programmes were to strengthen the rural base of the economy, specifically the primary sector comprising agriculture, animal husbandry, etc., and employment through labour intensive works that would create the infrastructure of roads and other community assets for the benefit of the rural people.

It was recognized that the skewed pattern of land holdings stood in the way of creating an egalitarian society and obstructed modernization and intensification of agriculture. Land reform measures for abolition of intermediary tenures, tenancy reforms, imposition of land ceiling on agricultural holdings, distribution of surplus land to the landless agricultural workers and consolidation of land holdings were introduced through a series of State Legislations under Central guidelines.

Certain areas of the country are characterized by soil erosion, water stress and environmental degradation. The Drought Prone Areas Programme was started in 1973 aiming at an integrated area development for optimum utilization of land, water, livestock and human resources through a watershed management approach to mitigate the effects of drought. A few years later the Desert Development Programme, a wholly centrally funded scheme, specifically to cover extremely and areas for controlling desertification and restoration of ecological balance, was also started.

The emphasis shifted to fulfilling minimum needs of the people during the Fifth Five-Year Plan.

A systematic analysis and examination of the status and role of women within the agriculture and rural development strategies in India started with the National Plan of Action (NPA) for women which followed the report of the Committee on the Status of Women in India (CSWI). Subsequently, efforts of women activists, social science institutions and researchers produced enough documentary support to persuade the Sixth Plan document to include a chapter on 'Women and Development' for the first time in the country's history of planned development.

A strategy of direct attack on poverty was adopted in the Sixth Plan as the theory of trickle down benefits of general development programmes had not proved as a successful strategy for the removal of poverty. Forty-eight per cent of the population were found to be living below the poverty line at the beginning of the Sixth Five-Year Plan.

One positive outcome of these developments has been the recognition that rural women are not a homogeneous group to justify a uniform development strategy. The development plans in the case of women must be based on the assessment of their actual role and participation in socio-economic activities.

Women's employment has been recognized as the 'critical entry point' for women's integration in mainstream development. The low and deteriorating status of rural women is attributed to their declining economic participation and other factors like the modernization of the agricultural sector. The need for giving a better deal to the rural women is beginning to be widely recognized. It is now accepted that the participation of women themselves in development activities is the most effective tool for the promotion of the access of women to the benefits of development. A working group set up by the Department of Rural Development, Ministry of Agriculture and Rural Development in 1978 recommended that the major objectives of the development plan for rural women should be (i) the improvement of their economic status; and (ii) the promotion of women's organization to have the collective strength to articulate their needs and promote their participation in the development process.

The Integrated Rural Development Programme initiated in 1978-79 and extended to all the development blocks in the country in 1980-81 was conceived as one of the instruments for a direct attack on poverty. It dealt with individual rural families below the poverty line. Credit from banking institutions and subsidy from the Government were given to the families for self-employment and income generation. Under IRDP, a special place was accorded for training rural unemployed youth for employment with the introduction of TRYSEM. An extensive scheme for the social and economic uplift of women belonging to families below the poverty line, DWCRA (Development of Women and Children in Rural Areas) was launched in 1982 as a sub-component in IRDR.

The Sixth Plan accepted poor rural women to be targets of rural development strategies. The specific problems identified concerning rural poor women were (i) marginality of attention and services to them in rural and agricultural development (ii) special constraints that obstruct their access to available assistance and services such as, lack of training to develop their awareness and skills; lack of information and lack of bargaining power; (iii) low productivity and narrow occupational choices; (iv) low level of participation in decision-making; (v) inadequate finance and expert guidance for promoting socio-economic activity of rural women and their participation; (vi) inadequate monitoring of women's participation in different sectors; (vii) wage discrimination; (viii) inadequate application of science and technology to remove drudgery; and (ix) low health and nutrition status.

The Sixth Plan document stated that one of the most important means of achieving improvement in the status of women would be to secure for them a fair share of employment opportunities, to earmark a percentage of allocation for women, and to fix for them a quota in all the poverty alleviation programmes. The Seventh Plan reiterated the strategies suggested in the Sixth Plan with a sharper focus on the increased coverage of women in various rural development programmes.

Simultaneously, the National Rural Employment Programme (NREP), assuring wage employment to the unemployed rural population was introduced in 1980. Subsequently, concentration on the rural landless was attempted to the introduction of the Rural Landless Employment Guarantee Programme (RLEGP) in 1983. The Indira Awas Yojana was added as an important component of the programme in the Seventh Plan for constructing houses for SC/STs and freed bonded labourers. Social Forestry was added as another component of the RLEGP with national emphasis on greening fuel and fodder.

The establishment of the Technology Mission on Drinking Water and Related Water Management gave a new thrust to the Rural Water Supply Programme. Safe and adequate drinking water is to be provided to the entire rural population by the end of the Seventh Five-Year Plan.

The impact of the poverty alleviation programmes coupled with the development in various sectors reduced the rural population below the poverty line to 37 per cent by the beginning of the Seventh Plan. The target is to bring this down to 28 per cent by the end of the Seventh Plan Period.

Agriculture and allied fields provide the largest sector to women's employment. It largely determines the rural women's socio-economic status. This is the sector where women's role as unpaid labour in productive activities is most prominent and is responsible for conferring women a non-working status. In case of both agriculture and animal husbandry, development strategies have provided very little attention to women in comparison to their active involvement in both the sectors. Some training is imparted to women in agriculture and animal husbandry under the programmes for Farmers' Training and Krishi Vigyan Kendras. But the Farmers Training Programme has lost much of its importance after the introduction of the new extension system of Training and Visit (T&V). Though women constitute a major work force in agriculture which with regional variation is estimated to be around 60 per cent, they are invisible in the T&V system. Currently there is one major extension programme for women in Karnataka and 2-3 such programmes on the anvil in other States. There is an in-built resistance observed in them in viewing women within their home making role. Even the visual presentations (slides, filmstrips and films) which are used for the orientation of the functionaries often depict the women in the field and the extension agent talking to the contact farmer on the field, fail to project the full dimension of women's role.

While rural women have become marginally visible in the anti-poverty programmes, they have not been adequately recognized in agricultural development, land reform, or rural industrialization. Non-recognition of women in agriculture has many implications. Intensive agriculture and the green revolution have reduced women's participation in on farm activities but the work load related to the home based farm activities has increased considerably. That has only reduced them from the 'working' to a 'non-working' status. Limited employment opportunities created by technology resulting in the means of production being concentrated in the hands of a few, and increased landlessness for the poor led to men replacing women in many of their traditional areas of employment. But women have had to work and survive. They are thus found gradually moving to the non-traditional sectors seeking employment for survival.

Following the Sixth and Seventh Plans, the Department of Rural Development issued directives to the State Governments to give priority to women headed households, enhance the share of women under the anti-poverty programme (IRUP), and the programme of Training and Self-Employment (TRYSEM). Guidelines for NREP and RLEGP envisage increasing participation of women in wage employment and creation of assets specific to the needs of women's groups. At present the share of employment generated under NREP for women is approximately 20 per cent. A special programme for women entitled Development of Women and Children in Rural Areas (DWCRA) was also introduced in 1982, as a sub-component of IRDP to accelerate the process of integration of women in the rural development programmes. Up to 1987, 11,533 groups are reported to have been organized in 106 districts under this scheme.

The Integrated Rural Development Programme meant for the poorest in the rural areas has been formulated for creating assets with a view to increasing the productivity and income generation abilities of the beneficiaries. Efforts have been made under this programme to select female headed households. The scheme of DWCRA could be strengthened and modified in order to ensure that the benefits reach more target groups. The National Rural Employment Programme (NREP) and Rural Landless Employment Guarantee Programme (RLEGP) would generate additional employment to women in the lean season. Under Training of Rural Youth in Self-Employment (TRYSEM), one-third of the beneficiaries were expected to be women and special attention was to be given to improve existing skills of women and imparting to them new skills under the programmes of farmers training, fodder production, post harvest technology, application of pesticide, budding and grafting, training in horticulture, fisheries, poultry, dairy and social forestry, etc. The training of women under TRYSEM has exceeded the target to 44 per cent as of January 1988. Out of a total of 37.23 lakh families which received benefits under the IRDP during 1986-87, the number of women headed families was 5.67 lakh which amounts to only 15.23 per cent as against the target of 30 per cent. On assessment of the programmes, it is observed that considerable efforts are required to elicit the participation of women in these activities. The training provided under TRYSEM and DWCRA is not always viable and there is a tendency to limit to a few traditional crafts, though the Department of Rural Development is laying greater stress on taking up innovative activities too. Therefore, a fresh look is needed to be given to identification of trades and activities which may gainfully be taken up by women. Many income-generating programmes have not succeeded due to full thought not being given to the input availability, training and marketing of products.

Special development projects linked to certain ongoing activities need to be taken up on a project basis to improve the effectiveness of the programmes related to women. Specific projects such as sericulture for tribals in certain states like Bihar and Orissa, development of dairy units linked to Operation Flood areas, fruits and vegetables cultivation linked to marketing through Mother dairy, prawn farming and fishing in the coastal region were commended. Agro-based industry schemes, etc., are essential.

The scheme of Training of Rural Youth for Self-Employment (TRYSEM) should be revamped with a view to organizing training in trades with assured employment potential to women in rural areas, as well as for wage employment in peripheral metropolitan and urban areas. State Emporia, marketing channels of KVSIC, etc., should be tapped, to ensure elimination of middlemen and better process.

The Accelerated Rural Water Supply Programme (ARWSP) and the Minimum Needs Programme (MNP) are of special significance to rural women who are the victims of drudgery, such as fetching water from distant locations. The Technology Mission on Drinking Water and Related Water Management lays emphasis on purification of water to make it potable, training in the use of water and maintenance of water sources. Women are the target of the awareness creation programmes as well as agents for creating awareness in conservation of water and maintenance of water sources. The low cost sanitation programme is also of great importance to women, who are otherwise subjected to a lot of privation due to lack of appropriate sanitation facilities. Rural Technologies and innovation promoted by CAPART aim at relieving the drudgery to women in several areas of their households and economic activities. They include the improved varieties of stone grinder, wheel barrow, ball-bearing pulley, ground nut sheller and smokeless chulhas.

The limited performance of the programmes introduced to achieve the integration of women in the development process suggests that only policy directives do not achieve the desired objectives. Programmes do not get implemented due to the lack of comprehension of the relevance of women's contribution to national development. Although the concern for development of women is well articulated at the central policy making level, an ambivalence is observed at the implementation level. The policy directives issued by the Government of India for the increased share for women in the development programmes and the promotion of a participatory approach, do not provide for corresponding development in the infrastructure, extension, training information support and a strong monitoring system which is particularly lacking at the State level. The programmes for rural women still continue as a separate exercise within the sectoral programmes with marginal attention, resources and inadequate monitoring.

The major shortcomings noticed in the implementation of the programmes for women with development objectives are: (i)

Perpetuation of the concept that women need only welfare services; (ii) That the developmental benefits will automatically accrue to the women as a result of economic development of the family; (iii) Inadequate knowledge and skills for designing socioeconomic activities for women and in group organizations; (iv) lack of supportive services such as credit, child care, marketing, training and technology for reducing the drudgery.

The approaches used for integrating women in the mainstream of development have raised some methodological issues. These relate particularly to the organization of groups, involvement of the voluntary sector, and the household approach in development programmes for rural women.

The organization of women's groups is considered to be one of the most effective tools for integrating women in the development process. Yet it has raised several issues which are not fully resolved. Some of the questions which are being asked repeatedly are:

(i) Who will organize the groups (the role of intermediaries)?

(ii) What will be the size, structure and status of groups — formal or informal?

(iii) Should the groups be organized first and the choice of activities to be undertaken by the groups come next?

(iv) Should women be assisted individually under the IRDP, etc., or be formed into groups.

Apart from these unresolved issues, there are problems in selecting and working out economically viable group projects. Women activists argue against giving individual projects to be carried out within the household as it would only perpetuate their subordination in the household hierarchy. They claim that assistance to the voluntary agencies, which was expected to provide grass-roots structural support in this regard, is either not forthcoming or has not been sought.

It is logical that the size of the group to be mobilized should be such as to enable close interaction amongst the members which is only possible when they come from the same background and from one cluster of villages. It is also evident that poor women acquire confidence when they get organized. The delivery system will respond positively even if they are informally grouped. But in the interest of economic viability, and to strengthen their earning capacity, it is desirable for the group to be formalized. It is however, not possible or advisable to suggest one organizational model for all situations. The experience by and large is that the organization based on personal interface and on localized issues is more effective, more flexible and functional than the highly structured and impersonal form of organization.

Some of the processes under IRDP, such as identification of beneficiaries/productive activities, preparation of loan application, sanction of the same and procurement of assets have not been given much attention in terms of proper planning, particularly of the linkage required after the asset is given, to make the same optimally productive. Such linkages include most critically the supply of raw materials and facilities for marketing. These processes and linkages are more effective when implemented through the group approach.

The crucial question in the field of land reforms is how rural poor women should get land and have access to land. Power structures in the villages are dominated by the relatively better off classes. Considering that implementation of land reform measures leaves much to be desired, there is an urgent need for people's participation more specifically of the women, by promoting their groups organizations and through Panchayati Raj institutions. Each village should have a village plan which should include land used for cultivable lands, gochar lands and forest lands with clearly demarcated boundaries.

The involvement of intermediaries in development programmes for rural women has been considered vital, particularly in demonstrating and, promoting the participatory model and to provide support to the grassroots structure. Here too, there are basic issues which need to be carefully resolved. Among others, it is queried whether the role of the intermediary organizations has been understood by the Government, or whether it is feasible for the voluntary organizations to function in partnership with the government, given the differences in approach.

There is no uniform understanding and acceptance of the role of the voluntary agencies in the States. In some cases, there is a complete lack of rapport between the Government and voluntary agencies. In others, there is the tendency of associating the women's programmes entirely with voluntary action, showing a lack of initiative on the part of the Government. There is little doubt that the voluntary agencies are committed to the cause of women and have expressed a real concern for the enhancement of women's status. They have also demonstrated skills for mobilizing women, and in trying innovative projects. In view of this, the association of the voluntary agencies with the programmes is bound to enrich the programmes as well as the delivery mechanisms. Yet, they cannot be a substitute for Governmental action. To end women's isolation from rural development, the Government must work in partnership with voluntary agencies.

Currently debated issues in the context of women in rural development and in the anti-poverty programmes, is the household versus group approach; some argue in favour of ensuring a share of developmental resources and benefits to women in all sectoral programmes, while others argue in favour of having separate investments for women.

In India, the family is hierarchical, traditional and the status in the family is determined by sex and age. In the patriarchal society, it is the man who holds the position of the head of the family and the bread winner. Therefore, it is the man who gets attention in the investment of developmental resources, training, extension and other supports. Women's contribution to the family's earnings goes unrecognized. This bias, in fact, is responsible for the earlier programmes not taking note of women headed households whose number is currently estimated at 30-35 per cent of all rural households. In mounting pressure on the government to give priority to this group, it has been convincingly argued that an improvement in the income of the household does not necessarily mean development for women. The household approach instead of creating equitable conditions, perpetuates the subordination of women and limits their opportunities for self-growth and self-expression.

Having a special component within sectoral plans can stimulate action for women provided the components are monitored separately. The introduction of the scheme of DWCRA within the programme of IRDP was aimed at stimulating the response of the State Governments to integrating women into anti-poverty programmes. Therefore, in case of women, it can be contended that a combined approach is desirable. This would allow women to be adopted as a target in all sectoral programmes, with earmarked resources along with special component plans aimed exclusively at women. Such dual approaches can be continued until women acquire sufficient power to articulate their needs and demands and until such time as women's concerns get to be internalized in the planning and administrative structures.

In the economic sphere and in particular in the rural sector, the 'empowerment' of women relates mainly to their access to means of production and control over the fruits of their labour. The access to the means of production implies ownership of land, other productive assets, access to capital and access to technology and acquisition of various skills required to make labour power more productive.

The aspect of ownership of land relates to rights of inheritance which are governed by personal laws of different communities. These personal laws at present are discriminatory against women and have a bias in favour of the male heirs. The State Governments of Kerala and Andhra Pradesh have sought to remove some of these discriminations with a view to give daughters in the family, co-parcenary ownership in the family property on the same level as the sons. But even these changes do not go far enough and still discriminate against a married daughter and a widow and do not apply equally to the separate properties of the father in the Hindu Customary Law. There is discrimination against women of different types in the personal laws of other communities also. In the customary law of certain tribes, only male agnates in the male line are recognized as valid heirs and an unmarried daughter is only entitled to maintenance. It would be necessary to introduce correctives to overcome the discrimination in order that the gap between the State's proclamation to achieve equality of the sexes and its laws which deny it, is bridged. Women's undiluted access to land, the most productive resource, would undoubtedly bestow on her necessary economic independence and power and would improve her social position in the family as well.

Regarding access of women to land, the land records do not incorporate the rights of women in the landed property shown in the name of the husband or the father. Only where a woman is a widow and happens to be the 'karta' of the family, her name may figure in the record of rights as the owner of property.

Co-ownership of property by women, should not merely be confined to land but also to other productive assets like house, family wealth, shops, factory or any other income generating establishment or asset. This would provide sufficient conditions for women to participate in and influence the decision concerning the use and disposal of such properties.

As regards access to capital, there is a general reluctance on the part, of the public financial institutions to extend credit to women independently of the male head or guardian of the family.

The existing land ownership pattern in India is largely male oriented except in some areas of the north-east and a few other places where matrilineal system is in operation and inheritance of property passes through the institution of the mother. The land records, to the extent they reflect the ownership and other interests in land, only record the names of men. Similarly, where shareholders of such lands are recorded, it is usually the male shareholder who finds mention in the land records. The processes of preparation of land records, i.e., the survey and recording of rights also deal with such male holders of interests in land. The only exception would be in such cases where a widow with no other male person, manages the land. Her name is recorded as the owner and manager of land. Land reform measures have also not taken into cognizance interests of women as co-owners or cultivators of land, and to this extent land reform measures seem to have by-passed the women. The most prominent example where this inherent discrimination in land reforms has been noticed is the case of ceiling laws where most State laws have provided for a separate unit of ceiling for major sons in the family but not major daughters married or unmarried. Although from the point of view of implementation of such ceiling laws, addition of yet another unit in the name of major daughters would have further defeated its objectives, nonetheless, the discrimination cannot be denied. Further, in the matter of distribution and allotment of various lands, it is usually the male head of the family who gets the patta in his name. Recently, of course instructions have been issued to give joint patta in the name of both husband and wife while allotting land and house-sites. Similarly, in the matter of collection of minor forest produce and enjoyment of rights over common property resources, the rights of women are not focused, even though it is the women who have to collect fuel-wood and fodder and minor forest produce from such lands.

Tribal social structures are more egalitarian and open and less stratified than social structures of larger and more advanced communities in India. The status and position enjoyed by tribal women in society, is therefore, in certain tribes, much better than their counterparts in other communities. This is on account of many reasons. Tribal society has a tradition of both men and women working on an equal footing whether in agriculture or in other vocations. Thus tribal women have access to income and are therefore, economically independent. There are also no restrictions on women going out for work independent of men, and not necessarily along with them. Usually, tribal women go out for work in large groups. In social matters and family life also tribal women are far more emancipated. They have a much greater say in the decision making in family and community matters and are not subjected to the same degree of social control by male members of the family as women in other communities are.

Despite this, in matters of inheritance of father's/ husband's property and in access to land, there is a certain built-in discrimination against women in some tribal communities. The customary law of some tribal communities excludes women from inheritance rights, such inheritance rights being restricted to "male heirs in the male line". These customs are even enshrined in tenancy laws wherever enacted and applicable to these communities. This discrimination against women has a harmful effect on their lives, rendering them economically and socially powerless and driving large numbers of them into destitution. In fact, in certain tribal communities, for example, the Ho Tribe in Singhbhum district of Bihar, a large number of women remain unmarried so as to ensure to themselves usufructuary rights available to them as unmarried daughters. Many of them are harassed by their husband's and father's male agnates who wish to deprive them even of this usufructuary right. A number of women are forced to migrate in order to earn their livelihood, since their hold over the family land is so insecure and dependent on the attitude of their male relatives even though these women do the bulk of agricultural work. Sometimes, the women are declared witches, the concealed motive being to drive them out of the village or even to kill them in order to usurp the family property.

The married women also enjoy limited usufructuary rights in the deceased husbands' property. Even these usufructuary rights cannot be freely exercised by them since the husbands male agnates often harass them and try to get rid of them in the hope of asserting their inheritance claims to the land. If the married woman has a son, the latter inherits the land from his father, and she has no legal claim to it. If the husband has one or two or more wives, the sons of other wives have inheritance rights to the land, and she is dependent on them for maintenance. In case, the marriage breaks up, or a man remarries or deserts his first wife, the woman is absolutely without land rights, since she has, by marriage, lost the usufructuary rights in her father's house, and she is also deprived of rights in her matrimonial home. Since tribal communities have their customary laws, the Hindu Succession Act, the Indian Succession Act, or any other succession Act do not apply to them.

The discrimination against women in the customary law of tribal communities, historically speaking, may have evolved with a view to preserve the integrity of the tribe and to prevent land passing from the tribal to persons outside the tribe which would have the effect of disintegrating the tribal society. While, it is necessary to preserve the integrity of the tribe and to protect the interest of tribals in land against any encroachment by non-tribals, it is also necessary to protect the interest of tribal women in land by giving them rights to inheritance in father's and husband's property. But safeguards will have to be provided in the event of marriages outside the tribe.

Therefore, provision in law and customary practices which discriminate against women in matters of inheritance of property and restrict such inheritance to male agnates in male line should be changed while at the same time preserving the integrity of the tribe and preventing alienation of tribal land to non-tribals.

Women, especially tribals, migrate in search of work. They are employed in large numbers in the unorganized sector like brick-kiln, road construction, irrigation works, agricultural operations, forestry operations, stone-cutting, domestic labour, etc. They are subjected to brutal exploitation at places of work by contractors and the middlemen who recruit them. The exploitation is not merely confined to payment of low wages, long hours of arduous work and other dismal working conditions. They are also subjected to sexual exploitation. It is necessary, that for each category of employment in the unorganized sector, specific institutional mechanisms be built-in to protect women's interests.

Rays of Hope

The Seventh Plan is set within a 15 years' perspective in which poverty alleviation in the rural sector remains central. It is targeted to bring down the percentage of rural poor below 10 per cent by 2000 A.D. The Department of Rural Development has already suggested that in case of women, poverty alleviation goals for 2000 A.D. should be to:

(i) Bring all women- headed households (estimated to be 30-35 per cent) above the poverty line; and

(ii) Attain the target of having women constitute 30 per cent of all beneficiaries to be assisted under IRDP.

In addition, the endeavour should be to bring in the women's development dimension into sectors which have hitherto not responded adequately to women's needs. Women's access to productive resources must also be ensured.

Political power and access to positions of decision making and authority are critical prerequisites for women's equality in the processes of nation building. Hence it is crucial that the representation of women in local bodies up to the district level be ensured.

1. In view of the inter-linkages of the economic and the social sectors and their supportive role in strengthening each other, the rural development agencies should function in the direction of convergence of the services of education, health, child-care technology and other developmental measures. For maximizing impact wherever possible programmes must adopt the group approach to mobilization of women.

2. The Minimum Needs Programmes should be strengthened and expanded. Efforts should be made to achieve the objective of water for all by the beginning of twenty-first century. Increasing involvement of women in the selection of sites for the installation of water sources, maintenance, utilization, etc., should be aimed at. Fuel, fodder, creche, sanitation should also be included in the Minimum Needs Programme.

3. Emphasis should be given to higher growth rate of industry in rural areas and expansion of housing programmes to generate a large volume of employment in the non-agricultural sector.

4. Land reform and redistribution are basic prerequisites for increased economic outputs and gains. Women's access to productive resources such as land for cultivation and credit inputs must be ensured.

5. Regarding access of women to land, the land records do not incorporate the rights of women in the landed property shown in the name of the husband or the father. Only where a woman is a widow and happens to be the *karta* of the family, her name may figure in the

record of rights as the owner of property. Therefore, in order to give the women genuine economic power through access to land, the following steps are necessary:

(a) Where a woman has brought some property to the family through marriage, this property must be exclusively recorded in her name.

(b) Property which is acquired during the subsistence of marriage should be recorded in their joint names.

6. Regarding women as co-owners of property should not merely be confined to land but also to other productive assets like trees, animals, house, family wealth, shops or any other income generating establishment or asset. This would instill confidence in women to participate in and influence the decision concerning the use and disposal of such properties.

7. Wherever shareholders in land and other assets are recorded in the record of rights, the shareholding must necessarily record the shares of female right holders also as per their entitlement. Existing records need to be reviewed and methods to revise entries to indicate joint ownership evolved.

8. Wherever other interests in land like cultivating possession, share-cropping, tenancy rights, rights in common property resources, rights of collection of minor forest produce, grazing and usufructuary rights, etc., are recorded, such rights must be recorded in respect of both male as well as female spouse.

9. The allotment of Government wastelands, village common land, developed house-sites, allotment of Indira Awas Tenements should invariably be done in

the joint names of the husband and wife or single title of ownership given to women heads of households, tribal women and Scheduled Caste, particularly those who are widows, unmarried or victims of harassment.

10. There is no reason why land, house sites, dwelling units should not be allotted exclusively to 'women' as eligible categories. This will give greater strength and confidence to women and will prevent men from disposing of the land without her consent. In future, as a matter of policy in the allotment of Government land and surplus ceiling land and house sites, at least 40 per cent women members of the eligible categories may be given pattas.

11. Apart from ownership, certain interests in land are heritable, as for example rights of share-cropping and cultivation on certain lands. This heritability does not usually devolve on the female spouse after the death of the husband but gets shifted to the male agnates of the family: The recording of joint interests should ensure that the female co-owner of such holdings inherits the interest after her husband dies.

12. Personal laws of many communities discriminate against female members, particularly married daughters in regard to share in the father's property. A review of property laws is essential to extend the principles of inheritance to women as they are applicable to men.

13. In customary laws of many tribal communities, women do not have any right of inheritance in father's or husband's property, although they are entitled to maintenance during their lifetime. This discrimination should be ended and safeguards should be provided that this process should not lead to non-tribals usurping tribal landed property.

14. Tree 'pattas' should be issued in the name of Women as a matter of preference. Social forestry schemes on Government or village common and forest lands should be allotted exclusively to women's groups. This is particularly applicable to tribal and Scheduled Caste women.

15. Productive assets under Integrated Rural Development Programme such as ploughs, bullocks, hand pumps, etc., should be issued in the name of husband and wife and, in the case of women headed households, to the women exclusively.

16. In dairy cooperatives or similar activities, the name of the female spouse should also be recorded as a shareholder along with her husband.

17. An effective support mechanism is a watchdog committee at village/panchayat, tahsil level to ensure that rights admissible to women are not deprived to them by members of the family and other vested interests should be developed so that their assistance can be taken by women in distress.

18. In implementation of land reform measures, potential women beneficiaries should be associated with any committee or representative groups set up to aid and advice the implementation machinery. The enforcement machinery for implementing land reforms needs to be made more effective.

19. In some communities, there are customs whereby if a tribal woman is raped by a non-tribal or lives with a non-tribal, she becomes automatically outcast from the tribal society and even deprived of the minimal usufructuary rights in land available to other women. It is necessary to make appropriate changes wherever such

practices exist, and provisions under the customary law for their maintenance should be made available to them.

20. Tribal women who are accused of witchcraft should be given legal, social and economic protection.

21. The rights of collection of minor forest produce by tribal women should be specifically recorded in the record of rights, along with their rights to collect fuel-wood, fodder and raw material for their employment from the forest.

22. The migration of women labour needs to be regulated to protect their interest by effective enforcement of existing legislation and other administrative measures wherever possible, rural development programmes for women must recognize seasonal migrant labourers as a special category.

23. Mining leases for such activities as brick-kilns, stone crushing, contracts for road construction, etc., where women are employed in large numbers, should be issued in the name of women applicants.

24. Programmes of creating awareness, organizing of labour camps, helping tribal women to organize themselves into collective groups for better bargaining and improving their skills should be the key to the future strategy of their development and physical and social protection. This training should also teach them how to cope with various exploitative situations including those of the marketing. Support systems should be built up with the help of traditional tribal community organizations. Legal aid, para legal training to educate tribal women and spread of legal literacy, among tribal women in general and migrant labourers in particular, should be important components of the support structure.

25. Women members of households should be entitled to credit, independent of the male head of the family or without his endorsement, where no mortgage of his property or joint property is required.

26. Since women constitute a substantial proportion of the self-employed categories, requiring, credit assistance, credit societies exclusively for women members need to be organized.

27. In terms of credit as a development input, the banking system is not sufficiently responsive to social banking needs and has not been able to deal with barriers that hinder women from using or gaining access to credit. Priority sector lending of banks must be extended to women as a group. Special counters for women in banks may also be initiated. Particular emphasis should be placed on institutional credit mechanisms at differential rates of interest for women in the unorganized sector.

28. Women's Development Corporations should be established in all States. They should obtain banking support to provide credit at national and local levels. The National, Commission on Self-Employed Women has in its recommendations also suggested that the terms of reference of Women's Development Corporations be expanded to play an effective role.

29. A number of existing models in the voluntary sector provide examples of alternate strategies for providing credit to women in the unorganized sector coupled with effective interventions required to utilize the credit, which can be replicated on a large scale. In this context, it is recommended that the DWCRA programme that has been modelled on voluntary approaches should be extended to all districts. It should also be expanded during implementation to encompass adolescent girls.

30. In selection of income generating activities, both under IRDP and TRYSEM, the banks and the rural development agencies should have committed involvement in helping and guiding the women in the selection of viable activities with local markets.

31. National Wasteland Development Programmes of social and agro-forestry must become more women oriented in their priorities and implementing strategies. Social Forestry Schemes formulated by the Women's Development Corporations should have a built-in provision for employing and training women extension workers.

32. The training of women members of panchayats should be undertaken to enable them to understand their role and responsibilities and to equip them with information on their rights. Women's concerns should be included in the training programmes for male panchayat members as well. A committee including the district coordinator for women's programmes (proposed) should be formed to look into the training needs of men and women panchayat members, and to help in designing the training programmes. The proposed Resource Centre could assist in evolving suitable training modules.

33. Provisions and infrastructures created under NREP and RLEGP should be closely linked so as to optimize their impact on rural women's development. The linkages with the funds and other infrastructural facilities available for the line departments is to be ensured in this regard. The plans for the creation of infrastructural facilities should be devised locally, in consultation with the women, instead of waiting for a centrally prepared blueprint. The appointment of district coordinators for women's programmes would expedite this process.

34. The Agricultural Extension System (T&V) should include women that work on family farm within its purview. Food production, nutrition, population education, etc., should form the extension service package for women. Simultaneously, agriculture extension programmes for women must be initiated in all States.

35. An impact study of the Farmers' Training Programmes and Krishi Vigyan Kendras should be routinely made. The syllabii of these institutions should be geared to the productivity role of women. They should collect area specific information on women's activities, assess the training and information needs of women, as well as provide feedback to the media for dissemination of information on women's role in agriculture and allied activities. The Kendras need to be extended to all districts.

36. Women's role in animal husbandry should be approached in a more pragmatic way. They should be trained in the management of cattle, veterinary care and fodder production. Production of fodder, collectively or individually, by women is to be included as a must in self-employment projects in animal husbandry. A cadre of para veterinarians from among the beneficiaries should be created.

37. Efforts for increasing the membership of women in existing dairy cooperatives, training of women for taking up managerial responsibilities, and separate cooperatives for women should be aimed at.

38. Voluntary organizations and educational institutions should be increasingly motivated to take up micro studies and action programmes in mobilizing and organizing women, and encouraging them to avail of the provisions of various programmes.

39. There is need to organize and conscientize the women under DWCRA, TRYSEM, STEP, etc., in order to get higher benefits from these schemes. The TRYSEM schemes should recognize literacy as a skill since it is an essential input for participation in various schemes. The 30 per cent target stipulated for women in various schemes should be strictly met by the officials.

40. There should be proper publicity about various programmes meant for rural women. Awareness camps should be organized in order to make rural women aware about the various schemes and programmes by voluntary and government organizations.

The vital role of women in the Indian labour force and their contribution to the national economy has been established beyond doubt. Women engage in a wide variety of occupations, especially in the unorganized sector. In the rural unorganized sector, women care for cattle, sow, transplant and harvest, weave and work on handlooms and produce handicrafts mostly as low paid wage earners, or as unpaid family workers.

In the urban informal sector, women work as petty traders and producers selling and producing a wide variety of goods, such as vegetables, fruits, flowers, cooked food, groceries, etc., or work as domestic workers. In both the rural and urban areas, they are engaged as construction workers. In addition, women spend on an average 7-10 hours a day on domestic chores as well as collection of fuel, fodder and water, and child care. The large amounts of time and energy expanded on these domestic chores, however, remain invisible as no productive economic value is attached to these tasks. Nor has any major effort been made to improve women's access to technology aimed at reducing drudgery in the domestic chores performed by them.

Accurate data on the extent and nature of women's work is an essential pre-requisite in the development of employment policies and programmes. Data relating to the employment of women in India is currently available from six major sources. These are: (i) the decennial population census; (ii) surveys undertaken by the National Sample Survey Organization (NSSO); (iii) Studies conducted by the Directorate General of Employment and Training (DGE&T) and Labour Bureau; (iv) Annual surveys of industries compiled by the Central Statistical Office (CSO); (v) Periodical reports from the State Governments; and (vi) Individual studies conducted by the Central and State Governments universities and research organizations.

The decennial population census provides valuable information on important aspects such as work participation rates by age, sex and occupation for both rural and urban areas. These data are available on as all India basis and for individual States up to the village level. The Census also provides information on the levels of employment and other work related aspects. NSSO produces comprehensive and detailed data on structure and changes in the labour force by relevant socio-demographic variables through a series of quinennial surveys from 1972-73 onwards. The Thirty-second (1977-78) and Thirty-eighth (1983) rounds have collected valuable data on the attitudes of women towards work and other related aspects. The DGE&T and the Labour Bureau have continuously collected vital information related to the organized sector and the implementation of labour laws. The latter also conducts occasional field studies on selected topics of national importance. The Labour Bureau has brought out a useful reference document entitled "Statistical Profile on Women Labour". It gives details regarding the population of workers, their average daily employment, sex-wise employment in factories by special/ normal weekly hours, live register and placement data, minimum and maximum wage rates for workers by sex and age based on occupational wage surveys, statistics on social security and information on factories providing creche facilities. The annual survey of industries (CSO) gives information on employment by sex and data on emoluments with respect to large factories. Some organizations under Central or State Governments, universities, research organizations and individual scholars have also been conducting micro studies concerning the socio-economic characteristics of workers and other problems.

The comparability of data on employment from these sources is, however, limited due to conceptual differences in the definition of workers and lack of uniformity in classification of workers by educational level, sex, etc. The workforce participation rates given in successive census are not comparable either as the definition adopted in each census has been changing. In the 1961 census, any person engaged in gainful work for even an hour per day of the greater part of the working season was counted as worker, whereas in 1971, the person was asked as to what his/her main activity was and he/she was classified as worker or non-worker accordingly. This main activity concept of workers brought down substantially the participation rate of females. In 1981, the concepts of 'main worker' and 'marginal worker were adopted. According to the 1981 census, the main worker has been defined as a worker who has worked for the major part of the reference period, and the 'marginal worker' was one who had worked not for the major period but nevertheless had done some work during the reference period.

The standard definition used by the NSS provides figures for 'usual status,' 'weekly status', unemployed. 'Usual status' measures the usual activity status-employed or unemployed or outside the labour force of those covered by the survey. Thus the activity status is determined with reference to a longer period than a day or a week. 'Weekly status' is determined with reference to a period of preceding seven days. A person who reports having worked at least for one hour on any day during the reference period of one week while pursuing a gainful occupation was deemed to be employed. A person who did not work even for one hour during the reference period but was seeking or available for work has deemed to be unemployed. In 'daily status', activity of a person for each day of the preceding seven days is recorded. A person who worked at least for one hour but less than four hours was considered as employed for half a day. If the person worked for four hours or more during a day, he/she was considered as employed for the whole day. Those with jobs for less than half the days in the preceding 365 days are considered unemployed with 'usual status'. The 'weekly' employed are those with less than one day's job in the preceding seven days and the 'daily' unemployed with less than half a day's work in the week preceding the survey.

The employment of women is generally underestimated in many of these sources. Often women themselves would report unemployed if they were not cash wage earners. The manner in which women's productivity is interpreted is also responsible for under enumeration of the female workforce participation. In quantifying labour days of employment, female and child labour are often converted into equivalent adult man days, though the converse factors vary from source to source and region to region. Such an assumption is totally untenable. A woman often earns half the wage earned by a man for an equivalent of a day's work, but not because her productivity is less. The wages paid to women is determined not by economic criteria but is a result of the cultural attitudes, social practices and power structures in society. Some review of the relative evaluation of various operations in any sector is called for to redefine equal remuneration for work of equal value.

11

New Perspective

Poverty alleviation in the rural sector remain central. It is targeted to bring down the percentage of rural poor below 10 per cent by 2000 A.D. The Department of Rural Development has already suggested that in case of women, poverty alleviation goals for the new millennium should be to:

(i) Bring all women-headed households (estimated to be 30-35 per cent) above the poverty line; and

(ii) Attain the target of having women constitute 30 per cent of all beneficiaries to be assisted under IRDR.

In addition, the endeavour should be to bring in the women's development dimension into the sectors particularly, agriculture and allied sectors which have hitherto not responded adequately to women's needs. Women's access to productive resources must also be ensured.

Political power and access to positions of decision making and authority are critical prerequisites for women's equality in the processes of nation building. Hence it is crucial that the representation of women in local bodies up to the district level be ensured.

Safeguards for the Family

Women's health status is basic to their advance in all fields of endeavour. Any serious attempt to improve the health of women must deal firstly with biased social customs and cultural traditions that have an impact on their health status. Though the health problems of women have been identified for priority attention and efforts made for maternal and child services since the beginning of planned development in India, much remains to be done to improve health care for women both in qualitative and quantitative terms. However, in subsequent plan periods it has been observed that resource allocations for health have been decreasing. There is need for a more comprehensive integrated approach to health issues if there is to be a significant impact on the present conditions of Indian women.

The cultural norms that specially affect women's health are the attitudes to marriage, age of marriage, the value attached to fertility and sex of the child, the pattern of family organizations and the ideal role demanded of women by social conventions. They determine her place within the family, the degree of her access to medical care, education, nutrition and other accessories of health. Improvements in female health status are, therefore, critically dependent on a number of non-health development components such as education, opportunities for skill-building, income generation and decision making and the availability of basic support services to carry out women's multiple roles. Thus it is essential to address the causes of women's ill-health. Measures to improve the social and health situation would have to form an integral part of a multi-sectoral package operationalized simultaneously, in complementary thrusts. Earlier analysis have emphasized this aspect. But gaps have existed in preceding plans and even more in the implementation of strategies.

Clear Signs

The demographic trends are important indicators of women's health status. The sex ratio which illumines the survival scene for women versus men was 933 females per 1000 males in 1981. Not only is this ratio unfavourable, but its steady decline from 972 in 1902 to 930 in 1971 is a cause for great concern. Marginal improvement has taken place in the last decade, but even today fourteen States and Union Territories have less females per 1000 males then the national average and in eleven States and Union Territories, the ratio has further declined.

Life expectancy has increased over the decade from 44.7 years in 1971 to 54.7 in 1980 for women. It was estimated to be slightly higher in 1980 for women than men: 54.7 and 54.1 years at birth respectively. A general reduction in female mortality, as well as the greater differentials in death rate was observed over 1970-82 in both rural and urban areas. However age specific death rates indicate higher mortality for female children and women for every five-year period till 35 years of age. This higher mortality experience of female children and younger adult women during the prime reproductive years is largely preventable through appropriate health and other interventions, and points to the continuing neglect of female health.

Women face high risk of malnutrition, retardation in growth and development, disease, disability and even death at three critical stages in their lives, viz., infancy, early childhood and adolescence and the reproductive phase. In old age, they face threats of cancer, breast cancer and uterus cancer and menopause related problems.

Discrimination starts even before birth in the form of sex determination tests misusing the high technology of amniocentisis, resulting in a new kind of femicide, i.e., abortion of female foetuses. A survey carried out in Bombay during 1984 revealed that out of

8,000 abortions 7,999 were of female foetuses. Considering that this test facility has spread to even small towns and people from rural as well as urban areas are utilizing it, the magnitude of the problem can be imagined.

Micro studies have shed light on the fact that sex is the main determinant of infant nutrition, irrespective of economic development. It is worse in a situation of poverty. Studies indicate that while both boys and girls get less than recommended daily dietary allowances, girls are more deficient and suffer more from related disorders and illnesses. However, more girls go without treatment when ill, than boys.

Boys are breast-fed longer, given more of weaning foods, and get a bigger share of whatever food is available. Consequently, although the female children are biologically stronger when born, their morbidity and mortality rates are worse than that of male children. Age specific death rates are higher for female children, as noted earlier. Whereas, no male/female break-up is available for immunization rates, the total figures themselves are low. By 1982, only 25 per cent of all children below 3 years were given DPT, 5 per cent of infants were immunized against Polio, and 65 per cent were given BCG.

The shadow of the girl child's deprivation looms throughout her later life, but most particularly increases her vulnerability to the risks of child bearing, which in turn create risks for the child to be born. Thus is set into motion the vicious cycle of deprivation, debilitation, disease and disability. Leading to greater deprivation and debilitation and often death. That is the depressing lot of a significant numbers of mothers and children today.

As girls attain puberty, they go through a second spurt of growth when their bodies grow much more rapidly to prepare them for child-bearing. But unfortunately, in addition to the poor economic conditions, their gender denies them proper nutrition.

Even in situations where food is available, girls are taught to eat less so that they remain slim to rate better in the marriage market. Nutritional deprivation at all growth stages gets compounded during the inset of puberty resulting in severe growth retardation in girl children.

The half grown, uneducated, adolescent girl is married early and becomes pregnant soon. Teenage pregnancy interrupts the physiological growth spurt which brings a girl to her genetically determined maximum stature. As of 1981, 7 per cent of girls in the age group 10-14 and 43 per cent in the age group 15-19 were already married. They enter into sexual life and child bearing with no knowledge about sex and the reproduction process. As estimated, 10-15 per cent of all the annual births (around 25 million) are attributed to these teenage mothers. With their malnourished status, small pelvis, under-nutrition, and overwork during pregnancy, these adolescent mothers run a high risk of life. Their babies are of low birth weight and suffer risk of mortality many times higher than those of fully grown, well nourished, educated mothers.

Girls who marry before the age 18 are twice as likely to end up with a large family than those who marry after completing 20 years, and therefore not only face much higher risks in pregnancy when they first conceive, but also compounded risks and related ill-health over their lifetimes.

Mother's Welfare

The Indian woman on an average has 8-9 pregnancies, resulting in a little over six births, of which 4-5 survive. She is estimated to spend 80 per cent of her reproductive years in pregnancy and lactation.

Dietary surveys have shown that the intake of women in low income groups is deficient by 500 to 600 calories. The corresponding findings for pregnant and lactating women reveal daily deficiency of 1100 calories and 1000 calories respectively. Deficits in nutrient intakes have been observed in various occupational groups, particularly in those without land and are labourers. Women belonging to the lower socio-economic groups gain around 3-5 kgs. during pregnancy as against 10 kgs. in the developed countries. Over 50 per cent of pregnant women have a haemoglobin level of less than 10 grams. Anaemia in pregnancy accounts directly for 15-20 per cent of all maternal deaths in India, and indirectly for a much larger proportion.

With the fairly high fertility levels during the reproductive span prevailing in India, maternal mortality accounts for the largest to near largest proportion of deaths among women in their prime years. Official estimates place maternal mortality at 400-500 per 100,000 live births but figures as high as 1000-1200 have been reported from certain rural areas. A woman in the subcontinent runs a lifetime risk of 1 in 18 of dying from a pregnancy related cause. Anaemia, haemorrhage, toxemia, sepsis, and abortion are the major causes of maternal deaths in India. It has been estimated that 70 per cent of these deaths can be prevented. Multiparity increases maternal illnesses and deaths which rise significantly with the fourth pregnancy and reach very high levels after the fifth. In India, 38.4 live births in rural areas and 33.0 live births in urban areas are of the fourth order and above.

Accurate assessments of maternal morbidity are unavailable but evidence from available studies point to an appallingly high incidence of pregnant women not in contact with health services.. Around 71.1 per cent of deliveries in rural areas and 29.2 per cent of deliveries in urban areas are conducted by untrained personnel outside the health system. In Rajasthan, one-third of pregnant women reported illnesses lasting on an average for over two weeks. The maternal mortality rate was 592 per 100,000 live births; for every maternal death some 60 episodes were related directly to pregnancy and childbirth and together represented both the leading cause and over a quarter of overall morbidity.

Abortion has been legalized in India as a health measure since 1972 by the Medical Termination of Pregnancy Act, 1971. Even so, because of non-availability of MTP services within easy reach for most of the rural population and ignorance of the law, 'illegal' abortions continue to be performed by incompetent persons under unhygienic conditions. As a result, abortion-related mortality and morbidity remain major problems. Only 507,719 terminations were performed through the health services in 1986-87 which is around 9 per cent of the induced abortions that were likely to have been performed during the same period. Since the inception of the programme, 5.1 million abortions have been performed under the MTP programme, which is less than the total number of induced abortions likely to be performed in one year. Induced abortions indicate an unmet need of women for family planning, highlight a gap between the availability of services and their accessibility to those in need, and demonstrate women's inability to make use of the services they need acutely.

Respite from pregnancy, and rest and care during pregnancy emerge as major needs. Studies have clearly shown that women engaged in hard physical labour during pregnancy did not gain much weight, and delivered low-birth-weight babies, as compared with women doing less work but having the same food intake. One study on energy consumption and expenditure per household per day, found the energy expenditure to be 5.68 units for men, 9.69 for women and about 3 for children. The major part of domestic energy consumption was for survival-cooking, fetching water, firewood, etc. Technology for reduction of drudgery in women, and providing water, and fuel within the easy reach of all, could go a long way in energy conservation for women.

Hardly any information is available for the health hazards of women engaged in different occupations, in agriculture and industries, birth during pregnant and non-pregnant states. In agriculture, they are exposed to heat and rain and have to work in standing and bending postures for long hours, which are hazardous to health. They also work in large numbers in industries such as beedi, carpet, jute, coir weaving, slate, electronics, etc. Micro studies have indicated that workers of these industries suffer from several health hazards.

The health services for children and women, particularly during pregnancy, childbirth and after are inadequate. About 40 per cent of pregnant women receive tetanus toxoid. Although data are unavailable separately on the proportion of pregnant mothers receiving iron and folic acid, it is roughly estimated that around 25 per cent of pregnant and nursing mothers receive iron and folic acid. About 46 per cent of pregnant women are estimated to register for antenatal care. Facilities and basic equipment for mid-wives have been found to be grossly inadequate.

The situation regarding women's health may be summarized as:

(i) Major disparities in health care in population groups in rural and urban areas; remote, backward, hilly and desert areas; and in socio-economically deprived groups.

(ii) Social attitudes and prejudices inherent in our milieu which are unfavourable towards girls and women, effect their health and nutrition negatively.

(iii) Poor health of women due to the synergistic effects of high levels of infection, malnutrition and uncontrolled fertility extending over a prolonged span.

(iv) Inadequate basic health care facilities (including facilities for MCH, family planning, MTP and nutrition) for women and children, in terms of outreach, range of services, quality, availability, etc.

(v) Inefficient use of resources available for health care of women, resulting in a slower pace of health development for them.

(vi) Ignorance and lack of knowledge related to health nutrition and family planning, affecting self-help efforts in health; and resulting in underutilization of existing resources.

(vii) Absence or inadequacy of essential non-health facilities which affect health, such as potable water, sanitation; female education; food supply, etc.

Health care has been accepted as an important intervention for women's development since the First Five-Year Plan. It was recognized that the high infant and maternal mortality would have to be reduced through the provision of maternal and child health services and family planning. The basic strategy for providing health care to the general population as well as women, in the 1950's during the first and second plan periods included:

(i) Expansion of physical infrastructure for health (including opening MCH centres);

(ii) Initiating the family planning programme;

(iii) Communicable disease control (for malaria, filaria, tuberculosis, leprosy and venereal diseases); and

(iv) Establishing facilities for training (attention was given to training female health personnel including nurses, auxilliary nurse midwives, health visitors and dais) and having more manpower.

The need to link hospitals at different levels into an effective coordinated hospital system, and correlate their functions with those of "clinics, domiciliary care services and public health activities", was recognized. The maternity centres which were established during the first two plan periods, were to be linked up with district and referral hospitals. MCH services in urban areas were generally provided through maternity and child health centres, in isolation from the rest of the services. 4500 maternity centres had been established, one-third of which were in urban areas; and about 2800 health units were also established in rural areas. In rural areas, the "health units" in the block were expected to provide MCH services in addition to other health services. During the decade 1950-60, female health personnel were increasingly trained and employed, which resulted in availability of 27,000 nurses (from 5,000 in 1950); 19,900 auxiliary nurse midwives (from 8,000 in 1950); 1,500 lady health visitors (from 52 in 1950) and 11,500 nurse-dais and dais (from 1,800 in 1950). From the First Plan itself, family limitation and spacing of children were noticed to be "essential steps for securing better care in bringing up children, and therefore, as an important part of public health." Though initially, family planning services were provided primarily through specialized family planning clinics, the need to integrate it with the general health services was realized; and when the fourth plan was put forth, maternity and child health services were stated to be integrated with family planning.

The basic strategies for health care in terms of expansion of physical infrastructure, training more female health personnel, communicable disease control and family planning were continued during the Third and Fourth Plan periods. Specific prophylaxis programmes were initiated to prevent anaemia in pregnant women, and vitamin deficiency in children 1-5 years of age during this period. Also, programmes were started to control smallpox were also formulated, which included a component for instruction of school teachers.

The primary objective of the Fifth Five-Year Plan was to provide minimum public health facilities integrated with family planning and nutrition for vulnerable groups - children, pregnant women and lactating mothers. The accent during this period was similar to previous plan periods - increasing the accessibility of health services to rural areas; correcting regional imbalances; development of referral systems for health care; and communicable disease control. The need for qualitative improvement in the education and training of health personnel was also recognized. Several schemes were initiated during this period to give increased emphasis to the health of mothers. The Integrated Child Development Services Scheme was accepted for countrywide application in 1977. Though primarily for child development, this scheme provides a package of health, nutrition and family planning services for pregnant women and nursing mothers who are socio-economically deprived. Since a large proportion of deliveries are conducted by traditional birth attendants (TBAs) particularly in rural areas, a scheme was initiated during this time to train them for safer mid-wifery practices; the target was to have atleast one TBA per 1000 population. In order to involve the community in health care, and to further promotive and preventive health care at village level, the health guides scheme was initiated. The norm of one health guide per 1000 population was suggested.

The guiding principles for the first two and a half decade of planned development in health in India included measures to:

(i) Make health services more accessible to the population;

(ii) Developing the needed human resources;

(iii) Provision of services for health, including maternal and child health, and family planning.

Over time, the need to interact more closely with people has been felt, and somewhat more emphasis was given to preventive and promotive aspects of health care.

Official Steps

The Committee on the status of women in India highlighted the impact of social attitudes on the health of women, which clearly revealed the poorer lot of women, from the time of birth. The demographic analysis brought into sharp focus the deterioration in the condition of the majority of women despite the advances in medical care and the general improvement in health services, pointing to the criticality of the social conditions.

On the health side, it was pointed out that more resources were being spent for curative than preventive and promotive services; and that major rural/urban and regional disparities existed in health care was noted to be an unfortunate distortion. The report further underlined that lack of security and mobility are major problems of female health personnel in rural areas.

However, their recommendations, while emphasizing the need for an integrated thrust for MCH, nutrition and family planning, were limited mainly to upgrading the posts of MCH officers at Central and State levels; the provision of a separate budget for MCH and separate units for MCH at primary health centres. Some modifications in the MTP Act were also recommended. However, while the legislative aspects were gone into detail, the main problems with medical termination of pregnancy, that is the wide availability of services and ignorance of the law, did not get sufficient attention. Altogether, while the analysis of problems was a powerful indictment of the existing situation, this was not matched by comprehensive suggestion to bring about the desired changes in women's health.

Particular Schemes

The National Plan of Action recognized that the health profile of women (and girls) in India was poor. While giving attention to the salient issues in the social and health areas, it did not however, develop the needed coordinated thrust for actions in each sector converging to achieve common goals. In fact, while emphasizing that the plans of action would have to cover a wide spectrum of programmes and needed to integrate with other strategies, it did not even attempt to provide any directions and made the action plans for health under six separate categories, namely: (1) Provision of Services; (2) Development of the needed human resources; (3) Mass Education Programmes; (4) Legislative Measures (5)Role of Voluntary Organizations; and (6)Areas of Research

Broadly, it stated that services for women, including mothers and female children, should be part of the general health system. It was recommended that the physical infrastructure be expanded and manpower for health care be augmented. However, their emphasis on the qualitative aspects of maternal care as well as training was inadequate. The necessary infrastructure strengthening at village, primary and secondary levels, linked by an affective referral system, did not receive much attention. Instead, they recommended the establishment of various types of clinics. The need to modify medical undergraduate curriculum, in order to cater to the needs of mothers and children in rural areas, was rightly stressed, so also, the need to orient doctors in services. The TBA was identified as one of the most important person, in the provision of maternity services, and steps to involve her were outlined. The Committee underlined the need to have mass education programmes for mother and child care. Several legislative measures were suggested.

They referred to the MTP Act, age of marriage, and provision of MCH services in municipalities and local bodies. However, the main issue remains operationalizing the law, ensuring that the necessary developments take place. This includes better services for MTP, specially in rural areas; more resources for MCH services through local bodies; and providing education as well as income generating opportunities to women to raise the age of marriage. Some legislative measures have been taken to ensure that advertisement of baby foods is curbed - this was also a recommendation. The committee suggested some areas, in which the voluntary organizations could be involved, such as school health services, MCH care in urban slums, training health workers and information dissemination. Though some efforts have been made to involve them, much more remains to be done on this aspect. Areas for research were suggested, on which only limited action has, followed.

Women's Welfare

During the Sixth and Seventh Plans, the major strategies for health care, including that for women, continued to be: (i)Expansion of physical infrastructure; (ii)Increasing the availability of trained health manpower; (iii)Strengthening services for communicable disease control, as well as other diseases; and (iv)Provision of family planning as well as MCH services.

During the Sixth Five-Year Plan period, in 1983, the National Health Policy was formulated and accepted for implementation. The policy for the first time, defined goals for women's health; reduction in maternal mortality, crude rate and crude birth rate; coverage with antenatal care and immunization of pregnant mothers, and the control of leprosy, tuberculosis and blindness (from which women also suffer), were specified. The levels to be achieved over time were also specified. The policy stated that:

"the highest priority" would have to be given to "efforts of launching special programmes" for the improvement of maternal and child health, with a special focus on the less privileged sections of the society. Such programmes would require to be decentralized to the maximum possible extent, their delivery being at the primary level, nearest to the doorsteps of the beneficiaries. While efforts should continue for providing refresher training and orientation to the traditional birth attendants, schemes and programmes should be launched to ensure that progressively all deliveries are conducted by competently trained persons, and that complicated cases receive timely and expert attention, within a comprehensive programme providing antenatal, intra-natal and postnatal care. Also, organized school health services, integrally linked with a general, preventive and curative services, would require to be established within time-limited programmes.

The Seventh Five-Year Plan clearly stated that primary health care will be the main sphere of action in health. It was stated that 'women would be organized around available economic activities to enable them to actively participate in the entire process of socioeconomic development, including health.' Care of pregnant and nursing mothers, young children and school-age children (both in and out of school) was stated to be a priority.

Significant Problems

Some of the critical factors and issues related to women's health have evidently not received the necessary attention in the existing health programmes, Girls need adequate care so that they can enter motherhood without physical and social inadequacies. Optimal reproductive and child-bearing patterns (age of the mother at first childbirth - 20 years; interval between pregnancies at least 3 years; a small family; and no pregnancy after 35 years of age, which influence the health of mothers and their children) need to be advocated, and backed by policies that make them feasible for women. Measures to reduce the workload of women have to be promoted to conserve their energy. Adequate and appropriate information for decision-making, particularly during pregnancy and lactation, needs to be made available.

Recognizing that the renewal of the human race is the unique contribution that women make at considerable personal cost to the nation's existence and productivity, it must be taken as a national obligation to ensure that the fulfilment of this role occurs with minimum personal risk to women's lives and health. Control, over reproduction is a basic right for all women, as this right forms an important basis for the enjoyment of other rights. The enormous wastage of female life and well-being occurring at present has, however, been demonstrated to be containable within human capacity and existing resources.

Women are victims of possessive syndrome and many other kinds of neurosis. The majority of women face mental depressions due to family related problems which are the outcomes of the present social attitudes. Particularly, in the rural areas, such depressions are believed as "possessed by spirits". This encourages many cruel practices and treatment which often lead to physical harm to the women. The primary health centres are ill-equipped to deal with even simple mental disorders.

With rapid urbanization and commercialization, the nutritious foods produced in the villages like fruits, vegetables, milk and so forth are being exported to urban areas thereby denying them to the rural poor. Growing poverty in the countryside is also encouraging such exports. This results in a further drop of nutritional levels of the rural poor.

The Bhore Committee way back in 1946 recommended establishing one Primary Health Centre for each 30,000 population which has not yet been achieved.

Health for All goals and indicators have already accepted and accorded primacy to maternal and child health care inter alia including a halving of maternal mortality, hundred per cent coverage for ante-natal care and delivery by trained birth attendants by year 2000 A.D. The health services programmes are already committed to work towards the achievement of these goals. The Technological and Societal missions for eradication of illiteracy, immunization and safe water supply include certain critical indicators that will have impact on maternal and child care. However, as in the past, the present efforts lack in scale and systematic organization of the various components that together could radically alter the situation for women and children. Therefore, a comprehensive programme of health care of women needs to be developed with a special technological and societal mission to halve maternal mortality and morbidity and ensure optimum child bearing patterns by the year 2000. This mission, the details of which would have to be worked out by an expert working group, would need to, simultaneously gear the health services to reduce maternal, infant and child mortality and address the conditions that can assist women not to bear a child when this event will increase the risk to the health of the women and/or the child to be born/already born. Inter alia, the observance of the small family norm through proper education of its impact on the health of women and children, will be an integral part of this mission.

Shield for the Household

It is unfortunate that the family planning policy is oriented towards fertility control and not concerned with providing a means for women and men to have control on their own bodies. A reflection of this policy is the encouragement of injectable contraceptives like Net-en which have been banned in most developed countries.

Though the family welfare and planning programmes have been a part of development planning since the First Five-Year Plan, actual achievements are below expectations. By March, 1987, the effective couple protection rate was only 34 per cent. From the beginning, emphasis has been placed on sterilizations rather than on temporary methods. Whereas in the early phases more vasectomies were performed, during the last decade, female sterilizations have been promoted at a very high rate. With the introduction of laproscopy, female sterilizations have reached high numbers amounting to almost 90 per cent of all sterilizations.

Research studies have shed light on the fact that the knowledge regarding family planning/methods is low despite the huge amounts of money spent on propaganda. The only method known to all is sterilization. The higher rates of abortions show the desire and need of the women for family planning and the failure of the family planning information and services to reach them in time. Laproscopic operations are being performed in several family planning camps without proper care and follow-up. Consequent problems tend to create apprehension among people. More intensive propagation of spacing methods together with innovative strategies for delivery of supplies has to be, taken up and spread of information about temporary methods accorded high priority.

The shift towards female sterilizations has to be reversed. Ironically, while that programme mainly provides female centred methods most of the women using these are not really happy due to the side effects. Hormonal reactions to oral pills, pain and heavy bleeding due to IUD, etc., are common complaints. In many areas women suffer from post-operative problems following tubectomy. The health personnel also concentrate most on' sterilization (female) as it helps them to realize their target and earn cash rewards.

1. Using amniocentesis for sex determination tests should be banned as in Maharashtra. Practitioners indulging in and abetting such acts should be punished severely and their medical licenses should be revoked.

2. Incentives should be considered to encourage parents to have female children. A couple who opts to limit their family to one female child may be given a regular monthly

cash subsidy to attend to the girl child's needs. The amount must be given to the family over a period of time and not in a lump sum, as this might result in misuse of the female child as an instrument for getting easy money and later to neglect the child.

3. Infants and small children's growth and development should be monitored by recording their weights and heights at regular intervals. Proper corrective interventions should be made wherever necessary.

4. Universal immunization should be enforced to encompass all children.

5. Oral Rehydration Therapy (ORT) should be widely disseminated. ORT salts in packed form should be made available at a large scale in order to reduce the mortality from diarroheal diseases.

6. The ICDS should be strengthened and priority access should be provided to the girl child. Higher participation of women would also result from expansion of the programme.

7. Efforts should be made to bring a qualitative change in the attitudes against girl children. Media should be used for this purpose aiming to get the girl child to be accepted in the family and the society as an equal to the male child.

8. Focus is needed on the adolescent girl (12-18 years), so that she attains her maximum physical and mental capacities. It is necessary to provide alternative options to an early marriage. This can be ensured by a mix of education and employment opportunities and enforcement of the law on minimum age of marriage (18 years). The younger girl child needs to utilize health and

education programmes more fully. It has been proposed that the ICDS will also address this issue in specific areas.

9. Adequate nutrition should be ensured for adolescent girls during the pre-puberty and pubertal growth phase to ensure 'catch up' on physical development by providing supplements to deprived groups.

10. Health and nutrition education should be promoted to ensure that preventive and promotive measures are adopted. The necessity of safe water, sanitation and personal hygiene also should be advocated.

11. Immunization against tetanus and rubella should be introduced for this age group.

12. Linkages with basic health care must be developed at the village level in the view of the special problems of mobility faced by young girls.

13. A massive communication campaign to create widespread awareness of the law prohibiting the marriage of the girl before 18 years and boys before 21 years and generate consciousness on the severe health implications in children and women of such early marriages must be launched.

14. The aim should be to implement the present legal minimum age of marriage effectively by creating a social consciousness for the desirability of marriage for girls only after 20 and for boys at 25. Preferential employment for unmarried males and females and priority in other developmental schemes for such youth, need to be seriously examined.

15. The comprehensive school health scheme which is being formulated, should be speedily implemented. Special

efforts must be made for the health services to reach girls of the school-going age who are out of school. Each child should be examined and screened at least three times at primary school entry, before leaving primary school and at completion of high school. Similarly, a girl child out of school should be examined and screened three times - at around 6, 10 and 15 years of age. Screening kits and medicines should be made available. School teachers and non-formal education functionaries should be trained in the required areas of health care. The health programme for school and non-formal education systems should be integrally linked with the general health services.

16. It is necessary to impart information about reproductive processes, ways to prevent conception, need for spacing between children, optimum age of child bearing, necessary care for pregnant women and lactating mothers and small family norm, etc. This may be introduced as a part of the regular curriculum in school, colleges and universities. For girls/boys who are not in school, Anganwadi workers/female CHWs may impart this knowledge.

17. To improve women's health status, there is no doubt that the general health services have to be made to respond to women's specific problems. A strategy for improving the health of women in the reproductive age group would be to reduce the risk of death and illness associated with pregnancy as well as to reduce the exposure to pregnancy itself. Comprehensive minimal care during pregnancy, childbirth and thereafter, steps to ameliorate malnutrition as well as decrease the workload of women, and improved access to health services, particularly family planning services, should be the salient instruments for improving the health of women.

18. Since women are severely restricted in their mobility, basic health care services must be made available to them

as close as possible to their homes. Therefore, resources should be allocated as a priority to health services at the village, as well as at the first level of referral. The services would be provided by the female health workers, supported by the functionaries and the community from the village, as well as supervisory echelons within the health sector. Measures should be taken to reduce the incidence of low birth weight babies.

19. A minimum package of services should be available for pregnant women at village level. This should include at least:

- Facilities for early detection of pregnancy, with low cost pregnancy detection kits;
- Antenatal registration;
- Minimum of three antenatal check-ups in the second and third trimester;
- Screening of high-risk cases;
- Anaemia prophylaxis with iron and folic acid tablets; Tetanus toxoid coverage;
- Prophylaxis against malaria in high endemic areas; Advocacy of adequate rest;
- Health and nutrition education;
- Priority attention to locally endemic diseases affecting women; and
- Adequate safe drugs for her illness.

20. ANMs should be trained to assess pelvic proportions of pregnant women to identify the high risk cases and refer them to competent institutions. This will help in saving women from maternal deaths and also to reduce the incidence of still births.

21. The emphasis will have to be on providing better care to the pregnant woman in her home, as well as to ensure that adequate facilities are available at the first level of referral to deal with obstetric emergencies such as toximias, sepsis, obstructed labour and haemorrhage. In order to improve village level care during childbirth, the following are suggested:

    - Continuous training, supervision and support for better mid-wifery practices to the TBA and female health workers;

    - Provision for sterile delivery kits to the TBA, health workers and even to mothers;

    - Stocking adequate drugs and supplies with the health workers, and providing a restricted number to the TBA; and

    - Pre-arranged transport (or reimbursement of transport costs) for any emergency, when a woman has been registered for antenatal care.

22. Post-natal services should be available as close to the homes of mothers as possible. In rural areas in several, parts of India, women do not leave their homes for 40 days after delivery. Post-natal care should include:

    - A minimum of three contacts with the mother by the TBA and/or female health worker within the first 10 days after child birth;

- One massive dose of vitamin A within one month after delivery to all mothers;

- Iron and folic acid for 50 per cent of mothers;

- Adequate drugs to deal with puerperal sepsis;

- Education for the mother's nutrition and contraception as well as for infant feeding and health care, particularly immunization.

23. The health of women who are not pregnant or nursing, is án area which has received inadequate attention so far. Interventions thus made can cause a significant difference to women's health status not only between pregnancies, but also improve the outcome of future pregnancies. Moreover, the woman's right to health care as an individual must be promoted.

24. Women with chronic or serious illnesses, such as tuberculosis, leprosy, viral hepatitis, anaemia, sexually transmitted cases, etc., should be promptly treated and advised to postpone their pregnancy for a suitable safe period.,

25. High priority should be given to women for treatment/ control of all endemic diseases, specially those which have a harmful effect on the next generation (for example, goitre, sexually transmitted diseases, etc.)

26. Doctors of the Primary Health Centres be given in-service training to handle the cases of possessive syndrome and neurosis. Mass education programme be taken up to change the negative attitudes prevalent against mental illness.

27. Nutritious foods produced in the villages should be primarily utilized to cater to the nutrition needs of the rural poor. Only the surplus should be allowed for export to urban areas. A widespread public distribution system would be essential to make basic foods available at affordable costs.

28. Emphasis should be placed on Science and Technology research pertaining to sex linked diseases, occupational hazards, and indigenous methods of family planning as affecting women. Undergraduate level programmes should introduce courses relevant to women, i.e.

    (i) Work physiology (ergdonomics) as related to health, and occupational hazards.

    (ii) Basic tenets of genetics, related to family studies, genetic disorders and environmental effects.

    (iii) At the postgraduate level and above, research needs to be conducted in ergonomic abnormalities in women such as spinal strain after carrying loads. Also, work is needed on sex-linked, genetic disorders like muscular dystrophy and haemophilia, where women are the carriers.

29. More Primary Health Centres should be set up in the rural areas to achieve the target of having one Primary Health Centre for each 30,000 population as recommended by the Bhore Committee.

30. The timings of the dispensaries and hospitals should be fixed in a way which would be convenient to working women.

31. There should be a 24 hours creche facility for women patients with children in every hospital and PHC.

32. There is a need for a humane Drug Policy and check on the pharmaceuticals industry that at present operates on the profit principle like any other industry.

33. It is necessary to provide safety equipment including powerful exhausts to remove harmful dust from the work environment and, personal protective equipment like masks, feet protectors, eyeglasses, ear muffs and gloves and strong contraceptions for the safety of women workers.

34. There should be Refreshers /Orientation courses for the doctors on the subjects of women's work and health.

35. Family planning policy should be such that it will help women have greater control over their bodies and enable them to make conscious choices on having or not having children and declining the number of children they want.

36. Injectible contraceptives as well as other contraceptives banned in developed countries should not be permitted in the country.

37. More research needs to be carried out to develop contraceptives that can be used by men and they should be propagated more widely.

38. Family Planning counselling needs to involve married and older women, selected from local surroundings for effective transmission of the concept and its urgency.

12

Conclusion

In India, nineteenth century may be noted for the most abominable conditions for women as well as the initiation of their emancipation. At the beginning of the century, the women were humiliated and tortured, kept illiterate, tradition bound and in complete subjugation to the men's will. As time passed, people began to rebel against this state of affairs.

The impact of western culture created a desire among many Indians to examine their beliefs and ideals. The scientific approach of the west initiated a search of Indian scriptures and mythologies for the causes of maladies that existed in society. A critical outlook among educated Indians aided the reinterpretation of religious texts and rational approaches replaced emotional reaction. These approaches led to the conclusion that blind faith, inability to discern right from wrong, and propagation of erroneous interpretations by decadent priestly class and immoral feudal lords had all been responsible for the existing web of subordination around women.

Reformers began their work in the direction of women's emancipation in the late nineteenth century, This work was continued in the twentieth century. In spite of great zeal and enthusiasm, the reformers achieved little success in breaking the strong notions of women's inferior status. However, the process of awakening to reality was initiated and India passed to an era in which myth around women began to be seriously questioned in terms of realities of human existence. Women started regaining their freedom of will and intellect. Still with the majority of women a major problem remained. They had for long believed that they were emotionally, morally, biologically and intellectually inferior to men and so were unable to contemplate their equal status with men. They failed to realise their full potential and high abilities. To alter this situation it was required that not only women, but the whole society should undergo a transition in its outlook towards them.

Let us now examine the movement for the emancipation of women, which was initiated in the nineteenth century.

It was largely through the efforts of Raja Ram Mohun Roy (1774-1833) that in 1829 Lord Bentinck decreed for the abolition of the sati system. He worked towards widow remarriages, inter-caste and inter-racial marriages, abolition of child marriages and polygamy. He founded a new religious order called the Brahmo Samaj. This reformed order became well known for the privileges it gave to women.

Keshab Chandra Sen (1838-1884) became Roy's spiritual successor and worked tirelessly for women's education. The Civil Marriage Act III of 1872 raised the minimum age for marriage to fourteen, gave permission for widow remarriage and inter-caste marriage and penalised polygamy. This reform was applicable only to members of the Brahmo Samaj and was brought about by Sen's courage and perseverance.

Many other prominent Indians were motivated by the example set by Keshab Chandra Sen. They led a vigorous struggle against child marriage and advocated widow remarriages. Ganga Ram at Lahore, along with others, started campaigns for women's emancipation. Mahadev Govinda Ranade (1842-1901) led a movement in Poona. He was a great patriot and social reformer who worked against existing Hindu customs, which made the life of the Indian women one of sorrow and hardship. It is notable that his reforms started with his own wife whom he taught himself.

In the north, Śwami Dayanand Saraswati (1827-1883) founded a religious order named Arya Samaj. The basic tenet of this order advocated equality of opportunity for all irrespective of caste, colour, or sex. In a very active manner, this society worked for women's education. Dayanand broadened the scope of women's education by emphasising education for self rather than linking it to their efficiency in familial roles. The curriculum for education devised by Dayanand was similar for both boys and girls. Hence Dayanand emerged as the first reformer who advocated and evolved a comprehensive scheme of education for raising women's status not only at the level of family and society but for her own development as an individual.

Another prominent person of the nineteenth century, Ishwar Chandra Vidyasagar (1820-1891) helped the British Government to establish the first girl's school in Calcutta in 1849. He was further responsible for the establishment of forty girls' schools in Bengal between 1855-1858. The Government Act of 1856, which legalised widow remarriage for Hindu women, was passed largely because of his efforts.

A brilliant national leader Gopala Krishna Gokhale (1866-1915) worked relentlessly towards raising the status of women in Indian society. He founded "Servants of India Society" in 1905 and established as its main objective the education of women. Two religious leaders who helped in bringing about the renaissance in the Hindu religion were Rama Krishna Paramahansa (1833-1866) and Swami Vivekananda (1862-1902).

Pandita Ramabai (1858-1922) was the most prominent of women of the nineteenth century who fought the battle for her own and her sisters' emancipation. Her book *The High Class Hindu Woman* was published in 1888 and highlighted the burdensome life of the caste Hindu women. She made a fervent appeal to the American (men and women) to render help for the enlightenment of Indian women and society. The last words of her book state:

> "In the name of humanity, in the name of your sacred responsibilities as workers in the cause of humanity, summon you, true women and men of America, to bestow your help quickly, regardless of nation, caste or creed."

American admirers sent Ramabai Rs.6000 to aid a widows' home, Sharda Sadan (home of learning), which she opened.

Another woman closely associated with education for women was Ramabai Ranade (1865-1922) who was the wife of Justice Ranade. She established an educational institution called Seva Sadan. Anandibai Joshi (1865-1887) was the first Hindu woman to take a Degree of Doctor of Medicine in America. Because she died very young, she could not provide a much-needed influence on education in medicine for Indian women. However, her life and work inspired women of late nineteenth and early twentieth centuries. Francina Sorabji (1833-1907) with her daughters, particularly her fifth daughter Cornelia planned and organised the establishment of schools for girls in the Western region of India. Cornelia was awarded a Law Degree from England.

Mohan Das Karamchand Gandhi, a shrewd politician and advocate of the righteous path, raised his voice against injustices to women of India in the 1920's. He took up many causes, including widow remarriage, and drew many women into his fight for freedom. His writings, speeches and private advocacy of the women's cause were attended to with great respect. In an article in a publication called *Young India* on November 18, 1926 he made it clear that if a man could remarry after the death of his spouse, a woman should also have this right: "What is considered desirable for man should be equally so for woman, and therefore, a widow should have the discretion as widowers about remarriage". In the same article he made the following comments:

> "I look to every youth in India to resolve not to marry a girl under sixteen. Let us tear down Purdah with one mighty effort. All that I have said about the wife applies equally to the husband-. She is a co-sharer with him of equal-rights and of equal duties."

Gandhi's approach towards women was idealistic. Though he was aware of their woes, he didn't think they had the same failings as men. He believed that their potential goodness incapacitated by years of bondage would, once freed, alleviate all the ills of society. He wrote that woman is sacrifice personified. His ideal of love was feminine as he identified that the greatest asset of a female was the ability to give motherly love. He saw the family as the nucleus of all Social Life and believed that women best functioned at home rather than in the work force. He saw the ideal of women with strong characters tending their families with peace and harmony and leading the world in this direction. He addressed a meeting of mill workers in 1920 at Ahmedabad:

> "It is not for women to work in factories. They have plenty of work in their own homes. They should attend to the bringing up of their children. If women go to work, our social life will be ruined and moral standards will decline".

Although Gandhi's efforts favoured the traditional role for women, he believed they deserved equal recognition for a job well done, just as men received. Gandhi's struggle for women's rights was that of dignity and humanity, rather than one of role differentiations. Certainly, in the tradition bound society into which his ideas were received they were quite revolutionary. His zeal led people to a realisation of injustices to women and prepared men to be more realistic in their attitudes towards women.

However, Gandhi still maintained the goddess image on a pedestal while exploding the myths about the witch like nature of women. He believed in the basic goodness of human nature and propagated the ideal of complete man and complete woman, both able to offer unconditional love while working for a common goal.

Gandhi's influence helped women assert their will. It was due to his leadership that women were given rights equal to men in India's Constitution. The history of the women's participation in the freedom struggle in response to Gandhi's call is one of the most fascinating stories of the rise of the Indian female, The Indian women of the late nineteenth century and early twentieth century who had led a life of drudgery behind purdah finally emerged free of the web that had held them captive for centuries.

Great reformers like Gandhi drew attention to the goodness inherent in women and made an appeal for an understanding of their human need. Men became aware of the love and affection which women were capable of bestowing. Many women realised that they were not inferior beings and were proud of the key role they played in the survival of human race. An important Muslim reformer of the early twentieth century, Sir Sayyid Ahmad Khan, began a movement for the education of Muslims under the western influence.

However, he excluded women from his scheme and firmly opposed their education. In contrast Molvi Nazir Ahmad and Hali were in favour of education of women. Perhaps, because of the influence of his mother on his early life Sir Sayyid saw no need for women's education other than home learning. He opposed starting schools for girls but emphasised the education of Muslim boys at Aligarh. On the other hand, Hali had his women characters reflect on the backward condition of Muslim community, the stagnation of vernacular learning, and the need for girls to be educated in order to fulfil their household and family duties. He did not go to extremes; however, the reforms he advocated were justified in terms of women's traditional role. In a magnificent poem called *Homage to Silence* Hali versified the role of women and their right to education.

Among the foreign women who came to India to serve the cause of women's emancipation, the names of Margaret Noble, later known as Sister Nivedita, Annie Besant and Margaret Cousins stand out. These women of Irish origin and former participants in Irish Home Rule agitation took up the cause of the downtrodden and underprivileged in India.

In 1917 the question of women's franchise was mooted. A deputation of women headed by Sarojini Naidu as spokesperson presented a memorandum to the British Secretary of State in 1919. The deputation demanded women's suffrage as well as increased educational and health facilities. The decision about the franchise was left to the Indian legislatures. With little opposition from these legislatures, thanks to the influence of the reformers, by 1929 women were enfranchised equally with men.

Although women were granted political rights equal to men, much reformative work was still needed to be done, as purdah and child marriages continued to be the dominant traditions. The laws of inheritance and divorce to assert their will legally restricted women. Illiteracy was predominant and so also the dowry customs. Women's organisations raised these issues for review. Enlightened Congress leaders like Nehru, Patel and Rajendra Prasad gave their full support for removing social and legal inequalities, which had been put upon women. Some of the women leaders who deserve acknowledgement for their efforts in achieving higher status for women in Indian society are chronologically: Annie Besant, Sarojini Naidu, Muthulakshmi Reddi and Raj Kumari Amrit Kaur.

Some interesting events occurred in 1929 when Gandhiji started Satyagraha, a freedom movement into which many women entered whole-heartedly. Mahatma's Dandi march which was in defiance to the salt law, had the full support of women. Within the next three years of this march, over five thousand women served terms of severe imprisonment suffered from lathi blows, cruelty, loss of livelihood and ill health. They picketed wine shops and shops that sold foreign clothes. They faced trials in law courts, suffered atrocities in prisons and were defamed for denouncing purdah and other evil social customs by the orthodox community leaders. Society came to realise, to some extent, the capacities of women as wilful responsible persons. Men and women began developing mutual respect. The prominent women of this period were neither an enigma nor a myth but were real people fighting for their independence. Sarojini Naidu, Kamla Nehru, Rukmani Lakhshmipathi, Hansa Mehta, Nellie Sen Gupta, Satyavati Devi, Miraben (Ms Slade), Durgabai and Kuttimala Amma all contributed richly to the destruction of the many strands of the web, which had dictated that women were either goddesses or witches. The above mentioned women were compassionate people who worked very hard for the good of all and for the betterment of their country.

In the general elections of February 1939, nearly five million women voters participated enthusiastically in electioneering. The majority of their votes were cast for Congress. It became clear that women could responsibly vote and the doubts of the orthodox men that the enfranchisement of women would bring their country to doom were quickly dispelled. The women who contested on the Congress ticket were extraordinarily successful. In ,one constituency, a woman elementary school teacher defeated the Vice-Chancellor of the University of her Province. In another, the wife of a doctor overthrew the President of a District Board who had represented the constituency in Parliament for twelve years. In thirty-nine years, India underwent such sweeping changes that by 1939, the political, educational and social position for women had risen so high that eight women were members of provincial and state legislatures. India ranked third among the nations of the world in regards to the political influence and position secured by its women. The United States and Russia were first and second respectively.

Viney Kirpal in her introduction to the edited book, *The Girl Child in 20th Century Indian Literature* writes about the depiction of the girl child in the literature of pre-independence period that "as in ancient literature, girl children are not presented as girl children. Their chronological age might place them as children but they appear in those works as 'miniature women-child brides, child wives, child widows'. The girls may be young in age but the responsibilities they are depicted to be taking up are those of grown up women." She further reports that "the period of adolescence and the transition to womanhood is like a blank page in these texts"

After Independence in 1947 most of the evils in Indian society were vigorously brought to the focus of attention of the nation. The principle of equality among the sexes was effectively put into law. Those ideas were constitutionally accepted by the Indian people who had been prevalent in the advanced nations for a long time. When the Constitution of India was framed in November 1949. Its Preamble stated that equality among the sexes was a fundamental right. Many other laws were enacted, intense efforts were made to remove the long-standing legal disabilities around women. It is worth noting that equal voting rights for women were given the very day the Indian Constitution was adopted.

Presently, the government offers incentives to women to enable them to obtain an education that will remove sex discriminations. No woman can now be refused employment because of sex. At present quite a number of women hold jobs in top administrative and managerial services. Almost all the services are open to women who are involved in serious competition with men for the topmost positions in foreign services, police and engineering. They have also found employment in areas such as nuclear engineering, flying and paratroops.

The Hindu Marriage Act of 1955 gave women the legal right to divorce. The daughter who was completely excluded from the inheritance of property among Hindus after the Vedic period now has this right which was granted by The Hindu Succession Act of 1956. In 1961 the Dowry Prohibition Act was passed. The Government began the family planning incentive programme as a social welfare measure to release women from unlimited child bearing responsibilities.

In spite of these measures to ensure equality, most women of India are sill tradition bound. Cormack, Rama Mehta, Promilla Kapur, Goldstein and others who have studied the thinking and the outlook of modern Indian women through questionnaire and Interview techniques found that the women, even the highly educated ones, are still completely rooted in their families. The unmarried still depend on their fathers for advice and guidance as well as for the choice of their husbands. The married depend on their husbands for advice about their careers, life-styles and future life plans. These women have identities, which have meaning only in terms of men in their lives. Independence as is found in Western women is lacking in most of Indian women who are willing to sacrifice their independence and identity for the family and for their men who get precedence over their own selves. Since society as a whole accepts this orientation, those who challenge this notion have a difficult time. Divorce is still a hated word in most of the Indian families. Nearly ninety per cent of all marriages among the middle classes are the arranged marriages. The choice of marriage partners depends on the parents.

The education of women is now considered as an essential feature of our national life. The point worth consideration is that: "should education strive to change this situation or strengthen these practices?" Many scholars are of the opinion that the stability of the Indian society is due to the prevalent practices while the exponents of the Women's Liberation Movement are very much against the undermining of women's position in any respect. They want them to be assertive and the determiners of their own destiny.

The Webster's New World Dictionary of the American language defines aspirations as "strange desire or ambition, as for advancement?" What are the ambitions of the Indian women? What are their desires? What do they consider as advancement? How do they strive to fulfil their ambitions?

Motivation can be viewed as one class of determinants of behaviour. What motivates the Indian woman? Her behaviour may give the key to this question. Since psychological determinants cannot be completely isolated from biological, cultural and situational factors, these factors must be taken into consideration while analysing her behaviour pattern of the Indian women. Thus Indian feminine behaviour is the chief concern with motivation as its determinant, and aspirations a secondary factor, which influence both but is not so easily observed.

Both Indian men and women believe that females are the weaker sex—weaker physically, emotionally and in the opinion of some, intellectually as well. Most parents do not want girls because they are considered liabilities. They must be protected, given a dowry and married in a good family. Hence during childhood girls hold an inferior position in the family. The differential treatment they receive develop within them the typical qualities or characteristics of Indian womanhood. The Indian girls upbringing determines their aspirations and motivations. They desire a virtuous, modest life centred around their husbands and children. They aspire for men of good character and education who can maintain them decently as their husbands. In a study by Cora Vreeda de Stuers, girls responded that their parents educated them so that they would be able to marry well. Girls by and large drop out of school as soon as their marriages are arranged unless their betrothed or in-laws wish them to continue their studies. In such cases they continue studies to fulfil the aspirations of others, rather than their own. To another question of Cora put to 203 postgraduate women students of Jaipur the answers were on traditional lines. The women reported that: "a woman's main destiny to be is marriage and motherhood."

The themes of the popular films, modern novels, love songs and other works of art all portray the Indian girl as a modest, shy, beautiful and delicate being who often dreams of a prince charming rather than a career. The aspirations of a woman after her marriage are confined to her family's welfare and needs. Even working married women are more concerned about their families than their jobs. If a conflict occurs, the family comes first. They welcome pregnancy as a chance to bear a male child. Cora wrote, "the girls had difficulty in imagining their married lives other than in serving their husbands and the children they would bear them."

Why is the Indian woman so rooted in her family? It may be said that it is centuries of socialisation, which has shaped her behaviour. 'Modern Indian writers point out that women of Vedic times had high status, but her position has degenerated since then. However, in the Vedic times also the woman's husband and offspring were her major concern. This may be attributed to the division of labour, which the society had approved in the very beginning of civilisation. Women were given the task of tending the homes and men the fields and arms. This division of labour was further made rigid when women were put behind purdah and men became absolute lords of their lives. Till recently the Indian woman was not allowed the opportunity to expand her horizons. Unfortunately even today very few models exist to show her how to develop her personality beyond the home environment.

Two studies done in sixties and seventies indicated a changing trend regarding the motivation for marriage. Kapur's two-phase, ten-year study found that women in the sixties married for social, economic or emotional security. In the seventies they responded that mutual companionship and satisfaction of needs were as important considerations as the earlier ones. At the beginning of twenty first century the motivations for marriage may still be in the direction of personal satisfaction and mutual companionship. The security aspect may further be undermined because the women of the middle classes are joining the world of work in larger numbers and the enrolment of girls in higher education is increasing very rapidly and not only this the women are excelling in all the fields of work, may it be Army or Police.

Another study by Barot reported in 1972 also revealed that the women's attitudes towards marriage had undergone change in that the emphasis had shifted from self-sacrifice to personal and mutual satisfaction. Unfortunately the shift was more towards obtaining material comforts from marriage rather than affection and love. Some women might be cold and calculating in weighing the advantages of marriage. In sixties and seventies quite a large number of arranged marriages were taking place. Merchant examined some statistics regarding this practice. He found that in 1935, 78 per cent of the respondents favoured marriage by their choice. Hate found that in 1946, 74 per cent of her unmarried respondents wished to choose their own partners. Kapur's 1959 study revealed that only 48 per cent preferred marriage based on love. Other studies by Jauhari, Mehta and Cormack during decades up to seventies also show the trend towards the liking of arranged marriages. All these studies had educated women as respondents, therefore, it may be concluded that the Indian women of these decades wanted the best of both the worlds mutual acceptance, material comforts and parental approval. Kapur called it as a quasi-traditional type of marriage. This might be due to the transitional phase. But it may be seen that even now after the end of twentieth century, the preference for arranged marriages has not very significantly changed in spite of the girls becoming more assertive in exercising their choice in the selection of their life partners.

Women in the 40's and 50's were full of romanticism born of struggles for emancipation. They envisioned a society where men and women might mix freely socially and make choices based on love. In reality such choices were hard to come by. Women had to either depend on the choice of their parents or remain unmarried. Two other aspects that have affected this situation were the legal granting of equality which conflicted with the ideal as presented by the mass media and tradition. Even among the educated women very few worked to fulfil personal ambition or married for love. Second, very few career women had aspirations to reach to the top level of their profession if it involved in any way the interference with their normal domestic life. Jauhari found in her study that a majority of working women in her sample neither took their work seriously nor had developed any notion of a career.

In a study by Arora, Bhattacharya and others, which sampled unmarried typists, clerks, stenographers and telephone operators in Bombay, it was found that 60 per cent of the respondents worked only as a stopgap measure until marriage. Only 22 per cent had aspirations for higher official status. The rest expected to simply continue what they were doing without advancement or wished to quit soon and 48 per cent were in favour of employment because of the possibility that it would improve their prospects for marriage. According to this study no one wanted to be just a career woman.

The Indian woman's subordination of her aspirations to the good of her husband and children may indicate a tendency to masochism. Could it be that Indian men are more sadist and Indian women more masochistic than non-Indians are? The Sati system does support this supposition. The Brahman priests who tabooed killing of animals were not in the least perturbed when a woman's husband died and she was burnt alive. Some widows burned themselves with pomp and grandeur. This tendency still persists in some men and women as the sati ceremony of Roop Kanwar in Rajasthan in the late eighties show. There were people who not only witnessed the gruesome happening but also positively supported the cult of sati. This was a clear example of sadism of men and masochism of women.

The abolition of the sati system by law in the nineteenth century did not ameliorate the conditions of the Hindu widows. In 1939 Chattopadhayya observed: "Truly as some are reminded that the widow was lifted from the pyre but left in the cremation ground. Certainly in 2000 AD they are out of the cremation ground but are still moving in their own funeral procession with colourless dresses, frugal meals, toil and tears. While compassionless men praise this simplicity they seem to feel a strange masochistic honour in living in such a lifestyle.

In Sengupta's book *The Story of Women in India,* this masochistic tendency is explored. When she asked a woman how she accounted for this accepting, deterministic view of life, the woman replied, "We have this serenity because our sense of duty is so highly developed, our duty towards God, towards our parents, towards husband and children. We think of ourselves last.... And if we meet with misfortune, it is because of our Karma". Sengupta offers this comment, "So it may, for it is bound to make one's life limited to a narrow area—merely for the lack of ambitions... An Indian woman's ambitions are not so much her own but her husband's and children's and many an unobtrusive woman has given great men to the world".

Unfortunately somewhat deeper probing of the psyche of an average Indian woman uncovers a weak willed individual who leaves all decision making up to the man in her life. This woman is afraid to develop her own personality for the fear of offending her husband. From this perspective, it would also follow that such a dedicated woman may aspire to die before or with her husband. Her entire motivation to live is for her husband. It may be mentioned that the Indian women have suffered from mental slavery for centuries. Their indecision, unassertiveness and lack of will have been branded as emerging out of their Karma. These women live every moment of their lives in the blind faith in the theory of Karma. In fact they do not know or do not want to know the true meaning of Karma, which cannot be interpreted in terms of inaction as these women depict in their lifestyle.

The literature in most of the Indian languages propagates the ideal of silent, suffering women. Surrender and self-sacrifice are associated with the personality of the woman. For the housewife the ideal of Sita and Savitri is eulogised. The ideal of Shakti is not so frequently emphasised as that of suffering woman. This may be because the power in woman is less acceptable than her humility.

Whatever we have discussed above about the Indian women's psyche may not be very true. Is the Indian woman psychologically a weak creature? So far we have portrayed her as such. But the question raised herein needs much deeper and thorough probe. The Indian woman's psyche has become outwardly as depicted above due to the sociological factors operating in our land for centuries. What is her true nature and what she can become if there are brought about vital changes in our social environment? We will be seized with these questions in the next three chapters of the present book. It may, however, be mentioned here that the modern literature in India as well as the mass media is no more presenting the woman as a weak-willed individual.

The modern man in India wants equality between the sexes; in principle. But he feels much difficulty and pain in accepting equality with his wife, daughter, mother or sister. The women demand protection and security from him and in return for it he demands their loyalty and respect. The psyche of modern male seems to be that the be given their freedom to the extent that they respect wishes look after him well and remain loyal and faithful to him. The male wants woman to have aspirations as long as they do not come in conflict with his own whims. He may allow his wife to move out of the house or join the world of work but he is extremely jealous if she associates with any colleague or friend. On the other hand he feels as his right as a male to mingle with her female colleagues and co-workers. Thus he believes in the double standards of conduct for males and females. The significant difference between the modern Indian male and his ancestors is that he does acknowledge that women have the right to an equal and decent life but it must be lived under his supervision and protection. The modern Indian women do not suffer from as many indignities as the women used to suffer in the past. Still it is desirable that they aspire to be more than mere appendages of their husbands. They should seek a partnership relationship in which the question of superiority and inferiority does not arise nor does one individual engulf the individuality of the other. When a clash of opinion occurs it should be resolved through mutual love, respect and consideration.

The doctrine of Karma, which preaches action, is really one of inaction so far as it concerns Indian women. The women are made inert and dependent upon a husband they worship, even if he is unworthy or a parasite on society or is a criminal. This is not what Lord Krishna taught when he motivated Arjuna to fight. Much of the teachings of Gita have been twisted in a degenerative social system of the Indian orthodox family.

Spratt provides a psychological reason for this inaction among males as well as females. He believes that the Hindu culture is essentially narcissistic in the Freudian sense. Moddie agrees with him and describes the social consequences of this distinctive Hindu personality. Spratt stated that a greater gap between aspiration and achievement exists in Indian culture than in most others, but it causes less stress.

The Indian female must strive to understand this aspect of her culture. Highly narcissistic attitudes lead to inaction in the face of frustration in order to keep their mental balance in a society where woman's whole life revolves around her husband, woman becomes totally inert when widowed. But this is quite an undesirable situation. Even after her husband's death woman can do much. She must rise above her frustrations and turn inaction into action. She may remarry or she may devote herself to social or national service. Many modern women are doing so but a vast majority of illiterate and semi-educated women fall prey, to inaction or to a life of drudgery and toil. The worst aspect of the life of the widows one can see at the religion oriented towns of Varanasi or Brindaban. The relatives of the widows leave them in these towns, as they do not want to support them financially. Having no means of subsistence these widows in order to maintain themselves have no option but to beg and live in extremely inhuman conditions.

The education for the women must be so organised that there occurs a directional change in their aspirations. More avenues of employment must be opened for the women. Special vocational training centres should be established for the widows and the destitute women. The women must be encouraged through a vibrant educational system to be more self-oriented. No doubt such an orientation may lead a new form of frustrations but a good educational system may convert these frustrations as the basis of higher achievements in all walks of life. The danger of frustrations resulting in greater introversion is always present but this can be overcome by the cultivation of a positive and outward outlook towards life.

At present there are various agencies which are working in the direction of woman's empowerment. Their impact is certainly towards the achievement of higher status and position of the women in the society but mostly this impact is being felt in the case of the women belonging to the affluent sections of the society. The women belonging to the poor families or of rural areas are beyond their influence. It is, therefore, extremely desirable that educational effort be extended to these neglected sections of the womanhood. In providing education to them care has to be taken that it develops in them right attitudes, higher aspirations and motivations for better achievements. The education should equip the women for building a better world in which mutual love, respect and effort become the ideals for living.

avenues of employment must be opened for the women. Special vocational training centres should be established for the widows and the destitute women. The women must be encouraged through a vibrant educational system to be more self-oriented. No doubt such an orientation may lead a new form of frustrations but a good educational system may convert these frustrations as the basis of higher achievements in all walks of life. The danger of frustrations resulting in greater introversion is always present but this can be overcome by the cultivation of a positive and outward outlook towards life.

At present there are various agencies which are working in the direction of women's empowerment. Their thrust is certainly towards the achievement of higher status and position of the women in the society. But mostly this impact is being felt in the case of the women belonging to the affluent sections of the society. The women belonging to the poor families and rural areas are beyond their influences. It is, therefore, extremely essential that educational effort be extended to these neglected sections of the womanhood. In providing education to them care has to be taken that it develops in them right attitudes, higher aspirations and motivations for better achievements. The education thus will equip the women for building a better world in which mutual love, respect and affection become the ideals for living.

Bibliography

Aami Taylor, *Family Structure in India,* Society Publications, Chennai: 1999.

Altekar, A.S., *The Position of Women in Hindu Civilization,* Motilal Banarsidas, Varanasi: 1962.

Anshen, R.N., (ed.), *The Family: Its Functions and Destiny,* Harper & Row, New York: 1959.

Asthana, P., *Women's Movement in India,* Vikas Publishing House, Delhi: 1974.

Badel, Auguste: *Women: Past, Present and Future,* Bone and Liveright, New York: 1918.

Baig Tara Ali: *India's Woman Position,* S. Chand and Company Pvt. Ltd., Delhi: 1976.

Barot, Jyoti: *The Indian Family in the Change and Challenge of the Seventies,* Sterling Publishers, New Delhi: 1972.

Bebel, August: *Women in the Past, Present and Future,* ed. By Mukerjee, Subrata and Rama Swami, Sushila, Deep and Deep Publication, New Delhi: 1996.

Bhasin, K. (ed.), *The Position of Women in India,* Leslie Sawny, Mumbai: 1971.

Bhushan, Jamila Brij: *Muslim Women,* Vikas Publishing House, New Delhi: 1980.

Billington, Mary Frances: *Women in India,* Amarka Book Agency, Delhi: 1973.

Carden, Maren Lockwood: *The New Feminist Movement*, Russall Sage Foundation, New York: 1974.

Carstairs, G. Morris: *The Twice Born*, Indiana University Press, Bloomington: 1958.

Chakrapant, C. Kumar-S. Vijaya (editors): *Changing Status and Role of Women in Indian Society*, M.D. Pub., New Delhi: 1994.

Chattapadhya, Kamladevi, et. al: *The Awakening of Indian Women*, Everyman's Press, Chennai: 1939.

Chaturvedi, Geeta., *Women Administration in India: A Study of the Socio-economic Background*, RBSA Publication, Jaipur: 1985.

Cofer, C.N. and Appley, M.N., *Motivation Theory and Research*, John Wiley and Sons Inc., New York: 1964.

Cormack, Margaret: *The Hindu Women*, Asia Pub.. House, Mumbai: 1961.

Das, Ram Mohan: *Women in Manu's Philosophy*, ASB Pub. Jalandhar: 1993.

Deckard, B.S, *The Women's Movement*, Harper and Row, New York: 1979.

Desai, Neera and Patel Vibbuti: *Indian Women*, Popular Prakashan, Mumbai: 1975-85.

De'Souza Alfred: *Women in Contemporary India and South Asia*, Manohar Pub., Delhi: 1980.

Devasia, L. and Devasia, V.V: *Empowering Women for Sustainable Development*, Ashish Pub. House, New Delhi: 1994.

Drucker, P.F., *An Introductory View of Management*, Harper College Press, New York: 1977.

Engineer Asghar Ali: *Islam and Liberation Theology*, Sterling Pub., New Delhi: 1990.

Evan, M. William, *Organizational Theory Structure, Systems and Environments*, John Wiley and Sons Inc, London: 1976.

Everett, J.M.: *Women and Social Change in India*, Heritage Pub., New Delhi: 1979.

Friedan, Betty, *The Feminine Mystique*, W.W. Norton, New York: 1963.

Gandhi, M.K.: *The Role of Women*, Bhartiya Vidhya Bhavan, Mumbai: 1964.

Ghadially, Rehana: *Women in Indian Society*, Sage Pub., New Delhi: 1988.

Good, W.J., *World Revolution and Family Patterns*, Collier MacMillan, London: 1963.

Gorwaney, N., *Self Image and Social Change*, Sterling Publishers, New Delhi: 1977.

Gullahorn, J.E.: *Psychology and Women in Transition*, John Wiley, New York: 1979.

Gupta, A.K.: *Women and Society*, Criterion Pub., New Delhi: 1986.

Gupta, A.R.: *Women in Hindu Society*, Jyotsna Prakashan, Delhi: 1985.

Gupta, J.L.: *Challenges to the Fair Sex*, Gyan Pub., Delhi: 1988.

Hate, C.A., *Changing Status of Women in Post-Independence India*, Allied Publications, Mumbai: 1969.

Hate, C.A. *Hindu Women and her Future*, New Bombay Co., Mumbai: 1948.

Horney, Karen: *Feminine Psychology*, W.W. Norton & Co., New York: 1967.

Inkeles, A. and Smith, D., *Becoming Modern*, Heinmann Educational Books Ltd., London: 1974.

Jain, D: *Indian Women*, Publication Division, Government of India, Delhi: 1975.

Jain, Pratibha and Mahan, Rajan: *Women Images*, Rawat Pub., Jaipur: 1996.

Kapur, Promilla: *The Changing Status of the Working Woman in India*, Vikas Pub., Delhi: 1974.

Keeton Kathy and Basrin Yvonne: *Woman of Tomorrow*, Harvard Univ. Press, New York: 1985.

Kidwai, Shaikh M.H.: *Women under Different Social and Religious Laws*, Seema Pub., New Delhi: 1976.

Kuppuswamy, B., *Social Change in India*, Vikas Publishing House, Delhi: 1972.

Marshall, Katherine, *Employed Parents and Division of Housework, Perspectives*, Autumn Pub., New York: 1993.

Mehta, Hansa: *Indian Woman*, Butala & Co., New Delhi: 1981.

Mehta, Rama: *Socio-legal Status of Women in India*, Metropolitan Book Co., Delhi: 1982.

Mehta, Sushila: *Revolution and Status of Women in India*, Metropolitan Book Co., Delhi: 1982.

Mies, M., *Indian Women : Conflicts and Dilemmas*, Concept Publishers, New Delhi: 1980.

Mittal Mukta (ed.): *Women in India. Today and Tomorrow*, Anmol Pub., New Delhi: 1995.

Moddie, A.D.: *The Brahamanical Culture and Modernity*, Asia Pub. House, London: 1968.

Mohanty, Jagannath: *Education for All*, Deep and Deep Pub., New Delhi: 1994.

Moneil, Elton B.: *The Psychology of being Human*, Canfield Press, San Francisco: 1977.

Montagu, Ashley: *The Natural Superiority of Women*, The Macmillan Co., New York: 1968.

Myrdal, A., *Woman's Two Roles*, Routledge & K. Paul, London: 1968.

Nanda, B.R.: *Indian Women*, Vikas Pub. House, Delhi: 1976.

Pal. B.K.: *Problems and Concerns of Indian Women*, ABC Pub. House, New Delhi: 1989.

Pandey, Rekha: *Women from Subjection to Liberation*, Motilal Pub., New Delhi: 1989.

Pandit, S. K.: *Women in Society*, Rajat Pub., Delhi: 1998.

Phandis, Urnifla: *Women of the World*, Vikas Pub. House, Delhi: 1978.

Pujari, Premlata: *Women Power in India*, Kanishka Pub., Delhi: 1994.

Rajgopal, T.S.: *Indian Ideal of Womanhood*, Ramakrishna Mission, Kolkata: 1969.

Ramabal, Saraswati Pundita: *High Caste Hindu Woman*, Jas. B. Podgers Printing Co., Philadelphia: 1888.

Ranganathan, Sarala: *Women and Social Order*, Kanishka Publishers, New Delhi: 1998.

Rege, Y.M.: *Whither Women*, The Popular Book Depot, Mumbai: 1938.

Rohibaugh, Joanna Bunker: *Women: Psychology's Puzzle*, Basic Books Inc., New York: 1979.

Ross, Aileen D.: *Hindu Family in its Urban Setting*, Univ. of Toronto Press, Toronto: 1961.

Sachidananda: *Women's Right: Myth and Reality*, Printwell Pub., Jaipur: 1984.

Sengupta, Padmint: *Story of Women of India*, Indian Book Co., New Delhi: 1974.

Shridevi: *A Century of Indian Womanhood*, Rao and Raghavan, Mysore: 1965.

Sikkri, Rehana: *Women in Islamic Culture and Society*, Kanishka Pub., New Delhi: 1999.

Singh, Indu Prakash: *Women, Law and Social Change in India*, Radiant Pub., New Delhi: 1989.

Singh, Uttam Kumar: *Women Education*, Discovery Pub. House, New Delhi: 1996.

Sinha, Anjana, Maitra: *Women in Changing Society*, Ashish Pub. House, New Delhi: 1993.

Srinivasan, M.N.: *The Changing Position of Indian Women*, Oxford Univ. Press, Delhi: 1970.

Subbamma, Malladi: *Women, Tradition and Culture*, Sterling Pub., Delhi: 1985.

Suguna, B: *Women and Religion*, Discovery Publishing House, New Delhi: 1994.

Thomas, P.: *Women and Marriage in India*, George Allen and Unwin, Lord: 1939.

Thomas, P.: *Epics, Myths and Legends of India*, D.B. Teraporevala, Mumbai: 1961.

Thomas, P.: *Indian Women Through the Ages*, Asia Pub. House, New York: 1964.

Tikoo, Prithvi Nath: *Indian Women*, B.R. Publishing Corporation, Delhi: 1985.

Usha, Rao N.J.: *Women in Developing Society*, Ashish Pub. House, Delhi: 1983.

Vashishta, B.K.: *Encyclopardia of Women in India*, Parveen Encyclopaedia, New Delhi: 1976.

Vitels, M.S., *Motivation and Morale in Industry*, Morton, New York: 1953.

Vyas, Anju and Singh Sunita: *Women's Studies in India*, Sage Pub., New Delhi: 1993.

Zeitlin, Irving, M.: *Rethinking Sociology*, Appleton-Century Crafts, New York: 1973.

Zumurd, N.K.: *The Womanhood*, DBM Pub., Delhi: 1993

References

Government of India: *Fourth World Conference on Women, Beijing 1995. Country Report*. Deptt. of Women and Child Development, Ministry of Human Resource Development, New Delhi. 1995.

Human Development Report, UNDP, New York: Oxford University Press, 1996.

Report of the Committee on Status of Women in India (1974), *Towards Equality*. Department of Social Welfare, Government of India, New Delhi.

Status of Women in India, A Synopsis of the Report, National Committee on the Status of Women (1971-74). New Delhi: The ICSSR. Allied Pub., 1975.

Index

□□□